Oxford Modern Britain

Gender in Modern Britain

Nickie Charles

Series Editor: John Scott

OXFORD
UNIVERSITY PRESS

OXFORD
UNIVERSITY PRESS

Great Clarendon Street, Oxford OX2 6DP

Oxford University Press is a department of the University of Oxford.
It furthers the University's objective of excellence in research, scholarship,
and education by publishing worldwide in

Oxford New York

Auckland Bangkok Buenos Aires Cape Town Chennai
Dar es Salaam Delhi Hong Kong Istanbul Karachi Kolkata
Kuala Lumpur Madrid Melbourne Mexico City Mumbai Nairobi
São Paulo Shanghai Singapore Taipei Tokyo Toronto

with an associated company in Berlin

Published in the United States
by Oxford University Press Inc., New York

First published 2002

British Library Cataloguing in Publication Data
Data available

Library of Congress Cataloging in Publication Data
Data available

ISBN 0-19-874211-8

1 3 5 7 9 10 8 6 4 2

Typeset in Swift and Argo
by RefineCatch Limited, Bungay, Suffolk
Printed in Great Britain by
Biddles Ltd., Guildford and King's Lynn

This book is dedicated, with love and gratitude,
to Mary and Freddie Charles,
the best parents anyone could hope to have

Foreword

THE Oxford Modern Britain series is designed to fill a major gap in the available sociological sources on the contemporary world. Each book will provide a comprehensive and authoritative overview of major issues for students at all levels. They are written by acknowledged experts in their fields, and should be standard sources for many years to come.

Each book focuses on contemporary Britain, but the relevant historical background is always included, and a comparative context is provided. No society can be studied in isolation from other societies and the globalized context of the contemporary world, but a detailed understanding of a particular society can both broaden and deepen sociological understanding. These books will be exemplars of empirical study and theoretical understanding.

Books in the series are intended to present information and ideas in a lively and accessible way. They will meet a real need for source books in a wide range of specialized courses, in 'Modern Britain' and 'Comparative Sociology' courses, and in integrated introductory courses. They have been written with the newcomer and general reader in mind, and they meet the genuine need in the informed public for accurate and up-to-date discussion and sources.

John Scott
Series Editor

Contents

Detailed Contents

List of Tables

Preface

THERE are many books on gender which provide detailed descriptions of the state of gender relations and the direction of change. This book attempts to do something different. As well as describing some important aspects of gender relations in Britain at the beginning of the twenty-first century and charting changes since the 1950s, it provides a discussion of how sociological theorizing and research into gender have developed and changed in the half century since the ending of the Second World War. It also engages with current debates about gender, such as whether there is a crisis of masculinity, the problem of boys failing at school, the debate over the family and mothers' employment, and the best means of ensuring a more equitable gender balance in formal political representation. It does not attempt to provide an exhaustive account of gender relations in Britain at the beginning of the twenty-first century and there are, inevitably, aspects of gender that are not included or are only discussed in what may seem a rather peremptory way. I would have liked to include more but this would have made the book too long and I would have taken longer still to finish it, so there was nothing for it but to select what to include and what to exclude.

An important dimension of gender relations that I *have* included is the way they are shaped by ethnicity. There is a difficulty here in so far as different studies adopt different classifications. Rather than attempting to resolve this problem I have simply chosen to go along with the classifications used by the author/s whose work is under discussion.

Most of the material in this book is new and much of it is based on a course I teach at Swansea on gender, work, and households. Some parts of Chapter 1 have appeared in similar form in the first chapter of *Practising feminism: identity, difference, power*, a book I coedited with Felicia Hughes-Freeland and which was published by Routledge in 1996. Similarly, some of the ideas in Chapter 9 are derived from work I did for my book *Gender divisions and social change* (Harvester Wheatsheaf, 1993) and from the work I did with Helen Hintjens for our edited collection, *Gender, ethnicity and political ideologies* (Routledge, 1998).

This book has taken rather longer than expected to see the light of day. I therefore need to thank the series editor, John Scott, for his patience and forbearance; he must at times have wondered if it was ever going to materialize. I also want to thank my editors at Oxford University Press, Tim Barton, and latterly, Angela Griffin. Angela has been particularly understanding about the difficulties I have faced in meeting ever-extending deadlines. I also owe a debt of gratitude to Chris Harris, whose enthusiastic insights about the symbolic significance of the suit for him as a young man chimed in with what I was reading about masculinities, and who has read and commented on the entire manuscript. And, once again, Lis Parcell has ridden to the rescue with food and drink and a rash promise to read the manuscript. On her recommendation, it may be advisable for readers who are unfamiliar with sociological discussions of conceptual issues to begin their reading not with Chapter 1 but with the more familiar territory of Chapter 2.

Theorizing Gender

IN the past fifty years the study of gender within sociology has undergone several transformations, reflecting both theoretical developments within the discipline and political developments outside it. The most significant political development was the emergence of second-wave feminism in the late 1960s which has, arguably, resulted in the study of gender becoming central to the sociological enterprise. It has also been associated with profound social change, something which sociologists are concerned to understand and which I attempt to describe in the course of this book. In this chapter my focus is on shifts in the way gender has been theorized within sociology. In the chapters that follow I explore the effect of these shifts on the way sociologists have studied gender and the changes that have taken place in gender relations in the second half of the twentieth century.

I begin this chapter with a discussion of sex-role theory, which dominated the sociological study of gender in the immediate post-war years and was not displaced from its pre-eminence until the early 1970s and the emergence of feminism. I then consider attempts by feminist sociologists (influenced by Marxism) to develop structural explanations of gender divisions of labour. Such structural explanations ground to a halt in the early 1980s leading to pronouncements about Marxist feminist sociology being 'all but dead and buried' (Roseneil, 1995b:199). I explore the subsequent shift from studying 'things' to studying 'words'—which is how the influence of poststructuralism and the associated 'cultural turn' have been characterized (Barrett, 1992)—and argue that, alongside the 'cultural turn' with its focus on subjectivity and identity, there has been a continuing engagement with materialist theorizations of gender and, at the beginning of the twenty-first century, there is a tension between poststructuralist theorizations of gender and various forms of materialist feminism.

Sex-role theory

It has often been asserted that prior to the emergence of second-wave feminism gender was not taken seriously within sociology and women, if they appeared at all in sociological research, were present as wives and mothers in the sociology of the family. Studies of work, politics, and practically everything else focused on men. Part of the project of feminist sociologists from the 1970s onwards was to rectify this omission, to study women as workers and as political actors, and to problematize gender divisions which had heretofore not been conceptualized as a constitutive part of the social division of labour (Stacey, 1981). It is not strictly true, however, that gender was not studied before the advent of second-wave feminism. A considerable literature exists on sex roles which has been revisited recently by those interested in the study of masculinity (see e.g. Carrigan et al., 1985 and Chapter 6). Sex-role theory, which derives from structural functionalism, conceptualizes role as the 'active aspect of a status'. In Christine Delphy's words,

each status had roles which the individuals who held that status had to fulfil. This perspective is clearly sociological in the true sense of the word. Thus, people's situations and activities are held to derive from the social structure, rather than from either nature or their particular capacities. (Delphy, 1996:31)

A role is therefore associated with a particular position within the social division of labour. Furthermore social roles, of which sex roles are one type, provide scripts which are learned and followed by social actors; the process of learning being socialization (Connell, 1987:30). The concept of sex role was developed by Talcott Parsons and is associated with his analysis of the family in industrial society. According to Carrigan et al., Parsons derived sex-role differentiation

from a general sociological principle, the imperative of structural differentiation. Its particular form here was explained by the famous distinction between 'instrumental' and 'expressive' leadership. Parsons treated sex roles as the instrumental/expressive differentiation that operated within the conjugal family. (Carrigan et al., 1985:555)

And it was within the family (conceptualized as a social group) that socialization took place. This way of theorizing gender defines a norm for masculine and feminine personalities and, by implication, there can be deviation from this norm. Thus homosexuality or juvenile delinquency can be explained by a 'failure' in socialization and conceptualized as deviant (Connell, 1987:49). This approach also recognizes that in industrial societies the feminine sex role is unstable because it involves a tension between being a full-time mother and homemaker and wishing to participate in paid work outside the home as equals of men. Parsons argued that

the separation of home and work characteristic of industrialism generated a functional strain towards a gendered segregation of roles, with the man specializing in the instrumental roles of work in the formal economy and the woman concentrating on the expressive roles of homemaking in the family household. On the other hand, the universalistic values characteristic of industrialism generated a pressure for equal opportunities for all members of society to achieve any position consistent with their abilities and efforts, irrespective of any ascribed characteristic such as sex. (Stockman et al., 1995:2067)

This tension leads to instability and the possibility of change. It also (according to later theorists) can be and is resolved differently in different industrial societies leading to different balances between women's paid and unpaid work: in all, however, women experience the double burden of women's two roles (Myrdal and Klein, 1956). The main focus of research on sex roles was women within the family, but studies of men were also carried out within this theoretical framework. Thus young men who were 'deviant' were studied (such as juvenile delinquents and boys who underachieved in schools). Indeed, during 'the 1950s and 1960s the most popular explanation of such social problems was "father absence"' and the overwhelmingly feminine environment of the home which allegedly led to developmental problems for boys (Carrigan et al., 1985:560). These questions are high on the current gender agenda within and outside sociology, as I discuss in Chapters 4, 5, and 6.

Sex-role theory in particular and functionalist sociology in general have been criticized for failing to conceptualize gender relations in terms of power, seeing gender roles as complementary rather than involving hierarchy and as changeable through interventions in the socialization process. This latter charge can also be laid at the door of liberal feminism which is underpinned by sex-role theory (Barrett and Phillips, 1992; Connell, 1987). Furthermore, viewing sex roles as the outcome of a process of gender-specific socialization implies that the basis for gender socialization is provided by biological sex (Connell, 1987:73). Culture elaborates on a foundation that is provided by nature; this elaboration is not predetermined, however, so intervention in the process of gender socialization can affect the outcome.

Feminism and gender

In the late 1960s and early 1970s feminist theory began to make its mark within sociology and dislodged sex-role theory from its hegemonic position. In *Sex, gender and society*, Ann Oakley took sex-role theory to its logical conclusion, arguing that the variety of gender roles within society demonstrates that gender is culturally determined, defining gender as separate and separable from biological sex, and demonstrating that gender roles are learned rather than innate (Oakley, 1972). In order to do this she used ethnographic evidence from societies around the world and evidence from social psychology on the way gender roles are learned. But she retained the framework of sex-role theory although she substituted gender for sex and argued for a theoretical distinction between gender, which is socially constructed, and sex, which is biologically given. She did this in order to 'discuss men and women as social groups without lapsing into the common vocabulary of such discussion which utilizes sexuality as its organizing mode' (Oakley, 1989:445). Her book was also important in demonstrating the almost infinite variability of gender roles thereby confirming that they could not be understood as being determined by biology: gender was theorized as being socially constructed. She concluded that

If gender has a biological source of any kind then culture makes it invisible. The evidence of how people acquire their gender identities ... suggests strongly that gender has no biological origin, that the connections between sex and gender are not really 'natural' at all. (Oakley 1972:188)

Oakley's theorization of gender has come in for considerable criticism, most significantly because there is no notion of the relation between gender and power and no consideration of why it is that, despite the almost infinite variety of gender roles in human societies, positions of power are almost universally occupied by men. Indeed her analysis, like the functionalist role theory in which it is embedded, does not include any consideration of hierarchy or asymmetry 'between the two groups, or roles, or sexes, or genders' (Delphy, 1996:32); it does not tackle the issue of male power over women. However, it was theoretically important that a conceptual distinction was made between gender and sex because, according to Christine Delphy,

We had first to demonstrate that 'sex' is applied to divisions and distinctions which are social. Then we had not only to separate the social from the original term, which remains defined by naturalness, but to make the social emerge. This is what the notions of first 'sex roles' and then 'gender' did. Only when the 'social part' is clearly established as social, when it has a name of its own (whether it be sex roles or gender), then and only then could we come back to the idea we started with. (Delphy, 1996:36)

In the 1970s sex-role theory was displaced by a 'political economy' approach which was heavily influenced by Marxism. Within this approach the term sexual divisions was used rather than gender in order to conceptualize social relations between women and men. This was because of its association with 'the division of labour problematic and the mutual definition of two groups (classes)' which meant that it introduced questions of 'power and control, oppression and exploitation' into theorizations of relations between women and men and within these categories. Indeed gender, which at the time was more widely used in social anthropology than in sociology, was associated with 'cultural relativism' and 'neglected power relations' (Allen and Leonard, 1994:22).

Sexual divisions

Feminist sociologists, many of whom were active in the feminist movement, developed analyses of sexual (or gender) divisions of labour. It was argued that the social division of labour was gendered/sexed as well as classed and that it could not be fully understood without taking this into account. Attempts were made to explain this division of labour as arising from social structures. There was a theoretical search for the cause and origins of women's oppression which was located not only within the family but throughout society (Barrett and Phillips, 1992). It was important to explain women's oppression without recourse to biology, hence the cause was located variously in capitalism (and class), patriarchy (and men), or a combination of the two. The origin was more difficult to trace and much attention was paid to Engels's analysis of the origin of the family in which he links women's subordination with the emergence of class society, particularly his observation that the social organization of repro-duction as well as production is part of the material basis of society (Engels, 1972). Women's oppression was taken to be a universal feature of societies of whatever type and universal explanations were therefore sought. Thus Marxist feminists argued that capitalism caused women's oppression (in contra-distinction to functionalist arguments about industrialism and the separation of home and work being the cause) and that it was in the interests of capitalism to keep women at home engaged in unpaid domestic labour while men engaged in paid work outside the home. This was so because women's unpaid reproductive work within the home meant that labour-power (the ability to work) was reproduced on a daily and generational basis at little or no cost to capital and male workers were tied into wage labour by their financial responsibilities towards their wives and children (Wilson, 1977). Thus Marxist feminists conceptualized gender or sexual divisions of labour as arising from women's association with unpaid reproductive labour while men were associ-ated with paid productive labour. As money confers value in a cash economy the paid work done by men was valued more highly than the unpaid work done by women.

Social reproduction

Central to this analysis was the concept of social reproduction and the idea that it involved work outside the sphere of capitalist economic relations. Various arguments were advanced to explain the gendering of productive and reproductive labour, most of which theorized women's subordination as arising from a process of class struggle in conditions of class exploitation. The problem then arose of how to explain gender divisions of labour—how can they be related to class exploitation and the class dynamics that are characteristic of capitalism? One set of arguments developed which related the development of a particular form of the gender division of labour to class exploitation and to the biological 'fact' of women's capacity to bear children. It was argued that during the period of capitalist industrialization when fertility levels were high, the working class sought to establish the conditions for its own reproduction. Frequent pregnancies meant that women's participation in production was interrupted more than men's. During these interruptions they required support which could come either from within the working class, i.e. from the men to whom they were related, or from the capitalist class in the form of their (usually) male employers. The relative strengths of the working class and the capitalist class resulted in the costs of supporting economically inactive women being borne by men within the working class. Thus there is a struggle over which class (and gender) will bear the costs of the reproduction of labour-power (Vogel, 1983; see Charles, 1993 for a fuller account). In this explanation high fertility levels, taken to represent the material reality of biological reproduction, in combination with particular relations of production, lead to a specific gender division of labour which disadvantages women and the working class. A similar argument has been advanced which sees this arrangement as a response by the working class to capitalist exploitation and an attempt on the part of the class to improve its living and working conditions by withdrawing a source of labour (women) from the labour market. This withdrawal frees women from the demands of wage labour and enables them to improve domestic conditions for themselves, the men with whom they live, and their children (Humphries, 1977; Brenner and Ramas, 1984). Once again the imperatives of biological reproduction are conceptualized as constituting part of the material reality of working-class life and women's dependence on men within the family is the response. It provides a solution to the very real problems faced by women in attempting to combine domestic labour, frequent pregnancies, and childcare with highly exploitative waged work. The cost, however, was dependence on a man or the necessity of earning an independent living in a labour market which paid women at much lower rates of pay than men (a situation vividly portrayed in the film of Edith Wharton's novel *The House of Mirth*). In both these variants of the argument the materiality of biological reproduction is used to explain the form taken by class struggle and its outcome, which was women's dependence on men within marriage and their exclusion from the better paid and more highly skilled sectors of the workforce.

Gender ideology

Another set of arguments explains gender divisions of labour as arising from gender ideologies. Thus Michele Barrett argues that gender divisions of labour are not intrinsic to the capitalist mode of production but are imbricated in capitalist relations of production as they have developed historically within Britain and elsewhere. She theorizes gender divisions of labour as arising from a gender ideology which predated capitalist industrialization and shaped the form taken by gender relations. Thus the structure of the economy gives rise to class relations and is characterized by the capital-labour relation while gender relations emanate from the cultural forms and associated ideologies and practices within which capitalism developed (Barrett, 1980; Charles, 1993). In particular she defines various social practices wherein gender relations and identities are reproduced. These are the economic organization of the household and familial ideology, the division of labour and relations of production, the state and the education system, cultural processes and sexuality (Barrett, 1980). Analyses which link gender divisions to the social reproduction of the working class under conditions of capitalist exploitation can therefore be differentiated by the importance they attach to ideology. For some more weight is given to material factors such as high levels of fertility while, for others, it is an Althusserian concept of ideology (itself rooted in material practices) which has the explanatory power (Althusser, 1971).

Other solutions to the problem of the apparent gender neutrality of class relations and the difficulties of explaining gender divisions of labour solely by relying on the concept of class were provided by the development of a concept of patriarchy linked to a domestic mode of production. Authors such as Christine Delphy and Sylvia Walby analysed gender divisions of labour in terms of a domestic or patriarchal mode of production wherein men appropriate the labour of women; this exists alongside the capitalist mode of production providing the material basis for exploitative class and gender relations (Rubin, 1975; Delphy, 1984; Walby, 1986; Hartmann, 1986). Latterly Walby has developed this analysis to include six structures of patriarchy, all of which seem to have equal weight, thus moving away from the idea of a material basis for patriarchy (Pollert, 1996). Her six structures are the patriarchal mode of production, patriarchal relations in paid work, patriarchal relations in the state, male violence, patriarchal relations in sexuality, and patriarchal relations in cultural institutions. The similarity with Barrett's five areas needs no emphasizing: the only distinction between them is the inclusion in Walby's analysis of male violence.

Nature versus culture

Alongside these macro-structural analyses of women's oppression there were others that attempted to explain the similarity of women's position worldwide. It was noted that women the world over are the ones who are involved in feeding and caring for others—namely children and men. It was argued that patriarchy was a worldwide system which reduced women to the status of housewives and made them dependent on men (Mies, 1986). This dependence was reinforced and maintained by male violence towards women (Brownmiller, 1986). It was seen as significant that women everywhere are associated with the private, domestic sphere and men with the public sphere (Rosaldo, 1974). Early analyses also focused on the distinction between nature and culture, arguing that all human societies value culture above nature and associate women with nature. This leads to a devaluing of women and women's work and to their subordination (Ortner, 1974). These theories were all concerned to explain a phenomenon which was assumed to be universal—women's oppression. And they all located the source of women's oppression in structures; whether these be class structures, sex-gender systems, or the structuring of the symbolic order.

Postmodernism

With the increasing influence of postmodernism in the 1980s, this sort of theorization became problematic. Anthropologists working in the field of gender noted the cultural specificity of the terms within which these analyses were being conducted thus undermining their claims to universality (MacCormack and Strathern, 1980). Feminist sociologists developed analogous critiques of sociological theory (Stacey, 1981). Thus production, it was argued, was not a gender-neutral term but was associated with men and masculinity within western cultures. The same was true of terms like 'public' and 'culture' itself. The categories of western philosophical thought, rather than providing a universal structure for understanding cultures everywhere, were analysed as part of the symbolic order of western societies. Furthermore, this symbolic order is gendered and structured hierarchically. Thus, underlying the oppositions rationality–emotionality, culture–nature, production–reproduction, active–passive, dominant–subordinate, objective–subjective, aggressive–peaceful, etc., lies the dichotomy masculine–feminine. The structure of western philosophical thought in terms of gendered dichotomies was exposed, and it was within this framework that western feminists had been constructing their analyses and explanations. This implied that all such analyses were ethnocentric and therefore problematic.

The problematizing of this type of explanation was associated with the postmodern critique of universalizing discourses, their reliance on 'grand narratives', and the rationality of enlightenment thought. It was also associated with political developments such as the black women's critique of white feminism and the emergence of identity politics in Britain and elsewhere (Lovenduski and Randall, 1993; Moghadam, 1994; Charles, 1996). The gender dimensions of these political developments are explored in Chapter 8. The critique of universalist explanations meant that it could no longer be assumed that women everywhere shared a common oppression; similarly the assumption that being a woman had the same meaning in every society was shown to be based on essentialist ideas (Spelman, 1990). The notion of oppression was not abandoned but, instead of analysing it in terms of structures and systems, the construction of gendered subjectivities and identities was problematized: the focus shifted from class to culture, from structure to agency, from a concern with systematic gender divisions to a concern with gender identities based on difference (Barrett, 1992). Culture displaced society and the economy as a focus of theoretical concern (Moghadam, 1994:5). Within sociology attention turned to empirical studies of gender. There was a move from

grand theory to local studies, from cross-cultural analyses of patriarchy to the complex and historical interplay of sex, race and class, from notions of a female identity or the interests of women towards the instability of female identity and the active creation and recreation of women's needs and concerns. (Barrett and Phillips, 1992:67)

Although this has been seen as a turn away from theory, it has also been argued that it is theory

pitched at a less abstract level . . . 'middle range theory' . . . The point of such analyses is not simply to describe the 'facts' of women's . . . situations, but to explicate and understand, at a theoretical level, the processes and mechanisms . . . through which men are able to exert power over women. (Maynard, 1990: 273)

This reflects an ongoing concern within sociology with the ways in which social actors in their daily lives reproduce and/or challenge the social relations which structure their experiences. This approach to the study of society and gender was eclipsed during the 1980s and for much of the 1990s by a focus on culture and identity, subjectivity, sexuality, consumption, and style, and a theoretical engagement with poststructuralism and postmodernism.

At this point it is useful to consider Sandra Harding's proposition that the study of gender should involve three dimensions, gender symbolism, sociosexual divisions of labour, and gender identities or, to use other terms, structure, culture, and agency (Harding, 1986). The shift in focus marked by the 'cultural turn' can be understood as a shift from studying sociosexual divisions of labour towards a focus on gender symbolism and gender identities. Studying sociosexual divisions of labour was informed by sociological theories which focus on social structures. Such theories tend to be materialist and, in the 1970s, downplayed gender symbolism and gender identities. Studies of gender symbolism, gender identities, and culture lay claim to a different theoretical heritage which informs many of the studies of education, masculinity, and sexuality which I discuss in Chapters 5, 6, and 7. During the 1980s, the challenge mounted by poststructuralism had an important influence on the study of gender.

Deconstruction, feminism, and Foucault

As well as being critical of theoretical universalism, poststructuralism deconstructs the humanist notion of a 'conscious, knowing, unified, rational' subject (Weedon, 1987:21) and mounts a profound critique of rationalism (Barrett, 1992). Poststructuralists argue that far from being unitary and fixed, the subject is discontinuous and fragmented. This conceptualization of subjectivity questions the possibility of any essential self or essential identity; the subject is constructed within discourse/language and is contingent. More specifically it problematizes the construction of the rational, knowing subject. Feminists gendered this critique, pointing out that within western philosophical thought the knowing subject was always male and that objectivity and rationality represented a white, masculine, Anglo-European perspective on reality. So-called objective and rationalist argument was neither dispassionate nor disengaged (Collins, 1991), it was the product of observers with specific gender, racial and class locations, and identities (McCall, 1992:853). The attempt to create a neutral observer was predicated on the existence of a privileged gendered subject which, by virtue of the labour of others (women and labourers of both genders), could abstract themselves from the material world and interpret it as if they were not themselves implicated in it (Smith, 1988; Haraway, 1988). Knowledge, rather than being objective and impartial, was subjective and partial because it was produced by social actors located in specific social contexts.

The argument that all knowledge was subjective and partial led to a claim that the knowledge of subordinate groups (such as women, ethnic minorities, the colonized, the working class) was more complete than that of dominant groups because subordinate groups have an insight into the operations of power (Griffin, 1996; Ardener, 1981). Poststructuralist and postmodernist feminists were mounting an epistemological challenge to the truth claims of science. Such challenges 'are situated within a field of struggle over the legitimate claims to knowledge derived from the social processes of social research' and are fundamentally political (McCall, 1992:853). They have given rise to a continuing debate and voluminous literature on the nature of feminist social research, whether there is a feminist epistemology and methodology, and the ethical and political basis of feminist research (Harding, 1986; Haraway, 1988; Sherwin et al., 1998). Here, however, I want to consider the influence of Michel Foucault's poststructuralism on the sociological study of gender.

Identities

For Foucault subjectivity exists only within discourse and as a product of technologies of power. If there is no subjectivity outside discourse and subjectivities are constructed within and by means of discursive practices, then an important focus of attention becomes the process of construction of gendered subjectivities and the engagement of individual subjects within this process. Empirical research influenced by this approach has focused on lifestyle, identity, and consumption and the way subjects construct their identities through buying particular commodities rather than others, adopting certain sartorial or behavioural styles: by choosing freely certain commodities, styles, and behaviours rather than others subjects locate themselves within particular discourses. They are also able to disrupt discourses by combining elements in transgressive ways.

This type of approach has been influential in recent studies of masculinity, but as I show in Chapter 7, there are problems associated with it because of the tendency towards voluntarism and a failure to link gender identities and subjectivities to social structure, however conceptualized. Furthermore, this tendency to focus on identity and the subjective is itself in need of sociological explanation.

To the extent that sociology has become focused on identity, emotion and the subjective, without reflecting critically enough on its material basis in social relations, it has become a part of the development of the mass culture of modernity which it ought to be analysing rather than uncritically adopting. (MacInnes, 1998:144)

The focus on identities and consumption is associated with the idea of gender as style and performance—something that can be put on and taken off at will—and echoes Goffman's much earlier conceptualization of role (Butler, 1990; Cornwall and Lindisfarne, 1994). Thus Goffman, in the 1950s, took 'role' and 'actor' in the stage sense of the words, and showed society as a pattern of performances. As compared with the way in which it had hitherto been treated, role for Goffman was much more a matter of play-acting. Parts could be changed and—an issue much discussed by Goffman—faked. (Dennis, 1989:429)

As I discuss in Chapter 7, this ability to fake roles and to perform gender is an influential strand in current debates on gender and sexuality.

Power

The theories of Foucault have also been influential because of his analysis of power as constitutive of social relations and intimately connected with every aspect of social life, even the construction of the self. Furthermore power may not only be oppressive, it may also be constitutive of pleasure. Thus feminist sociologists have studied sexuality and the dynamics of power relations in the kindling of desire (see especially Chapter 7). This conception of power enables an understanding of women's active involvement in power relations which subordinate them. Power, rather than being seen as something which is exercised over you, is seen as a set of relations in which we are all implicated. Power is not located in one place any more than another but is ubiquitous. As Barrett puts it:

[Foucault] developed a concept of power that did not locate it in agencies (whether the state, individuals, economic forces etc) but saw it in terms of 'micro' operations of power and by means of strategies and technologies of power. (Barrett, 1991:134)

This means that resistance to power is possible, not only through organizing to confront the might of the state, but also in daily interaction and in intimate relations. Indeed, according to Foucault, wherever power exists there also is resistance.

Foucault and feminism come together in the idea that power exists not only at an institutional level but also within daily lives. This has been an axiomatic tenet of feminism since the early days of second-wave feminism and was pointed to by the slogan 'the personal is political' and it may partly explain the attraction of Foucault's theories (Ramazanoglu, 1993). But it has also been highly problematic for feminists because of its apparent denial of any extra-discursive, material reality in which power is based; many feminists therefore distance themselves from Foucault's theorizations. Hartsock for instance argues that his theory of power is dangerous for feminism as a political project because 'systematic power relations ultimately vanish in his work' (Hartsock, 1990:168). She continues:

Domination is not a part of this image; rather, the image of a network in which we all participate carries implications of equality and agency rather than the systematic domination of the many by the few. (Hartsock, 1990:169)

This way of conceptualizing power informs much research on masculinities and I explore it further in Chapters 5 and 6.

Critique of materialism

Poststructuralism also involves a 'critique of materialism' which makes it problematic for many sociologists and feminists (Barrett, 1992:208). Indeed, the influence of poststructuralism within sociology highlights the existence of two 'traditions' within social thought.

Materialist assumptions . . . are common in the social sciences, and flourish particularly in the notion of a determining 'social structure' on which culture and beliefs, as well as subjectivity and agency, rest. Nevertheless, there has long been what one might regard as an alternative tradition within social theory, emphasizing experience and attempting to understand society without the aid of a social structural model. (Barrett, 1992:209)

It is this 'alternative tradition' in which poststructuralism is located together with the phenomenology and ethnomethodology of an earlier period which came under attack in the 1970s precisely for failing to locate social interaction in its wider social context. It had

no explicit conceptualisation of the supra-situational, of social structure or culture, as societal phenomena, even less of inter-societal cross-cultural or world-systemic relations . . . To work with a social theory that . . . has no concept of society . . . makes it impossible to produce a sociology which can answer to most of the major problems of understanding social life. (Worsley, 1974:9, cited in Allen and Leonard, 1994:27–8)

Similar criticisms have been mounted of poststructuralism and postmodernism, particularly from within sociology (see e.g. Allen and Leonard, 1994). Such criticisms illustrate the continuing importance of materialist approaches to the study of gender and their focus on social structure and systemic power relations as well as culture and human agency.

Many sociologists of gender have continued to concern themselves with divisions of labour as well as gender identities and subjectivities even in the midst of the 'cultural turn'. They have explored the ways in which women and men, as gendered beings, actively constitute and reconstitute the social relations within which they live. They are concerned with the relation between structure and agency, or individual and society, which is central to sociology. They also provide examples of the continuing vitality of materialist analyses of gender relations within sociology. Indeed, although such analysis has been eclipsed throughout the 1980s and 1990s, and has led to statements about the younger generation of feminist sociologists having cut their theoretical teeth in a 'post-Marxist era' and as being 'more interested in sexuality than in employment' (Roseneil, 1995b:202), there is also evidence that the shift from things to words is far from universal and that a concern with the materiality of gender relations is still central for feminist sociologists. At the beginning of the twenty-first century, however, the way the material is conceptualized is being transformed, a transformation that was called for more than twenty years ago (Stacey, 1981; Pollert, 1996; Glucksmann, 1995). This can be interpreted as the beginnings of the incorporation of gender into the way society and the social are conceptualized whereas, hitherto, although women as well as men have been studied and new areas of study have been opened up by the problematizing of gender, gender remained marginal to the core theoretical concerns of the discipline (Allen and Leonard, 1994; Maynard, 1990; Oakley, 1989). This reconceptualization involves a return to structure and a theorization of the relation between agency, structure, and culture (Halford et al., 1997).

Reconstruction and social practice

After the deconstructivism of poststructuralism there is a sense in which the study of gender is being joined up again. The three elements of studying gender identified above—structure, culture, and agency—are brought together in order to understand the ways in which social actors, engaged in the practices of daily life, are constrained by social structures which they themselves through their social practices reinforce or transform. This theoretical position can be seen as a product of middle range theory which pays attention to the ways in which gendered power relations constitute the way in which people interact.

This way of theorizing gender has emerged from a critique of what has been termed the mechanistic materialism of earlier approaches which tried to understand gender relations in terms of a non-gendered concept of the economy. Thus Marxist feminism ground to a halt when it theorized gender relations as arising from culture and/or ideology rather than being a constitutive part of the economic basis of society and was swallowed up in the 'cultural turn' (Adkins and Leonard, 1996), while theorizing gender, but not sex, as socially constructed left the door open for biologistic and naturalistic explanations to infiltrate any attempt at a materialist analysis of gender.

The 1990s saw the re-emergence of theorizations of gender which bring these three areas together in a materialist way. One dimension of this is that the split between gender and sex, between culture and nature, has been superseded and there has been a strong case made that hierarchical relations between women and men are structured by gender and heterosexuality and that sex is therefore fundamentally social. This case has been put most consistently by French materialist feminists but can also, in a different form, be seen in the work of Judith Butler which I discuss in Chapter 7. It is also apparent in attempts to transcend the public–private or production–reproduction split in theorizations of work (Pollert, 1996; Glucksmann, 1995) and in feminist appropriations of Bourdieu's theories of cultural reproduction (Moi, 1991; McCall, 1992; Gottfried, 1998).

Sex and gender

French materialist feminists have long argued that sex, as well as gender, is socially constructed: an argument which has only recently become influential in Britain (Allen and Leonard, 1994). Thus Delphy asks us to consider whether or not gender precedes rather than being based on sex. Perhaps it is the case that

sex . . . simply marks social division; that it serves to allow social recognition and identification of those who are dominants and those who are dominated. That is, that sex is a sign, but that since it does not distinguish just any old thing from anything else, and does not distinguish equivalent things but rather important and unequal things, it has historically acquired a symbolic value. (Delphy, 1996:35)

Sex is therefore 'the sign that marks out the dominants from the dominated' (Delphy, 1996:35). Furthermore both gender and sex may be social in so far as sex refers to 'the way a given society represents "biology" to itself' (Delphy, 1996:36). Delphy goes on to argue that gender difference is constituted by hierarchy, thus the elimination of gender hierarchy involves the disappearance of gender. This disappearance is, however, seen as problematic by feminists who attach value to women's 'nature' and their special capacities for caring and nurturing. But as she pointedly comments:

we might well ask how women who are 'nurturing' and proud of it are going to become the equals of unchanged men—who are going to continue to drain these women's time? (Delphy, 1996:38)

And she adds that 'if women were the equals of men, men would no longer equal themselves' (Delphy, 1996:39).

Anthropologists have also asked us to imagine societies without gender, as have some recent theorists of masculinity (Cucchiari, 1981; MacInnes, 1998). This is, however, difficult and it has been suggested that our attachment to gender arises from a fundamental confusion between gender and biological reproduction (MacInnes, 1998). As Delphy puts it:

commonsense and academic theories of sexuality . . . involve a double confusion: a confusion of anatomical sex with sexuality, and of sexuality with procreation. (Delphy, 1996:40)

A way out of this confusion has been provided for some theorists of gender by Pierre Bourdieu, for whom 'the sexual division of human beings into two fundamental categories is a thoroughly arbitrary cultural construction' (Moi, 1991:1030). Toril Moi argues that,

Bourdieu's analysis does not lose sight of the fact that if women are socially constructed as women, that means that they are women. Or to put it in terms of current theoretical debates within feminism: sexual differences are neither essences nor simple signifiers, neither a matter of realism nor of nominalism, but a matter of social practice. (Moi, 1991:1034)

Social practice

In the 1980s some feminist sociologists used Bourdieu's theory of social practice to understand the way food practices within families, for instance, 'symbolised, reinforced and reproduced' social relations of gender and class (Charles and Kerr, 1988:2). This type of approach also characterizes Cynthia Cockburn's analysis of the printing industry where she demonstrates that patriarchy, or the sex-gender system, both is a product of the interaction between gendered social actors and reacts back on them, setting limits to their actions (Cockburn, 1983; Gottfried, 1998). She also explores the way in which gender identities are dependent on the continued existence of particular material social relations rather than (or as well as) being defined discursively (Cockburn, 1983). The masculinity of the print workers, for instance, depended upon their involvement with dirty, noisy machinery which they could control. Computer technology threatened to undermine their masculinity hence making changes in gender relations and identities a real possibility. In this situation the men could choose either to reinforce those relations that supported a sexist, racist masculinity or to undermine them (see Chapter 2 for a fuller discussion of this study). In this way Cockburn demonstrates that, within specific sociohistorical circumstances, human agency has an effectivity through social practice. Anne Witz adopts a similar position in her analysis of professional formation in health care. She argues that women's and men's access to resources, of whatever kind, are systematically structured to advantage men and disadvantage women. This has historically enabled men to exclude women from the more desirable jobs (Witz, 1992). Men act so as to maintain these advantages, the structures have no existence apart from the social actors through which they are constituted. Indeed it could be argued that Bourdieu provides a materialist alternative to Foucault, focusing as he does on the way dispositions are a product of practice and how these dispositions predispose people to maintain social relations and structures as they are and as they have become familiar to them. Haug et al.'s analysis of the way female bodies are sexualized, which I discuss in Chapter 7, is an example of this way of theorizing the reproduction of gendered and sexualized relations of power. A gendered habitus is produced by and through the body: it is very much an aspect of material social relations. This is expressed clearly by Toril Moi:

To produce a gender habitus requires an extremely elaborate process of education . . . an important aspect of this process is the inscription of social power relations on the body: our habitus is at once produced and expressed through our movements, gestures, facial expressions, manners, ways of walking, and ways of looking at the world. The socially produced body is thus necessarily also a political body, or rather an embodied politics. Thus even such basic activities as teaching children how to move, dress, and eat are thoroughly political, in that they impose on them an unspoken understanding of legitimate ways to (re)present their body to themselves and others. (Moi, 1991:1030–1)

Cultural capital

Bourdieu's notion of cultural capital is also significant for theorizing gender and has been used to explain the greater success of men in being selected for political representation (see Chapter 8). Thus Moi argues that while those who are 'from disadvantaged groups require all the educational capital they can obtain if they are to advance in society', those who are from more privileged backgrounds 'can get further on less educational capital' because 'they have access to large amounts of other kinds of capital' (Moi, 1991:1024). Bourdieu uses this theorization to explain the persistence of class inequalities in education, those from more privileged social groups beginning with a considerable advantage because of the cultural and social capital to which they have access. This analysis can also be applied to gender. Thus being female is associated with negative capital as is being working class. Such a theorization may help to explain the fact that the same qualifications have different outcomes for women and men. At every level of the occupational hierarchy, for instance, women are better qualified than their male counterparts (Marshall et al., 1989). It also suggests that relatively better educational achievement for girls than boys will not necessarily mean that the gendering of paid employment is going to be transformed in women's favour. However, even if being female is associated with negative capital, this can be countered by access to high amounts of social or cultural capital (Moi, 1991:1038). Thus class privilege, connections with a privileged man, or high levels of educational achievement can cancel out the negative capital associated with being a woman. This sort of theorization allows for the effects of gender not being predetermined but being seen as an outcome of social practice; it also operates in combination with other dimensions of social reality which have implications for access to cultural capital such as ethnicity and class.

Bourdieu is also significant because of his concern with the 'struggle over scientific truth', which he defines as a struggle grounded in politics and ethics rather than epistemology (McCall, 1992:855). In common with many feminists he argues that reflexivity is an essential component of the sociological enter-prise. This reflexivity is a component of what Leslie McCall has called 'feminist habitus'; a disposition which enables feminist sociologists 'to reconstruct questions relevant to the lives of women and which challenge the gender order of social life' (McCall, 1992:859). Such a habitus or disposition is, arguably, what permits the construction of 'alternative visions' which were part of second-wave feminism and which led to the epistemological shifts which are an important outcome of social movements (Eyerman and Jamison, 1991). Recon-ceptualizations of the social world as fundamentally gendered can be seen as an outcome of these 'alternative visions' and are apparent in some of the more recent studies I discuss in the chapters that follow (see e.g. Adkins, 1995; Dunne, 1997; Adkins and Lury, 1994; Skeggs, 1997).

Sociology and gender

Sociological theorizations of gender at the beginning of the twenty-first cen-tury are therefore marked by a tension between materialist and idealist theor-ies and between those which take gendered power as fundamental to gender relations and those which focus simply on difference. Within sociology there is a reluctance to embrace the higher flights of poststructuralism and postmodern-ism and a continuing attempt to integrate the theorization of structure with practice. In what follows there are many examples of sociological studies of gender which theorize 'big structures from small acts . . . [and] . . . direct atten-tion to the efficacy of agency as well as structure' (Gottfried, 1998:455–6) and which operate in the middle range of theory (Maynard, 1990). We are only just beginning, however, to see attempts at reconceptualizing such fundamental categories of sociological analysis as class, work, and the state (Glucksmann, 1995; Charles, 2000) and sociological theory remains unreceptive to feminism (Allen and Leonard, 1994:23; Oakley, 1989). Thus, although the study of gender has been profoundly influenced by theoretical developments and shifts within and outside sociology, recognition of the consequences of taking gender ser-iously has been more significant at the empirical than the theoretical level. This is demonstrated by the fact that 'grand' sociological theory has to be critiqued by feminist sociologists before it can incorporate gender and in the gendering of theoretical production which remains overwhelmingly male; women are more likely to be engaged in the production of middle-range theory embedded in sociological research.

In the chapters that follow I describe changes in gender relations since the Second World War and then discuss how sociologists have studied these changes. Throughout I am concerned to highlight the way different theorizations of gender have influenced not only how gender is studied but also what aspects of gender are seen as important. For most of the book I concentrate on Britain but in the final chapter I attempt to put gender in Britain in a global context.

Chapter 2

Gender at Work

S INCE the Second World War there have been significant changes in the British economy which have had an impact on gender divisions of paid employment. In the immediate post-war years there was an expansion of the welfare state and the service sector and an increase in the availability of part-time employment. Latterly, with the decline of heavy industry, working-class jobs for men are disappearing from many areas while the continuing expansion of services is associated with increasing numbers of jobs for women. In this chapter I look briefly at changes in the British economy and how they have affected gendered patterns of employment in the second half of the twentieth century (fuller accounts can be found in Crompton, 1997; Pilcher, 1999; Walby, 1997). I then discuss the way sociological research and explanation have developed in response both to these changes and to the conceptual shifts outlined in Chapter 1.

Economic change and gender

After the Second World War the British economy experienced a situation of labour shortage. The newly established welfare state, together with the expanding service sector of the economy, led to an increase in the number of jobs available. This meant that government and employers had to look for new sources of labour which they identified as married women and Commonwealth immigrants (women and men). Attempts were made to attract married women into the workforce through the provision of part-time work while, in order to attract immigrants from the Commonwealth, the Ministry of Labour launched recruitment campaigns (Bhavnani, 1994:20). This phase of economic expansion and growth was marked by full male employment and an expectation that men would be in full-time paid employment from leaving full-time education until retirement. Although female employment was increasing, married women were expected to be financially dependent on their husbands and have no need to participate in paid employment. This reflects the assumption that men were the providers and women were their dependants: whether or not they also took up paid work outside the home was a matter of choice.

During the 1950s and 1960s the economy continued to expand but by the 1970s this situation was beginning to change; unemployment started to rise and the decline in heavy industry, which had been going on since the early years of the century, gathered pace. Coupled with this there was a move away from mass production to more flexible forms of production, a move which has been theorized as a move from Fordism to post-Fordism and which is marked by increasing levels of job insecurity and non-standard employment (i.e. part-time, temporary, casual work and self-employment). It has been argued that we are experiencing a shift from an industrial to a postindustrial society and that these new forms of work are part of this societal transformation. However, what concerns us here is the gender dimension of these changes and how women and men of different class and ethnic groups and with different sexual identities and orientations experience them.

The most immediate difference in experience between women and men is that traditional areas of male employment have been in decline for much of the post-war period while female areas of employment have been expanding. Thus agriculture and much heavy industry, such as coal mining and steel production, have suffered a catastrophic decline as have manufacturing industries, such as metal manufacturing and textiles (Wilson, 1994); these were the industries where full-time employment was the norm. In contrast, the service sector of the economy, initially health and education and later retail, banking and other financial services, and the leisure industry, have been expanding and have pioneered a variety of non-standard forms of employment and the '24-hour economy' (Glucksmann, 1998). It is these sectors of the economy where women are concentrated and which underpin the increased levels of women's economic activity. These developments mean that women's economic activity rates are increasing while men's are decreasing; indeed in September 1996 the number of women in employment exceeded the number of men for the first time (11.248 million women compared with 11.236 men) (*Guardian*, 30 December 1999; Wilson 1994: 19, 20). This was hailed as the 'feminisation of employment' by the media but, less dramatically, is to be expected given the trends in women's and men's employment since the 1950s and the structural changes in the economy. Thus in 1959 women constituted 34.1 per cent of all employees while in 1995 the figure was 49.6 per cent, or almost 50 per cent (Walby, 1997:27, table 2.1).

Changes in women's and men's economic activity rates have resulted in a more or less equal gender balance in the workforce. There is, however, considerable debate as to its significance given the fact that almost all the increase in women's economic activity rates can be accounted for by the increase in part-time employment amongst married women (Hakim, 1995). Thus, between 1971 and 1995 the percentage increase in women full-time workers was 3 per cent while the percentage increase in women part-time workers was 75 per cent (Walby, 1997:31–2). As Catherine Hakim has controversially argued, increased economic activity rates amongst women do not represent an increase in the volume of female employment but rather a switch from full-time to part-time employment. She is no doubt right to point to the expansion of part-time working and the erosion of full-time jobs by non-standard forms of employment; but whether this justifies a denial of the significance of women's increased economic activity rates, whether on a full- or part-time basis, is a moot point (see e.g. Ginn et al., 1996; Bruegel, 1996; Walby, 1997:34; Crompton and Harris, 1998). Male part-time work has also increased but much more slowly—11 per cent of male workers were working part time in 1994—and part-time working amongst men is concentrated amongst younger and older workers and is higher for ethnic minority men than for white men (Bhavnani, 1994:51), the highest rates being found amongst Bangladeshi and Pakistani men.

Economic activity and hours of work

Women's and men's economic activity rates are affected by factors such as class, ethnicity, and responsibilities for caring and domestic work. If we look at ethnicity, for instance, data from the 1991 census show that 88.7 per cent of white men of working age were economically active compared with 80.2 per cent of men in minority ethnic groups. In contrast it was Afro-Caribbean women who had the highest economic activity rates while the lowest were found amongst Pakistani and, particularly, Bangladeshi women (Bhavnani, 1994:47, 48, table 5.1; Modood et al., 1997:85, 87).

Ethnicity also affects hours of work. Thus, the propensity to work part time is a peculiarly white phenomenon and, crucially, depends on the presence of a partner who is in full-time employment (see Chapter 3). Thus, while the 1991 census showed that a little over a third (37.1 per cent) of white women in employment were working part time, the figure for ethnic minority women was lower (21.7 per cent). Conversely, a lower proportion (56.3 per cent) of white women than ethnic minority women (69.8 per cent) in employment were working full time (Bhavnani, 1994: 49).

Hours of work are also affected by caring responsibilities. Thus, on the birth of a child, mothers who are partnered by men are likely to withdraw from the workforce for a longer or shorter period of time while fathers increase the hours they work, either doing more overtime to keep the household income at the level it was before and to compensate for their partner's withdrawal from the workforce, or putting in more hours to further their career and promotion prospects thereby increasing their earnings. In contrast lone mothers, unless they are in relatively highly paid jobs, are likely to withdraw from the work- force and rely on state benefits for support and, in the 1990s, they were half as likely as married mothers to be in paid employment (McRae, 1999a:15; see also Chapter 4). There is therefore variation in the nature of women's and men's participation in the workforce which relates to class, ethnicity, their responsi- bility for children or other dependants, and whether they are in a heterosexual partnership (Dunne, 1997; Siltanen, 1994). The relation between paid work and caring responsibilities is discussed in more detail in Chapter 4 while the impact of institutionalized heterosexuality on paid employment is explored later in this chapter and in Chapter 3.

Gender segregation

There have been several important large-scale studies of gender segregation in the workforce since the Second World War, all of which show that women and men are concentrated in different industries and that within the same industry women are over-represented in the least-skilled and lowest-paid jobs (Hunt, 1968; Martin and Roberts, 1984; Scott, 1994). Indeed, in 1991 over half of all women in employment were working in routine non-manual jobs such as sec- retarial, clerical, and personal service work (Wilson, 1994:25). In contrast, men were more evenly spread throughout the occupational structure but were over- represented at the top of the occupational hierarchy (as managers and profes- sionals) and in skilled manual occupations (Wilson, 1994:26). There is some variation if ethnicity is taken into consideration with white men being more likely than men from any other ethnic group to be employers and managers of large establishments, Caribbean men being least likely to be in the top category of professionals, managers, and employers, and Bangladeshi men being over- represented in semi-skilled manual work (Modood et al., 1997:100–1). This can be seen in Table 2.1.

The variation amongst women is less, with over half of working women in all ethnic groups being in intermediate or junior non-manual work. As Modood et al. note, 'This reflects the economy-wide concentration of women in clerical/ secretarial and sales occupations' (Modood et al., 1997:104). Thus women are

Table 2.1 Job levels of men and women by ethnicity

Women (base: female employees and self-employed)

(column percentages)

Socio-economic group	White	Caribbean	Indian	African Asian	Pakistani	Chinese
Professional, managerial, and employers	16 (15)[1]	5 (5)	11 (7)	12 (10)	12 (6)	30 (25)
Intermediate non-manual	21	28	14	14	29	23
Junior non-manual	33	36	33	49	23	23
Skilled manual and foreman	7 (2)	4 (2)	11 (3)	7 (3)	9 (3)	13 (—)
Semi-skilled manual	18	20	27	16	22	9
Unskilled manual	4	6	4	1	4	2
Armed forces/inadequately described/not stated	0	1	1	1	0	0
Non-manual	70	69	58	75	64	76
Manual	29	30	42	24	35	24
Weighted count	734	452	275	196	60	120
Unweighted count	696	336	260	164	64	63

[1] The figures in parentheses exclude the self-employed.

Men (base: male employees and self-employed)

(column percentages)

Socio-economic group	White	Caribbean	Indian	African Asian	Pakistani	Bangladeshi	Chinese
Professional managers, and employers	30	14	25	30	19	18	46
Employers and managers (large establishments)	11	5	5	3	3	0	6
Employers and managers (small establishments)	11	4	11	14	12	16	23
Professional workers	8	6	9	14	4	2	17
Intermediate and junior non-manual	18	19	20	24	13	19	17
Skilled manual and foreman	36	39	31	30	46	7	14
Semi-skilled manual	11	22	16	12	18	53	12
Unskilled manual	3	6	5	2	3	3	5
Armed forces or N/A	2	0	3	2	2	0	5
Non manual	48	33	45	54	32	37	63
Manual	50	67	52	44	67	63	31
Weighted count	789	365	349	296	182	61	127
Unweighted count	713	258	356	264	258	112	71

Source: Modood et al., 1997: tables 4.10 and 4.12, pp. 100, 102. Reproduced with the kind permission of the Policy Studies Institute, London.

under-represented in the most powerful positions at the top of occupational hierarchies and in skilled, working-class jobs, and are concentrated in a much narrower range of occupations than are men (Marshall et al., 1989).

This vertical segregation goes hand in hand with horizontal segregation. The Social Change and Economic Life Initiative (SCELI), for instance, found that men were twice as likely as women to work in highly segregated jobs and half as likely to work in unsegregated jobs. A high degree of segregation for men was associated with highly skilled manual work (fitters, plumbers, carpenters) while for women it was associated with manual work (packing, sales) and low-skilled, non-manual work (clerical) (Scott, 1994). A recent study shows that 93 per cent of secretaries, personal assistants, and typists are women compared with 61 per cent of teaching professionals (Grimshaw and Rubery, 2001:5). This suggests the existence of clear gender boundaries in manual and relatively low-skilled, non-manual work which contrasts with more permeable boundaries in some middle-class jobs. Indeed, the only area where women are making inroads into 'mainly men's' jobs is the professions. Thus 37 per cent of professional women work in 'mainly men's' jobs compared with 5–6 per cent of women in most other occupational groups and between 1981 and 1996 'almost 70% of the 450,000 professional jobs created … have gone to women' (Scott, 1994; *Guardian*, 30 December 1999). However, although women now constitute almost 50 per cent of the economically active population and have increased their representation in the professions, they have not been so successful in entering the corporate world of management (Rees, 1999:37; Wajcman, 1998). Moreover, the SCELI research found that gender segregation was higher in the private manufacturing sector than in private or public services; manufacturing is precisely the area of production that, with the exception of food and textiles, has been historically heavily male dominated. Thus:

for men the most highly segregated industries are construction, energy and water, extractive, engineering and transport industries, and the least segregated are distribution, hotels and catering, banking, and other services. Women are less segregated than men in all industries, most of them being in moderately segregated jobs. Distribution, hotels and catering is the only industry where significant numbers of women are in mixed jobs. (Scott, 1994:12)

It seems, therefore, that gender segregation is more marked in some sectors of the economy than others and that these tend to be where so-called traditional working-class jobs are found and where men predominate.

Ethnicity and gender segregation

Ethnicity also affects the distribution of women and men between industries. Thus about a third of white, Caribbean, Indian, and African Asian men work in manufacturing industries but a higher proportion of Pakistani men and a lower proportion of Bangladeshi and Chinese men work in these industries (Modood et al., 1997). Reena Bhavnani comments that

Black people as a whole are likely to be over represented in particular industrial sectors by ethnicity, so for example, African-Asians, Indians and Pakistanis are over represented in the retail distribution sector, Chinese in hotels and catering, Pakistanis in transport and communications and Afro Caribbeans and Africans in health care and other services. (Bhavnani, 1994:72)

This distribution is shown in Table 2.2.

These patterns of industrial segregation partly reflect recruitment drives in the 1950s and the needs of the economy when different waves of migration took place. Thus recruitment in the Caribbean was aimed at finding transport, hotel, factory, and nursing staff and—significantly—domestic workers (Phizacklea, 1983). Many of those recruited were skilled and semi-skilled workers and women and men migrated separately as well as together (Bhavnani, 1994:18; Paterson, 1963). In contrast, migrants from South Asia tended to be men and to come from rural areas; they were recruited for work in metal manufacturing and engineering (Phizacklea, 1988:29) and it was not until later that women came to join their husbands as their dependents. As Bhavnani comments, 'the needs of the economy have been critical in the arrival of black people, pushing them into segregated patterns in the labour market' (Bhavnani, 1994:19–20). Migrant workers filled the jobs that white workers no longer wanted, such as work in the metal trades in the black country (Phizacklea, 1988; Brooks, 1975) and work in the textile industry of the north-west and north-east (Modood et al., 1997:184–5). They also developed 'ethnic enterprises' in the garment industry in London's East End (Shah, 1975). As a result the decline of manufacturing in the 1970s and early 1980s, particularly textiles and heavy engineering, hit some ethnic minority groups much harder than others. For instance, Pakistanis and Bangladeshis have experienced relatively high rates of unemployment because of their concentration in the textile industry in the Midlands and the North of England (Modood et al., 1997: 146).

Table 2.2 Employment by industry and ethnic origin, 1989–1991

	Men		Women	
	White	Ethnic minority groups	White	Ethnic minority groups
All industries: overall nos (000s)	13,276	580	10,600	393
				Per cent
Agriculture, forestry, fishing	3	–	1	–
Energy and water supply	3	–	1	–
Extraction of minerals, metal manufacture, etc.	4	3	2	–
Metal goods, engineering, and vehicles	14	13	5	6
Other manufacturing, of which:	10	11	8	11
Footwear, clothing, and leather goods	1	2	2	5
Construction	13	5	2	–
Distribution, hotels, catering, and repairs, of which:	16	30	25	24
Wholesale distribution	4	3	3	3
Retail distribution	8	15	15	15
Hotels and catering	2	9	7	7
Transport and communications, of which:	8	11	3	5
Postal services and communications	2	4	1	–
Banking and finance, etc., of which:	10	10	13	12
Business services	6	6	6	6
Other services, of which:	18	17	41	40
Public administration, national defence, etc.	6	4	6	6
Education	4	3	11	6
Medical/health/veterinary services	2	5	9	15
Other services to the public	2	3	11	10

Source: Labour Force Surveys 1989–1991; House of Commons Hansard, 21 May 1992, cols 248–50 (Amin and Oppenhein, 1992: 10) (Bhavnani, 1994: table 7.1, p. 72). Parliamentary copyright material from Hansard is reproduced with the permission of the Controller of Her Majesty's Stationery Office on behalf of Parliament.

Notes:
These figures exclude those on government employment and training schemes.
— indicates less than 10,000 in sample; estimate not shown.
The totals include those who did not specify industry.
'Other public services' comprises all other public services excluding sanitary, research and development, recreational and domestic services.
Percentages do not add up to 100 because of rounding.

Unequal pay

The Equal Opportunities Commission and the Labour government are exercised by the continuing existence of a 20 per cent wages gap between women
and men in Britain even though the Equal Pay Act was passed in 1970. The
'gender pay gap' is 82 per cent for full-time workers; this means that women
in full-time employment earn 82 per cent of the 'average pay for all male full-
time employees' (Grimshaw and Rubery, 2001: 3). The gap is greater if weekly
as opposed to hourly earnings are compared (due to men's propensity to work
longer hours than women) and if non-manual rather than manual rates are
compared. Similarly part-time women workers earn 60 per cent of men's full-
time hourly rates and 74 per cent of women's (Grimshaw and Rubery, 2001:3;
Walby, 1997:32–3). This is largely due to the fact that women working part time
are concentrated at lower levels of the occupational hierarchy in 'women's
work' and most high-status (and therefore highly paid) jobs are not associated
with part-time hours of work. Similarly there are differences in the hours
worked by women and men, with aggregate figures showing that men work
longer hours than women at all levels of the occupational hierarchy.

If full-time employment is considered, the gender pay gap advantages men of
almost all ethnic groups in relation to women. Thus, with the exception of
Pakistani and Bangladeshi men, all men in full-time employment have a higher
mean weekly wage than all women in full-time employment (Modood et al.,
1997:113, 114; cf. Higginbotham, 1997: xxvii for similar findings in the USA).
Conversely, there is less variation in pay amongst women of different ethnic
groups than amongst men and the biggest gap in pay is between white women
and white men; indeed, amongst women in full-time employment, white
women earn on average less than women in other ethnic groups with the
exception of Pakistani and Bangladeshi women (this holds true when hours
worked are taken into consideration). In addition, ethnic minority men in
manual occupations earn more than their white counterparts (Modood et al.,
1997:118). It is now only Bangladeshi men who 'have lower weekly earnings
than other men of the same age with similar qualifications, social class, family
circumstances and local labour market conditions' (Modood et al., 1997:117).
Similar processes seem to be occurring amongst women (Modood et al.,
1997:120). Clearly gender and ethnicity interact in complex ways to influence the
relative pay of different groups of workers although, on almost all dimensions,
Pakistani and Bangladeshi women and men come off worst.

Informal economic activity

Some argue that the employment situation facing ethnic minority women and men in Britain is improving in so far as they are increasingly to be found in jobs which reflect their qualifications (Modood et al., 1997:142). This is controversial, however, because it focuses only on those who are already engaged in the formal economy and employed full time. Others argue that ethnic minorities are concentrated in the worst-paying and least-skilled sectors of the workforce and are over-represented amongst the un- and under-employed. This interpretation is supported by the high rates of unemployment to be found amongst ethnic minorities. Thus Bangladeshi and Pakistani men have unemployment rates of 42 per cent and 38 per cent while the rate for Caribbean men is 31 per cent which is double that of white men (Modood et al., 1997:89). Low rates of employment amongst Pakistani and Bangladeshi women have been linked to their poor prospects in the formal economy and the discrimination they face. Indeed, self-employment (amongst men) and homeworking (amongst women) have been seen as responses, on the part of the ethnic minority population, to racism within the labour market (Bhachu, 1988).

Self-employment is more common amongst men than women and is highest amongst Indian, Pakistani, African Asian, and Chinese men and lowest amongst Caribbean men; white and Bangladeshi men are in an intermediate position. In all ethnic groups women are less likely to be self-employed than are men and when they are it is 'directly related to male self-employment' so they may be working in family enterprises and/or at home (Modood et al., 1997:123). It is ethnic minority women who are over-represented in homeworking, which is characterized by low rates of pay and irregularity (Felstead and Jewson, 2000:77–80). Many homeworkers do not know who they are working for, having contact only with the driver who delivers the raw materials and collects the finished product. There is considerable disagreement about the extent of homeworking and whether it is particularly prevalent amongst ethnic minority women. Thus Catherine Hakim's findings, which suggest that it is not (Hakim, 1987a, 1987b), are sharply contested by other researchers who argue that ethnic minority women are very unlikely to declare themselves as homeworkers to unknown researchers and that this leads to underenumeration in large-scale surveys. Thus even in the recent Policy Studies Institute study the proportion of homeworking amongst Pakistani and Bangladeshi women was not found to be high (Modood et al., 1997). This is a perennial problem in researching homeworking as much of it is of dubious legality and those who are engaged in it are amongst the most vulnerable of workers (see e.g. Brown, 1974).

Thus although formal economic activity rates are low, there is considerable evidence that Pakistani and Bangladeshi women are involved in economic activities which could be classed as informal and which would not necessarily be recorded in official surveys, such as homeworking and working in the so-called ethnic economy as family labour (Shah, 1975; Saifullah Khan, 1979; Phizacklea, 1990; Phizacklea, 1988; Phizacklea and Wolkowitz, 1995). Such economic activity can take place within the domestic sphere, thus facilitating adherence to cultural norms of seclusion practised amongst first-generation Asian Muslims at the same time as enabling women to make a financial contribution to their households (Modood et al., 1997:87).

Gender ideologies

Along with changing patterns of employment and women's increasing participation in the workforce have gone changes in attitudes towards women's, particularly maternal, employment. Here there is a major generational gulf with older generations adopting much more conservative attitudes, adhering to notions of the male breadwinner and female dependent family, while younger age groups are more inclined to adopt egalitarian gender ideologies. There are also important class variations and variations between different ethnic groups. Thus, more traditional attitudes towards gender roles within the family have been noted amongst Asians and, particularly, in Muslim households although here also there are generational differences, with younger generations in all ethnic groups demonstrating tendencies towards egalitarian gender ideologies (see Chapter 3; Scott et al., 1996).

Despite changing attitudes towards women's employment and the decline of male breadwinner ideologies, jobs are still seen as gendered. Thus 'men's' jobs are heavy, dirty, dangerous, involving outdoor work, and are associated with qualities such as aggression, ambition, an ability to exerise authority and cope with stress, a natural affinity with machines, and superior intelligence. In addition men's work tends to be more highly valued than women's (Scott, 1994; Martin and Roberts, 1984; Wajcman, 1998; Savage, 1992; Cockburn, 1983). 'Women's' jobs, in contrast, are associated with low pay, are boring, low grade, low status, involve subservience, and are jobs that men would not want to do. They are associated with 'feminine' qualities of caring, being good with people, and dexterity. There is a 'naturalistic gender ideology' underpinning these attitudes which 'identifies masculinity with physical strength, dirt and danger, and femininity with caring qualities and drudgery' (Scott, 1994:21). This ideology legitimates gender divisions in the paid workforce and, despite the considerable changes in women's employment, is still very widespread. It suggests that although there is now a gender balance in the paid workforce and women as well as men are expected to earn a living, gender segregation is more resistant to change and, as we shall see, it is the social processes which reinforce this segregation that have become the focus of research.

Studying gender at work

Changing gender divisions of paid work and the emergence of second-wave feminism have both influenced the way gender at work has been studied. In the early post-war years, when part-time employment for married women was increasing, studies explored 'women's two roles' and the problems associated with attempting to combine paid employment with domestic work (Myrdal and Klein, 1956; Jephcott, Seear, and Smith, 1962). It was assumed that women's primary commitment was to their families and paid work had to fit in around these prior obligations. Thus women, in government policy and in sociological studies, were defined first and foremost as wives and mothers. It was men who were the ideal typical workers and, in the 1950s and 1960s industrial sociology focused on them. Marxist-inspired studies explored class relations in factories and communities and investigated the extent to which increasing affluence was leading to the embourgeoisement of certain sectors of the working class (Goldthorpe et al., 1968). Interviews were with workers (male) and, possibly, their wives, but explorations of class consciousness and working practices which gave workers control in an alienating and exploitative environment were explorations of men and class relations between men (Beynon, 1975). The sociology of work was dominated by studies of industrial workers, the theoretical issues under exploration were those of class, and class relations were implicitly understood as relations between men: women as workers either remained invisible or were defined in terms of their familial roles. Studies of ethnic minority workers, although few and far between, included women as well as men but were located in the context of race relations rather than industrial sociology and a structural-functionalist rather than a Marxist theoretical paradigm (Paterson, 1963, 1968).

In the 1970s and early 1980s, with the growing influence of feminism within sociology, studies of women as workers replicated the industrial sociology tradition of studying workers in factories and exploring class relations, although now there was concern to understand the way gender and women's 'fractured identities' shaped their class consciousness (see e.g. Pollert, 1981; Cavendish, 1982; Hunt, 1980). These studies showed how women's attachment to paid employment was shaped by their expectations of marriage and how viewing their jobs as temporary interludes between school and marriage/ motherhood meant that they had a different relationship to work from their male peers. Very few studies explored race and ethnicity as well as gender and class (a notable exception is Sallie Westwood's ethnographic study of a textile factory (Westwood, 1985)) although homeworking amongst Asian women and their participation in the so-called ethnic economy attracted some attention (Saifullah Khan, 1979; Shah, 1975).

Gendered boundaries and skilled work

In the 1980s attention turned to the ways in which gender segregation was maintained despite the advent of equal pay and sex discrimination legislation which, supposedly, gave women equality at work. Studies of women in areas of work where they were in fact concentrated—such as secretarial and clerical work—began to address the ways in which sexuality operates at work and how gendered boundaries are maintained within the workforce (Pringle, 1989; Walby, 1986; Witz, 1992; Cockburn, 1983). These studies explore the way the gendering of jobs and gender divisions of paid work are associated with particular gender identities and how social actors on an individual and collective basis organize to preserve or challenge these identities. They focus on the way men have organized around masculine identities to protect their jobs in a context of capitalist exploitation and how, in the process, they have policed gendered boundaries which exclude women and other groups of workers—particularly ethnic minority workers—from the more highly skilled and highly paid occupations. In a study of these gendered processes within cotton textiles, engineering, and clerical work, Sylvia Walby argues that in the nineteenth century skilled workers (men) organized themselves into trade unions in order to 'control the price at which their members' labour was sold' and they did this by 'regulating entry to a particular trade or skill' (Walby, 1986:91). They regulated entry by excluding certain groups of workers, in particular women, and legitimating this exclusion by appeals to 'naturalistic' gender ideologies. Thus in 1877 the TUC Parliamentary Committee declared that it is

the duty of men and husbands to bring about a condition of things when their wives should be in their proper sphere at home instead of being dragged into competition of livelihood with the great and strong men of the world. (TUC, 1955:52 cited in Charles, 1979)

And earlier that century in the *Supplementary Report on Child Labour in Factories*, nature was invoked in support of women's exclusion from the workforce:

Nature effects her own purpose wisely and more effectively than could be done by the wisest of men. The low prices of female labour makes it the most profitable as well as the most agreeable occupation for a female to superintend her own domestic establishment and her low wages do not tempt her to abandon the care of her own children. (Cited in Charles 1979)

Walby argues that the monopoly of skilled, working-class jobs by men of the majority ethnic group was nothing to do with nature but everything to do with white, working-class men organizing to protect their own privileged position within the workforce and to maintain women and children at home. She calls this a patriarchal strategy of exclusion. This strategy, however, rather than excluding women from the workforce, resulted in their being confined to certain areas of work which were less skilled and lower paid than men's work and, as a result, employers were able to use them to undercut men's rates of pay. Not only had the strategy of exclusion failed in terms of protecting men's jobs and keeping women out of the workforce, but women were themselves challenging their exclusion from male trade unions and from the professions—a challenge which incorporated demands for political rights (Walby, 1990, 1986; Witz, 1992). In the twentieth century, in the face of women's winning the vote and the legitimation of their participation in the public sphere, the patriarchal strategy changed to one of inclusion. Thus women are now in the workforce but in positions where they are subordinate to men and under their control. Male control at work and at home is reinforced by women's pay being lower than men's and by women's continuing responsibility for childcare.

Whether or not one agrees with Walby's contentions about patriarchy, and she has been criticized for simplifying a complex picture of struggle and accommodation between women and men (Charles, 1993) and for developing an ahistorical and static concept of patriarchy (Pollert, 1996), it is clear that during the nineteenth and early twentieth centuries the labour movement pursued a strategy of a family wage for men to enable them to support a dependent wife and children at home and that this has contributed to women's concentration in low-paid, women's work (Charles, 1979).

Similar studies of the way gendered boundaries are maintained and challenged have explored men's control of resources, such as technology, and its relationship to gendered identities (see e.g. Witz (1992) for an analysis of gendered strategies of exclusion amongst health-care professionals). Thus Cynthia Cockburn studied a highly skilled group of workers in the print industry, the compositors, who had historically organized on the basis of a particular masculine identity (Cockburn, 1983). This was a path-breaking study in so far as it focused on men as gendered workers, thus insisting that gender shapes men's lives as much as it shapes women's. Cockburn argues that through their control of apprenticeships, which gave them a monopoly of the skills necessary to work the technology, compositors were able to control both the supply of labour and the labour process within the printing industry. Through controlling the apprenticeship system they excluded certain groups of workers from printing, notably women and ethnic minority men, and gained control over the labour process within the workplace, thus resisting capitalist exploitation. However, at the end of the 1970s new computer technology was introduced into printing which involved new skills which the compositors did not possess; the skills were 'women's' skills and women taught the men how to use the new technology. This undermined their sense of masculine identity because their new work was no longer dirty, noisy, and involving a close relationship with the hot metal technology. On the contrary, it was typing—women's work. In Cockburn's words:

The compositor, therefore, in this typing phase of his new labour process, feels reduced in sexual authority as well as in that initiative and control in work that has secured his class standing. (Cockburn, 1983:104)

Thus technological change has gender as well as class dimensions. As well as undermining the class power of this group of highly skilled workers it was also used to undermine their gender power and in so doing threatened their masculine identities, which were bound up with control over technology and the nature of the job. These changes created contradictions in the men's lives which, Cockburn argues, have the potential to lead to changes in gender relations and gendered boundaries. Thus a compositor who has always regarded women's work as unskilled now finds himself doing this work. But he is a skilled worker. Does this mean that women's work may after all be skilled? Will it call into question the association of skill and masculinity, thereby shifting the gendered boundaries between skilled and unskilled work? Or will it lead to further attempts to retain the association of skilled manual work with masculinity? It is through the responses of men and women—individually and collectively—to such change that the gendered nature of jobs and their association with specific gender identities can be contested or reinforced.

Gendered boundaries and authority

Gendered boundaries at work are constantly having to be reinforced and are constantly changing. What seems to remain the same, however, is that men retain their monopoly of positions involving power and authority. In order to explore the issue of vertical segregation attention has turned to the nature of organizations and the social processes which take place within them. According to Weber, bureaucracies are the ideal-typical form of organization in capitalist societies where rational-legal forms of domination and authority predominate. Large organizations approximate to this ideal type, which is characterized by hierarchies, clear lines of authority, specialization of tasks, and written rules. Such bureaucratic organizations came into existence at the end of the nineteenth and beginning of the twentieth century (Witz and Savage, 1992).

Feminists have argued that bureaucracies, in theory and in practice, are gendered. Thus when they emerged, career positions within them were the preserve of men and were predicated on the existence of an army of subordinate workers (usually women). These workers would carry out the routine tasks without which the organization could not function but would not themselves be eligible to progress up the organizational hierarchy (Witz and Savage, 1992:10; Savage, 1992; Zimmeck, 1992). Those pursuing careers were and are expected to be free to devote all their time and energy to furthering them; it is therefore easier for those without domestic responsibilities (usually men) to have organizational careers. As one researcher notes:

The managerial/professional career is a particularly telling example of the dependence of male workers upon their wives' domestic labour because it requires long hours, geographical mobility, considerable preparation for public participation, and high standards within the home. (Wajcman, 1998:43)

Thus as well as being based on a specific gender division of labour which frees men from routine tasks at work, bureaucratic organizations also assume a specific domestic division of labour which frees men from domestic and childcare responsibilities at home (Crompton, 1986).

These formal and hierarchical relations of power and authority coexist with informal 'networks and patterns of behaviour' (Wajcman, 1998:41–2). Thus while women are no longer formally excluded from any job there are informal processes which militate against women's advancement. Informal networks are important in facilitating or hindering career advancement within organizations and recent research points to their continuing importance in maintaining men's supremacy at work (Wajcman, 1998). These networks are often referred to as the 'old boys' club', conveying a sense of gender and class identity within networks which are also ethnically specific. They are important because it is through them, as much as through formal processes, that access to power resources can be achieved (Bradley, 1999). Successful careers are dependent on access to such networks but women find it very difficult to participate in them. This disadvantages them in promotion because they do not become visible to those who have the power to promote, and they do not have access to the knowledge and contacts that are necessary for corporate success. This is despite the fact that many employers have introduced equal employment policies in order to encourage women's careers within their organizations and that it is career women, rather than women in the routine, more working-class jobs, who benefit from such policies (Cockburn, 1991).

Gender cultures and gender identities

Furthermore there is evidence that the cultures of many organizations are masculine and that women often experience them as excluding and threatening (Cockburn, 1991; Charles and Davies, 2000; Wajcman, 1998). Men create this masculine culture by displaying page 3 pin-ups, for instance, or by engaging in conversations on 'masculine' topics such as technology or sports; such practices convey a message that women are out of place and studies have shown that women receive this message loud and clear (Blackaby et al., 1999). Furthermore men defend gender boundaries by various means, non-acceptance of women's authority for instance or sexual harassment—and women are reluctant to cross the boundaries and challenge the association of power/ authority with masculinity because to do so calls their gender identity and often their sexuality into question. This also happens to men who aspire to work in areas which have traditionally been defined as women's work. It may be assumed by clients and by other workers that men who work in the caring professions, for instance, are gay and research has shown that these assumptions, and the practices associated with them, lead to men's giving up non-traditional work and returning to more traditionally male jobs associated not only with masculinity but with heterosexual masculinity (Williams, 1993). Similarly women may experience being labelled as 'dykes' if they enter the male world of building sites or car mechanics (Dunne, 1997). Thus women and men can find it difficult to cross gender boundaries at work because of the threat this poses to their gender and/or sexual identities. This suggests that there is a sense in which we 'do' gender, that we enact our gender identity through the sort of work we do. For women to work in a man's job, and vice versa, creates an uncertainty about their gender identity; what they are doing, the activities in which they are engaging, are gendered and are in contradiction with their own gender identity. Often the only way of explaining this contradiction is by labelling them as homosexual; their sexual orientation is mobilized to explain away the inconsistency between gender identity and gendered job. By the same token, if a job is defined as masculine, such as most senior management jobs involving power and authority, and a woman succeeds in this sort of job, her ability to do the job can be brought into question by emphasizing her heterosexuality. The sexualization of women at work reduces their power and reinforces the disjuncture that exists between a job which is gendered male and the woman who is carrying it out. On the other hand women who have such jobs are often regarded as having sacrificed their femininity on the altar of success and are upbraided by men for behaving in a masculine way (Cockburn, 1991). Similarly women's bodily differences from men can be seen as rendering them unsuitable for 'men's' jobs. These arguments have a long pedigree and are related to those advanced in the nineteenth century to exclude women from higher education. Then education would divert energy from women's wombs to their brains thereby rendering them infertile (Sayers, 1982), now a too obvious sign of women's sexuality—such as pregnancy or dressing in a way which does not downplay bodily differences—is seen as inappropriate for those in positions of power and authority at work (Halford et al., 1997). Indeed, in order to be taken seriously women themselves ensure that their bodies are regulated so that their visual difference from men is minimized (Wajcman, 1998).

Orientations to work

There is a school of thought that argues that the gender patterning of paid work derives from choices made by individuals and in this context there has been considerable debate about the extent to which women's and men's commitment and orientation to paid work differs. Thus it has been argued that women can be differentiated according to whether they are career or marriage minded, the former leading them into full-time employment (the 'masculine' pattern) and the latter into part-time work (Hakim, 1995). This difference between women could be associated with class, with middle-class women who are committed to careers being more likely to be found in full-time employment than working-class women with jobs, but it has been found among middle-class *and* working-class women. Thus women in middle-class occupations in banking and medicine have been shown to have different work orientations, with those in banking prioritizing their career and those in medicine adopting a strategy of 'satisficing'—an orientation which prioritizes neither home nor work but attempts to maintain a balance between the two (Crompton and Harris, 1998b). Similarly the work orientations of working-class women working full time seem to differ from those of casual women workers (Glucksmann, 2000). Moreover there is also evidence that women's orientation to paid work changes over the life course (Crompton and Harris, 1998a) and that men's orientation to work and career is affected by family considerations (Halford et al., 1997): I explore this issue more fully in Chapter 3 where I discuss the gendering of the breadwinner role. Here I want to look at the way gender differences in workers' relation to the labour market have been theorized.

A gendered labour market

It has been suggested that women sell their labour under different conditions from men and that this is because of familial relations at work and the sexualization of women workers (Cockburn, 1991; Adkins, 1995). Lisa Adkins argues that capitalist labour markets are structured by family work relations and by heterosexuality; that is that gender and sexuality are just as fundamental as class to the way labour markets are structured. In her study of the leisure industry she explores the way the marriage relation and heterosexuality structure gender relations at work and how they operate to ensure that women sell their labour under different conditions from men. She found that companies running hotels and/or pubs prefer to employ married couples as managers and that hotel managers are usually required to be male and married. When married couples are used like this the employment contract specifies that both husband and wife are required to work in the establishment but the employment contract is actually between the husband and the company. The husband receives the wages. In Adkins's words:

Thus although the labour of wives is included in the contract, it is assumed to constitute part of husbands' labour by the hotel and catering companies. (Adkins, 1995:75)

And she notes that the companies pay only 1.25 as much to a married team as they do to a single male manager. Adkins argues that because of the nature of the employment contract husbands directly control the labour of their wives — as they do all the other employees in the establishment. Wives receive no wages in their own right, 'their duties are not specified by the companies', their husbands control their labour, and their work is open-ended (Adkins, 1995:83). Thus they are not working as employees of the company but for their husbands: the contract under which they are working is the marriage contract not the employment contract (cf. Delphy and Leonard, 1992). She comments:

Hotel and catering companies' extensive reliance upon this system of management within their establishments, and husbands' direct appropriation, control and exploitation of the labour of wives, shows clearly that both family production and the familial mode of control and exploitation of women's labour are actively operating *within* the contemporary labour market. (Adkins, 1995:84)

Such control is also apparent in family-based production where women work as family labour under the control of the male head of household rather than as 'free' labour (Josephides, 1988:43)

The sexualization of women's labour is evident in the fact that the companies regard wives as an attraction for male customers. This means that their sexual attractiveness is crucial to the work they do. Their husbands and the companies, but not the wives themselves, benefit from wives' sexual work. The sexualization of women's labour is also clear from Adkins's analysis of a large hotel where women's appearance was vital to their recruitment and their continued employment. Thus in order to be employed in catering women had to have an 'attractive' appearance; if they 'looked wrong' they would be offered a job in the parks department instead. Looking wrong was being 'too butch, too manly' or 'too ugly' (Adkins, 1995:106). If women failed to maintain their appearance they could lose their job but this was not the case for men; attractiveness was not a requirement for male employees. Adkins suggests that the stipulation of an attractive appearance indicates that women in the leisure industry are required to sell their sexuality as part of their labour-power.

Women's sexualization was also evident in the low-level sexual harassment they experienced from men who were co-workers, customers, and managers. This behaviour makes women feel as if they are on display—it objectifies them and produces what Adkins terms a 'sexually commodified workforce' (Adkins, 1995:133). This commodification takes place through 'attractiveness' being prioritized over all other requirements for women workers. Indeed the general manager commented that women employees should ideally look like Raquel Welch and the male bar manager required his staff to wear their dresses off their shoulders and 'he would often pull their dresses down into this position'.

On one occasion, a woman operative reported that she entered the bar at a moment when the bars manager was trying to pull a woman's dress down over her shoulders and the woman in question 'just turned round and screamed at him "I'm not a fucking prostitute, I'm here to serve drinks"'. (Adkins, 1995:126–7)

Defining women workers primarily in terms of their sexual attractiveness diminishes their status as workers. And the expectation that they would provide sexual services for male customers—in the sense of boosting male egos and giving them sexual thrills—reinforced heterosexual power relations between men customers and women workers. Women's sexualization also reduced their status in relation to their male co-workers: 'men did not have their status as workers undermined by a subordinate sexual status. Women did' (Adkins, 1995:137). Adkins argues that this is the result of specific work relations which operate only for women, i.e. that they are selling their hetero-sexuality rather than (or as well as) their ability to work in ways that men are not.

The women workers considered in this book were not exchanging sexual intercourse with men for money. But by responding to sexual innuendos and men's advances—by smiling, looking flattered and entering into it—they were, nevertheless, sexually servicing men. (Adkins, 1995:158)

A gendered and racialized labour market

Studies of gender at work have moved from explorations of gender and class to include considerations of the way sexuality shapes work relations and, with the emergence of non-standard working and the growth of the service sector, they have moved away from an exclusive focus on the factory. Relatively little atten-tion, however, has been paid to ethnicity (see Bradley, 1999, for a useful discus-sion) and this, together with the 'cultural turn' within sociology, means that attention has focused on cultural explanations for differences in employment between women from different ethnic groups. Thus studies of Afro-Caribbean women have focused on lone parenting and 'matrifocal families' as explan-ations for their full-time participation in the workforce, while studies of Asian women have focused on arranged marriages and religious observance as examples of patriarchal control within households which militates against their participation in paid employment (Bhavnani, 1994). Such explanations echo those of earlier decades which explained white women's participation in part-time work in terms of the male breadwinner family and women's responsibility for domestic and care work rather than (or as well as) relating to processes occurring within the labour market and within the workplace. As Bhavnani comments, such explanations 'problematise black women' and shift attention away from the 'gendered and racialised labour market' to the cultural and family practices of ethnic minorities. There are, however, some exceptions which combine cultural and economic explanations. One such is Naila Kabeer's comparative study of Bangladeshi women working in the gar-ment industry. She argues that their concentration in homeworking in London is due both to cultural practices within their community and to the limited opportunities, often due to racism, available in the labour market. She thereby combines a cultural and economic explanation for the nature of women's economic activity (Kabeer, 2000). Many studies, though, continue to focus on cultural difference, both as explanation and as object of study, despite the high-profile militancy of Asian women in disputes such as Grunwick in the 1970s

(Westwood, 1988) and in the West Midlands in the 1980s (Phizacklea, 1988:30; Bhachu, 1988; Bhopal, 1999; Bradby, 1999; Butler, 1999). Such militancy speaks of a strong presence of ethnic minority women in the workforce and the importance of a work identity to them.

Although explanations which rely solely on culture are problematic, cultural practices are undoubtedly important in affecting both women's and men's participation in economic activity and what goes on within the workplace. Thus studies have highlighted the significance of social networks not only for facilitating the development of careers within organizations, but also for finding work (see e.g. Morris, 1990; Pahl, 1984; Werbner, 1988; Westwood, 1988; Phizacklea, 1999:39; Kabeer, 2000). For instance, in Wolverhampton in the 1960s South Asian workers were recruited into metal foundries through networks of kin and friendship, both within Britain and between Britain and the Indian sub-continent, and Gujarati women found work in the knitting factory in Needletown through contact with other women (Westwood, 1988:108). Mobilizing what are often international or global networks to provide work and other forms of support is a feature of what has become known as 'chain migration'.

Kinship networks not only are important in enabling people to find jobs in the formal economy, they also facilitate the development of entrepreneurial activities among migrant groups; this is often achieved by guaranteeing men's access to family (i.e. female) labour 'subordinated to patriarchal control mechanisms' (Phizacklea, 1988:22, 1990). Thus, as we have seen, self-employment and entrepreneurial activity are higher amongst Asians than among Afro-Caribbeans and their enterprises are labour intensive and concentrated in retail, the service sector, and small-scale manufacturing such as the garment industry. The 'rag trade' in London's East End is particularly notable for its use of women homeworkers recruited through kinship networks and its reliance on family labour and has historically been associated with migrant entrepreneurs. In the early part of the century it was Jewish immigrants, now it is Cypriots and Asians who engage in this form of production (see Westwood and Bhachu, 1988). And as Shah comments in an early study:

Since the industry has a unique capacity in enabling people to quickly reach an employer or self-employed status, it has meant that alternative systems of employment (e.g. based on kinship) have been set up. In this way many of the problems and difficulties faced by immigrants in obtaining jobs through 'normal' channels can be avoided. (Shah, 1975:11)

This reinforces the significance of family labour and, in particular, the marriage contract, for determining the nature of women's economic activity and their participation in the labour market and underlines the ways in which work is structured not only by class but also by gender, ethnicity, and kinship.

Changes

As we have seen, there have been significant changes in the gendering of paid work in the second half of the twentieth century and in the types of jobs that are available. There are now far more jobs that are seen as 'women's' jobs and a 'feminizing' of the workforce has taken place. Despite this there has not been a significant decrease in gender segregation and men are still to be found at the 'commanding heights' of the economy.

There have also been changes in the way sociologists study gender at work. During the 1950s and 1960s paid employment was assumed to be a masculine realm and it was men at work who were the focus of research. Gender only entered the picture implicitly or when women were studied as workers *and* as wives and mothers. Then it was women's two roles that were problematized in contrast with men's sole role as provider. This was the period when married women's paid employment, particularly in part-time work, was beginning to increase and the difficulties of combining paid and domestic work were becoming an issue. With the impact of feminism the assumption that men went out to work while women stayed at home was challenged and women began to be studied as workers. Their secondary position within the workforce, however, continued to be explained in terms of their domestic responsibilities. This began to change in the 1970s and more so in the 1980s when attention turned to social processes within the workplace and the ways in which social actors created and reproduced gendered boundaries and gender identities. Workplaces were reconceptualized as gendered organizations with particular gender cultures, and factors such as ethnicity and sexuality were shown to be important in shaping women's and men's experiences of work. This reconceptualization can be seen as a response to the challenge of postmoderism and the 'cultural turn'.

At the beginning of the twenty-first century, processes within organizations and, particularly, informal cultural practices, have been identified as reinforcing gendered boundaries and gender identities. Labour markets are theorized as structured by gender and 'race' as well as class, women's labour is not 'free' in the way that men's is, and ethnicity and sexuality are seen as important in patterning women's and men's participation in paid employment. Attention has shifted to the informal networks in which power is located and away from structural inequalities; to the cultural processes within the workplace which maintain a situation where men who are white, middle class, and heterosexual predominate in positions of power; and to the actions of gendered social actors which maintain gender divisions of paid work.

In the next two chapters I continue to explore gender divisions of paid work, looking at them first in relation to domestic divisions of labour and then in relation to the gendering of parenting.

Chapter 3

Families and Households

THIS chapter explores domestic divisions of labour and their relationship to changes in women's and men's employment since the Second World War. I look first at the changes in domestic organization that have taken place and then focus on the way they have been studied and understood within sociology.

In the immediate post-war years married women were encouraged to return home and give up the jobs they had been doing in industry while the men were away fighting. This, however, did not have the effect of reducing women's economic activity rates; it merely served to reinforce pre-war gender segregation within the workforce which, in some industries, had been temporarily broken down (Summerfield, 1989). Wartime propaganda which had encouraged women to leave their children in nurseries and take up 'men's' jobs now stressed the importance of women's 24-hour presence in the home to care for children and husbands (Lewis, 1992). The expectation that men would be the breadwinners was enshrined in social security legislation and underpinned the newly formed welfare state. Despite women's increasing participation in the workforce, they were defined as domestic creatures who gave priority to their roles as wives and mothers. The male breadwinner role was reinstated, both materially and ideologically, and families were expected to conform to the institutionalized norm of male breadwinner, female dependent, and dependent children. But how far did this ideological definition of 'the family' reflect reality? Were family households composed of heterosexual couples where the husband produced and the wife consumed? Or were domestic arrangements, even in the 1950s, somewhat more varied than media images suggest?

The male breadwinner family

The Beveridge report was published in 1942 and assumed that women would ideally be full-time housewives, caring for their husbands and raising the next generation of British citizens. This prescription was for white women; black women were regarded as producers rather than reproducers and were valued as workers in the newly formed welfare state (Williams, 1989; Doyal, 1981). But even in the 1940s Beveridge's assumptions were wide of the mark. Indeed, in evidence to the Beveridge commission, Abbott and Bompas (1943) argued that the assumption that most women would marry and thereafter be financially dependent on their husband was inaccurate and, by 1951, 25 per cent 'of married women were economically active, double the proportion Beveridge had assumed in his report' (Land, 1994:104).

In the 1950s women and men married at a slightly younger age than they do now, fewer marriages ended in divorce, and, once married with children, more women were full-time housewives. In 1955, for instance, only 27 per cent of people aged between 25 and 64 were not currently married or in a long-term relationship compared with 36 per cent now (*Guardian*, 29 December 1999). In retrospect the 1950s and 1960s stand out as unusual for the high levels of conformity in family life. At the end of the twentieth century, although marriages were still contracted at a relatively young age, over 40 per cent were likely to end in divorce and the remarriage of one or both partners (McRae, 1999a:12; Finch, 1989:111). More people were cohabiting, many more children were being born outside state-sanctioned heterosexual marriage, more people were choosing to remain single, and fewer were having children (McRae, 1999a). These changes can be seen in Table 3.1 and most of them date from the late 1960s and early 1970s.

These patterns vary with ethnicity. Thus the highest rates of marriage are recorded amongst South Asians, particularly Pakistanis and Bangladeshis, and the lowest rate amongst Caribbeans. Of people aged between 40 and 49, 98 per cent of South Asians are or have been married/cohabiting, compared with 94

Table 3.1 Family change in Britain, mid-1960s to mid-1990s

	Mid-1960s	Mid-1990s
Mean age at first marriage	22	26
Mean age at first birth	23.9	26.5
Fertility rate (TFR)	2.93	1.8
Childlessness (%)	10	20
Divorces per 1,000 marriages	2	13
Births outside marriage (%)	5	35
Cohabitation before marriage (%)	5	70
Lone-parent families	570,000	1,500,000

Source: S. McRae (1999a) 'Introduction: family and household change' in S. McRae (ed.) *Changing Britain*, Oxford University Press, Oxford, table 1.1, p. 2. Reproduced by permission of Oxford University Press, Oxford.

per cent of the white population and 88 per cent of Caribbeans (Modood et al., 1997:25, table 2.5). Similarly, Pakistani and Bangladeshi young people (20–24 years old) are seven times more likely to be married than young Caribbeans (Modood et al., 1997:33). Separation and divorce are much more frequent amongst the Caribbean and white populations than amongst South Asians. In the population as a whole the trend to smaller families continues although South Asians, and particularly Pakistanis and Bangladeshis, tend to have more children than other ethnic groups.

These changes, together with married women's increasing participation in paid employment, gathered pace in the last decades of the twentieth century and have led many to argue that the male breadwinner family is in decline (Land, 1994). Thus, by the 1980s, families consisting of a male breadwinner, a female dependant, and 1.9 children accounted for less than a third of households and, at the end of the 1990s, it was a quarter (Brannen et al., 1998; Delphy and Leonard, 1992). This can be seen in Table 3.2.

However, even though it is only a minority of the population that lives in

Table 3.2 Household by type of household and family in Britain (percentages)

	1961	1971	1981	1991	1998–9
One person					
Under pensionable age	4	6	8	11	14
Over pensionable age	7	12	14	16	15
Two or more unrelated adults	5	4	5	3	2
One family					
Married couple,[1] with no children	26	27	26	28	30
1–2 dependent children[2]	30	26	25	20	19
3 or more dependent children[1]	8	9	6	5	4
Non-dependent children only	10	8	8	8	6
Lone parent[1] with dependent children[2]	2	3	5	6	7
Non-dependent children only	4	4	4	4	3
Two or more families	3	1	1	1	1
All households (millions)	16.3	18.6	20.2	22.4	23.5*

Source: H. Land (1999) 'The changing worlds of work and families' in S. Watson and L. Doyal (eds) *Engendering social policy*, Open University Press, Buckingham, table 1.2, p. 21; Cabinet Office, 2000: 12.

Notes:
[1] Other individuals who were not family members may also be included.
[2] Households may also include non-dependent children.
* This total is for 1995–6.

households which conform to the male breadwinner/female dependant plus dependent children norm, the majority live in a heterosexual marriage relationship with or without children. At the beginning of the twenty-first century further change is anticipated. Fertility rates have been relatively stable since the 1970s but the proportion of childless women continues to rise; thus 20 per cent of women born in the 1950s will choose not to have children (Coleman and Chandola, 1999). Single-person households are set to constitute 40 per cent of households by the year 2010 (*Guardian*, 18 October 1999) and there is increasing acceptance of same-sex couples as 'families' with the rights and obligations associated with heterosexual marriage. The male breadwinner family, if not in decline, is under threat with women increasingly able to earn a living wage and control their own fertility.

Families and households

While in the immediate post-war years in a situation of housing shortage it was common for newly married couples to share a home with their parents or parents-in-law and, on moving out of the parental home, to live in close proximity to their parents, at the end of the twentieth century increased geographical and occupational mobility means that families are living further apart (McRae, 1999b). In addition, families are smaller and three-generation households are comparatively rare. Household composition varies with ethnicity however. South Asians, for instance, are more likely than others to live in joint family households. This refers to a situation where adult children continue to live with their parents and a patrilineal marriage system operates, with adult sons moving their wives into their parents' home (Bradby, 1999). In contrast young adult whites and Caribbeans tend to move out of the parental home and live in nuclear family or single-person households; indeed Caribbeans are more likely to remain single than whites or South Asians (Beishon et al., 1998:84).

The number of single-parent households has also increased since the Second World War. In the 1960s there were 570,000 and by the late 1990s there were 1.6 million. Most of these are headed by women (McRae, 1999a). Again there are significant differences between ethnic groups with a quarter of all Caribbean women in their late 20s and early 30s being single parents compared with a tenth of white women of similar age (Modood et al., 1997:38). Or to put it another way, nearly half of Caribbean families with children are headed by single or separated mothers (Modood et al., 1997:40). In the population as a whole, the proportion is just over one in five (McRae, 1999a:14). Almost all (90 per cent) of South Asian families with children had 'formally married parents' compared with 75 per cent of white families with children and less than half of Caribbean families with children (Modood et al., 1997:39). This should not necessarily be taken to mean that children were living with a single adult, especially as rates of cohabitation for whites and Caribbeans are relatively high, but is an indication of the variation in household types between different ethnic groups.

Attitudes

It is also important to look at the way attitudes towards women's and men's roles within 'the family' have changed and their relation to how people actually live their lives. Thus the *Women and Employment Survey* published in 1984 found that 25 per cent of the women surveyed supported the idea that 'a woman's place is in the home' while 46 per cent thought that 'a husband's job is to earn the money; a wife's job is to look after the home and family' (Martin and Roberts, 1984:170, table 12.1). This contrasts with a survey done almost twenty years earlier where support for this gender division of labour was greater and with recent attitude surveys which show that support has declined even further (Hunt, 1968). Thus 83 per cent of women and 78 per cent of men aged between 18 and 27 in 1994 'disagree that the husband should earn the money while a wife's job is to look after the home . . . compared with only 27 per cent of women (21 per cent of men) over the age of 68' (Scott et al., 1996:487). As with attitudes towards women's employment, there is a generational difference in attitudes towards gender divisions of labour within the home, with the younger generation being far more egalitarian than the older generation. However there is still a 'strong conviction' amongst women and men (although men more so) that 'women's family responsibilities, particularly those involving young children, must come first' (ibid.: 490).

Ethnicity also seems to affect attitudes towards maternal employment although the data are sparse. What data exist suggest that there is a difference in atittudes between Pakistanis and Bangladeshis, who feel that a married woman's place is in the home and that she should not go out to work (Beishon et al., 1998:52), and the rest of the population who feel that women should go out to work and that two wages are essential to maintain a family's standard of living (Beishon et al., 1998:52; Thorogood, 1987). These attitudes tie in with the differences in economic activity rates noted in Chapter 2 and the proportion of women in different ethnic groups who are 'housewives'. Thus over 80 per cent of Bangladeshi women and 70 per cent of Pakistani women were looking after the home and children full time compared with 25 per cent of white and

African Asian women, 33 per cent of Indians, and 13 per cent of Caribbeans (Beishon et al., 1998:90). Other studies, however, suggest that a significant number of Bangladeshi and Pakistani 'housewives' may in fact be working as homeworkers (see e.g. Werbner, 1988:184 and Chapter 2). There is also evidence that the younger generation of South Asians, particularly those who have been brought up in Britain and are highly educated, hold more egalitarian attitudes than their parents (Bhachu, 1988:93; Bhopal, 1999). In this context it may be significant that many Pakistanis and Bangladeshis live in inner-city areas in communities which are characterized by close-knit networks: and, as we shall see, this is precisely the social environment which exerts strong social control over its members and maintains a high degree of conformity and gender segregation (Werbner, 1988 and cf. Bhopal, 1999:123; Butler, 1999:148).

It is difficult to gather evidence on the nature of domestic divisions of labour in the 1950s and 1960s except from sociological studies. These show that, even in the immediate post-war years, men 'helped' with domestic work. Thus in Bethnal Green in the 1950s and Swansea in the early 1960s:

The husband is expected to help with the household chores, to stay at home or go out for the evening with his wife, to help with the children, to push the pram ... to share the major family decisions. (Rosser and Harris, 1965:184–5, cited in Harris, 1983a:224)

A later study showed that 'a quarter of all husbands "participated to some degree" in doing shopping, two fifths in washing up and from almost a half to 80 per cent in *the more interesting* sorts of childcare' (Goldthorpe et al., 1969:108, cited in Harris, 1983a:226, my emphasis). For the later decades of the twentieth century official statistics are available. Thus in 1985 a majority of women, whether in full-time or part-time employment, were responsible for carrying out most domestic tasks with the exception of household repairs. This can be seen in Table 3.3.

The task which was most equally shared was shopping but this was only true for women in full-time employment. Men were least likely to be involved in washing and ironing. One of the most time-consuming activities in the home is childcare. Indeed a study published in 1984 claimed that looking after small children took over seven hours a day and that women were responsible for 89 per cent of the time spent on childcare tasks; men's participation was in the more enjoyable aspects of childcare like reading them stories at bedtime or taking them out (Piachaud, 1984). These distinctions are lost in more recent figures which show the average number of minutes per day spent on various household tasks by women and men (see Table 3.4).

However, even at the end of the twentieth century, 'Women spend almost twice as long on household chores as men' and there is a very clear gender division in the distribution of paid and unpaid work (*Guardian*, 7 October 1997).

Table 3.3 Households where women are mainly responsible for doing domestic tasks (per cent)

Task	Women in full-time employment	Women in part-time employment
Shopping	52	64
Preparing evening meal	61	79
Cleaning	61	83
Washing and ironing	81	95
Household repairs (men)	83	74

Source: Adapted from Henwood et al., 1987: table 1, p. 11. Reproduced with kind permission of the former Family Policy Studies Centre.

Table 3.4 Minutes per day spent on various household tasks

	Women	Men
Cooking	68	28
Childcare	86	55
Washing	25	3
Shopping	46	26
Cleaning	70	43
DIY	6	22
Paid work	127	212
Unpaid work	295	155

Source: *Guardian*, 7 October 1997; ONS statistics.

Although there has been little research on domestic divisions of labour in ethnic minority households, what exists suggests that similar patterns prevail (Modood et al., 1997; Beishon et al., 1998). Indeed, in comparison with other ethnic groups, one study found that white women 'appeared to be doing less domestic labour' (Beishon et al., 1998:68). This is allegedly because white households tend to employ cleaners and there is more sharing of domestic work, 'with men doing the cooking rather than the cleaning'; in only a fifth was there a 'traditional' division of labour with women undertaking the bulk of domestic work (Beishon et al., 1998). These findings are based on a small, qualitative study and need to be treated with caution; clearly more research is needed to verify these observations.

Studying 'the family'

Sociological studies have reflected these changes. Thus during the 1950s Eliza-beth Bott studied families and their social networks (Bott, 1957). Her under-standing of families was informed by structural functionalism which led her to formulate her problem in terms of roles, social groups, and networks. She was particularly interested to explore what it was that influenced the nature of the 'conjugal role relationship' and, from an in-depth exploration of 20 hetero-sexual couples, hypothesized that the nature of their relationship was affected by the density of their social networks. She set up two 'ideal types' of conjugal role relationship—segregated and joint. In the segregated type spouses had different spheres of activity and responsibility; husbands went out to work, earned a wage, and engaged in leisure activities with their friends rather than their wives. Wives were responsible for the home, looking after children, clean-ing, and cooking, and they may also have been in paid employment; they did not expect help from their husbands with domestic tasks nor did they get it. Even when they were ill it was their female kin who provided assistance. Their leisure time was spent with family and friends rather than with their husbands. This type of role relationship was to be found embedded in close-knit social networks, usually in stable communities where the men worked in the same workplaces as well as living in the same neighbourhoods. It was also associated with long-established, working-class communities in industrial societies. The joint conjugal role relationship was, in contrast, to be found in loose-knit net-works and was associated with geographical mobility. This type of relationship was characterized by an expectation that spouses would share leisure activities and have friends in common, although men were expected to be the breadwin-ners while women were the ones responsible for childcare and domestic work. Bott suggested that there was a move towards joint conjugal roles under way (indeed she found only one couple with a segregated role relationship in her sample of 20) but what she took for granted was that there was an underlying gender division of labour within nuclear families which defined women's and men's spheres of activity. The taken-for-grantedness of this basic gender div-ision underpinned other studies (see e.g. Goldthorpe et al., 1969:107; Young and Wilmott, 1973). Responsibilities for paid and domestic work were assumed to be gendered and were understood in terms of men's and women's roles. There was however some flexibility in the way these roles were carried out which reflected the changed circumstances in which couples found themselves and the loosening of the social networks in which they were embedded (cf. Harris, 1983a:231).

In a study carried out at the beginning of the 1960s, it was argued that women were becoming less domesticated, and that this, together with a reduction in family size since the early years of the century and increased geographical mobility, meant that families were less able to provide support for their members, particularly older people. Social change, through its effect on 'the social position of women', was thereby affecting the ability of families to carry out their functions, which were defined as 'that of social identification on the one hand and that of practical support in need or crisis on the other' (Rosser and Harris, 1983:175–6). Furthermore the shift from close-knit to loose-knit networks consequent upon industrial change was significant for 'the way in which women perceive their position'.

As long as women interact chiefly with women, as long as gender is more important than age as a determinant of interaction, it is likely that women will compare themselves with women of other ages and generations. The disruption of close-knit single-sex networks will not only isolate the housewife, it will also destroy (not the household division of labour) but the categorical division of the world into male and female domains. Once this has occurred, women will come to see themselves as deprived relative to men within marriage, rather than fortunate compared with their grandmothers among women. (Harris, 1983b: xv)

This study identifies the material changes which made possible the view that 'traditional' domestic divisions of labour were 'iniquitous' rather than the normal and expected way to organize domestic life. These changes created a situation which did not exist before, a situation in which women could contrast their lot with that of their husbands and begin to think in terms of gender equality within the domestic sphere as well as the sphere of paid work: they made possible the problematizing of previously taken-for-granted gender divisions of labour.

It is significant that this study was carried out in 1962 and it was towards the end of this decade that the women's movement, which was highly critical of women's position within the domestic sphere, emerged. Rosser and Harris were unusual in so far as they took ethnicity into account, exploring the significance of Welsh and English identities for the nature of kinship relations. 'Race', however, hardly features in these classic studies and where black families are the focus of research they are seen as deviant, being headed by strong, independent women who emasculate their men, or as based on arranged marriages (Bhavnani, 1994:7; Phoenix, 1988:155; Harley, 1997:39).

The emergence of the women's movement, together with the resurgence of Marxism in the late 1960s, marked the end of the hegemony of structural functionalism in sociological studies of the family (Harris, 1979:1). Indeed, it marked the end of studies of 'the family' and a shift towards studying families and households and problematizing the gender divisions of labour which characterized them.

Feminism and families

Feminism had a significant impact on sociological studies of families. Feminists pointed out that 'the family' was an ideological construct which was historically and culturally specific and that there was considerable variation in the ways that people chose to live together in family households; here they were influenced by increasingly sophisticated historical analysis of changes in families and households (Gittins, 1985; Morgan, 1979:3). They also turned their attention to what went on inside family households in terms of distribution of and access to resources: they opened up the 'black box' of the family and demonstrated that economists' assumptions that resources were distributed equally between family members were wide of the mark and that sociological assumptions about the existence of a symmetrical family overstated the case (Brannen and Wilson, 1987). Thirdly, feminists problematized the gender division of labour within family households, arguing that it was socially constructed and that it disadvantaged women because it denied them access to key resources thereby rendering them subordinate to men. David Morgan has argued that this constituted a shift to studying households as economic units rather than families as social groups where emotional, sexual, and caring activities take place (Morgan, 1996:33). Clearly both aspects are important, but here I focus on studies which explore domestic divisions of labour, the distribution of resources within households, the gendering of the breadwinner role, and the ways in which ethnicity and institutionalized heterosexuality affect domestic divisions of labour.

Domestic divisions of labour

Probably the first feminist sociological analysis of domestic labour was Ann Oakley's study of housework published in 1974. She argued, controversially, that housework should be conceptualized as work and that it was a proper topic for a sociologist of work to study. The 40 women in her study subscribed to the idea that housework was women's work. They felt that they were 'naturally' domesticated while men were not, indeed men were not real men if they did women's work (Oakley, 1974:155). In the words of one of her respondents,

I don't agree with men doing housework—I don't think it's a man's job ... I certainly wouldn't like to see my husband cleaning a room up. I don't think it's mannish for a man to stay at home. I like a man to be a man. (Oakley, 1974:156)

Despite the perceived naturalness of women's domesticity, women were dissatisfied with housework, finding it monotonous and lonely and the 'most disliked aspect of being a housewife'. They valued the autonomy they had in doing their housework but resented the low status associated with being a housewife. Oakley also found that women who had had enjoyable and relatively high-status jobs before becoming housewives were more dissatisfied with their current situation than others. Despite high levels of dissatisfaction with the work, however, there was acceptance that this was the way things were and a strong identification with the housewife role. If husbands did any housework they were 'helping out' and there was no hint that gender equality in the domestic sphere was seen as a desirable state of affairs, never mind one that had already arrived. Indeed Oakley notes an anxiety at any suggestion that expectations about domestic divisions of labour might be changed (Oakley, 1974:192). These attitudes persisted in the findings of the Women and Employment survey published 10 years later where 99 per cent of married women and 54 per cent of women in full-time employment were defined as houseworkers (the person with the major domestic responsibility); this situation was seen as satisfactory and even 'natural' by 80 per cent of the women (Martin and Roberts, 1984). Thus,

In only a small number of marriages is the husband notably domesticated, and even where this happens, a fundamental separation remains: home and children are the woman's primary responsibility. Doubt is cast on the view that marriage is an egalitarian relationship. (Oakley, 1974: 164)

Resources within households

As well as exploring domestic divisions of labour and demonstrating their 'iniquity', feminist sociologists were concerned to investigate the distribution of resources within households, particularly as access to and control over resources is a dimension of power relations and access to women's domestic labour was conceptualized as an aspect of patriarchal power (see Chapter 1). Thus in the 1980s considerable research was undertaken into the way resources such as money, time, food, and leisure were distributed within family households (Pahl, 1989; Charles and Kerr, 1988; Green et al., 1990; Brannen and Wilson, 1987). Jan Pahl's study of money and marriage, for instance, explored the way systems of money management related to power relations within marriage, arguing that they reflected the differential earning power of the spouses and their beliefs about the nature of marriage. Thus working-class couples on low incomes were likely to adopt a whole-wage system where, although the woman controls the household budget, it does not give her power because she is managing scarce resources and has all the worry and responsibility of making ends meet. The man's responsibility ends when he hands over his pay packet and receives back his spending money, something his wife is unlikely to allow herself. In households where the man is the breadwinner an allowance system is often adopted whereby he gives his wife a 'housekeeping allowance' on which she has to manage the household affairs. He is in control of the money coming into the household and the amount that is available for housekeeping, she has to manage the daily expenditure. These two management systems are associated with a male breadwinner ideology and a weak attachment of women to the labour market and are more prevalent within the working class.

The other two money management systems are associated with a more egalitarian gender division of labour and a greater attachment of women to the labour market, although women are likely still to be earning less than their male partner. They are also associated with higher incomes. The most widespread of these involves the pooling of household income in the form of a joint bank account or kitty and is associated with a commitment to sharing and egalitarian notions of marriage as a partnership. However, Pahl argues that this system masks continuing gender inequalities and power differentials which arise from the higher earning capacity of men (Pahl, 1989). Thus even in pooling households, and especially if they are temporarily out of the labour market, women can feel as if they are supplicants. Many regard the money coming into the household as not theirs and feel that they have no right to money they have not earned. As one woman said:

He regards it (his wage) as ours. I regard it as his. I never look at his wage slip or ask him how much he has earned. He gives me the housekeeping and takes care of the bills. If I run short I just ask for more and he tells me to help myself. I feel though that it is his money because I am not contributing any more. (Cragg and Dawson, 1984:53)

This highlights the contradiction between the fact that wages are earned by individuals in the labour market but distributed to non-earning members of the household; the non-earners do not feel the same entitlement as they would had they been the earners. And men's willingness to share their wage within the household does not negate the structural inequalities which confer upon the earner power and authority within the household; a power to which women are responding in their feeling that their husband's wage is not for them to spend as they wish.

The independent management system is associated with high-earning, two-income households and a commitment to independence, equality, and autonomy. It tends to be found amongst cohabiting (as opposed to married) heterosexual couples and is associated with a stronger attachment to the labour market on the part of women (as is the pooling system) and a commitment to gender equality at the level of norms and values. Both pooling and independent management systems are more common amongst middle-class than working-class couples. Moreover independent management systems tend also to be found amongst gay and lesbian couples where there is no predetermined, gender-based pattern which can almost automatically be adopted. Thus, in a study of 60 non-heterosexual women, Gill Dunne (1997) found that lesbian couples recognized that unequal access to resources could lead to power imbalances and was therefore undesirable. Consequently most of them adopted a system of independent money management. This recognition was also noted by Pahl amongst some of her heterosexual couples where pooling was adopted as a way of mitigating the effects of differential earning power (Pahl, 1989). Dunne compares her findings with those of Pahl and notes that in Pahl's sample there were very large income differentials between wives and husbands (79 per cent of the men earned more than the highest-earning wife in the sample). As Pahl comments:

Many couples wanted their marriage to be a relationship between equals and tried to express this equality in their financial arrangements. However, the results of this study showed that the greater earning power of husbands continues to be associated with greater control over finances and greater power in decision making within the family. (Pahl, 1989:169)

So structural inequalities between women and men in paid employment place limits on the extent to which they are able to have equal domestic relationships. In contrast, most of the lesbian couples in Dunne's study did not have large earnings differentials and efforts were made to minimize the effect of any income differentials by, for example, living at the level which the lower earner could afford or by each contributing to household expenditure in proportion to her income.

Ethnicity and sexuality

There are virtually no data on the distribution of resources or systems of money management within ethnic minority households. What few there are suggest that in South Asian households income tends to be pooled, with the most senior man being solely responsible for the household finances, while in Caribbean households the proportion of women taking financial responsibility is slightly higher than in white households (Modood et al., 1997:179). Similarly there is little research on domestic divisions of labour in ethnic minority households. In a rare study of 32 Afro-Caribbean women in London, Nicki Thorogood found that only the two women who were full-time housewives accepted that housework was their responsibility. Most of the women who had paid employment and husbands resented the fact that they had to carry the burden of housework. One woman, who was a single working mother of six, said:

If I were living with a husband I couldn't do all what I have to do. For instance now, he would come in now and I would have to go because he want his dinner. Right? You see, I do two work. I work in this school and I do dinner duty and I go to an institute or centre and tidy it up a bit . . . but if I had a husband I couldn't take two jobs. I would have to do just one because I would have to cook his food. (Thorogood, 1987:34)

Thorogood comments:

Thus what emerges is that . . . husbands, even those who earn, diminish these women's access to resources within the household. It appears that living with men generally increases women's domestic labour, that is, their contribution to the reproduction of the family, whilst decreasing their access to the material resources of money and time. (Thorogood, 1987:35)

This was recognized by several of the women in the study and led to a reluctance to compromise their freedom and independence by cohabiting or marrying.

This study clearly shows women's awareness of the way heterosexual marriage or cohabitation restricts women's access to resources and increases their domestic work. Indeed, in heterosexual partnerships women are generally responsible for the bulk of unpaid domestic work even when they are in full-time employment and it is usually women who have to balance the responsibilities of home and work. Their employment is adjusted to compensate and they experience fatigue, strain, guilt, and anxiety because they 'choose' to be employed (Dunne, 1997: 204). In contrast, in gay and lesbian households there is often a strong commitment to an equitable domestic division of labour although evidence is contradictory (Oerton, 1997). This may relate to an ideological commitment to feminism, as more egalitarian arrangements have also been observed between heterosexual couples who are feminist (VanEvery, 1995). In lesbian households, couples tend to spend less time on household tasks than is spent in heterosexual relationships. This is perhaps because women's identity and self-worth are not so tied up in housework and the housewife role (Dunne, 1997).

Women's full-time employment

This evidence suggests that the greater women's attachment to the labour market and the more control they exert over their own income, the less unequal are gendered power relations within households. Indeed, households where women are in full-time employment are significantly different, in terms of money management and domestic divisions of labour, from those where women are in part-time employment or are full-time housewives. Thus if women are in full-time employment they are likely to adopt a pooling system whereas if they are not they are likely to have a whole wage or allowance system (Vogler and Pahl, 1993:80). Conversely, where women are not earning or are earning substantially less than their partner, and where they do not have a strong attachment to the labour market, they have less access to resources and correspondingly less power. Part-time employment 'simply operates to reduce calls on the husband's wage, without ever increasing wives' influence over finances' (Vogler and Pahl, 1993:80; Morris, 1990). Thus equality in distribution of and access to resources within households is dependent on 'women's commitment to full-time employment' (Vogler and Pahl, 1993:81).

Women's participation in full-time paid employment also has an effect on domestic divisions of labour. The figures on the distribution of domestic tasks suggest that men whose partners are in full-time employment are more likely to participate in housework than those with partners who are employed part time. Conversely, women's participation in paid employment, if it is on a part-time basis, does not challenge 'traditional' domestic divisions of labour. Moreover it seems that women have had to take on an increased burden of work, both paid and unpaid, before men's participation in unpaid work shows any sign of increase: this has been termed 'lagged adaptation' (Gershuny, Godwin, and Jones, 1994). The experience of trying to combine paid and domestic work creates pressures on women which, through processes of negotiation and conflict within relationships, lead either to a redistribution of tasks or to relationship breakdown and reconstitution. Middle-class (especially higher-earning, white, middle-class) women can resolve this problem, to a certain extent, by employing other women to cook and clean and look after their children but this option is not open to working-class and ethnic minority women who are often those providing services to their career-minded sisters (Arber, 1999; Gregson and Lowe, 1994). Thus domestic divisions of labour, despite women's increasing participation in paid employment, have not changed significantly, and normative expectations about spheres of responsibility remain resistant to change. Women continue to carry the main responsibility for domestic work, their paid work fits in around this, and men carry the main responsibility for earning a wage. This is true even in dual-career households where the costs of childcare are met from the woman's salary and it is usually she and not he who takes time off work if children are ill (Brannen and Moss, 1991). This lagged adaptation suggests that there is resistance to change, a resistance already noted by Oakley as stemming from women's sense of self and their feminine identity being bound up with the housewife role and domesticity (Oakley, 1974:185). Indeed, there is evidence that both women and men are resistant to major change in domestic divisions of labour because of the ways in which gender identities are constructed within familial ideology and the emotional investments that are made in these identities (Barrett, 1980).

Gender identities

In the 1990s attention has turned to the ways in which gender identities, gender ideology, and institutionalized heterosexuality affect women's and men's participation in full-time employment and domestic divisions of labour. Resistance to changes in domestic divisions of labour has been noted amongst families of unemployed men. This is counter-intuitive in so far as it might be expected that if a husband is out of work it makes sense for him to take on unpaid domestic work and for his wife to increase the hours she spends in paid employment. Lydia Morris's research in South Wales and Durham shows, however, that this is not a widespread response to male unemployment. She argues that this is because unemployment undermines a man's identity as breadwinner and therefore his masculinity:

unemployment may undermine a man's gender identity and self-respect and sometimes, in consequence, his source of authority within the home. (Morris, 1990:28)

Morris found that both men and women felt strongly that it was a man's role to be the main wage earner and even when men were unemployed and potentially available for domestic work they did not increase their participation in domestic labour (Morris, 1990; Pahl, 1984). Domestic work is not seen as appropriate for men, it is women's work and if men do it, or perhaps more to the point are seen to be doing it, it can undermine their masculinity. So if their masculine identity is already undermined by unemployment men are arguably less likely to contribute to domestic labour than before. But it is not only men who are resistant to change, women also do not want men getting under their feet.

Sometimes he gets me mad when he's sat in and I'm doing it [the housework] and you've got to keep asking him to move. I mean he just can't sit in the kitchen while I do in here and then come in here while I'm doing the kitchen . . . In the end I told him I'd give him two quid and I said 'just clear off down to the pub'. I said 'I've had enough, just get out of my way so I can get it done'. (Morris, 1990:33)

Conversely men, even if they are willing to do a bit of housework, find it problematic:

It was alright for something to do, but just sort of when I felt like it. She'd keep on at me to get it done straight away and I couldn't see the point. (Morris, 1990:33)

Amongst working-class families the response to male unemployment is hardly ever for the woman to go into full-time employment, i.e. take on the breadwinner role. It is seen as unnatural, again underlining the 'naturalness' of gender divisions of labour and echoing Oakley's earlier findings:

it's not possible and it's not natural, I suppose it's class if you come down to it. For the working class it's our system, worked out over hundreds of years, and you can't change it. (Morris, 1990:31)

Despite this resistance, role reversal happens in about 2 per cent of British households (Brannen et al., 1998). Thus Jane Wheelock found in her study of households of unemployed men that in half the households there had been shifts in domestic divisions of labour (although this was not necessarily in the direction of more male participation in domestic labour) and that the degree of change was related to women's hours of work (Wheelock, 1990). This suggests that what leads to change is not men's lack of participation in paid employment but women's increased commitment to paid work. In a fascinating study of a former mining community Stephanie Jones found similar processes at work. Even though male unemployment was high, men's masculine identity was preserved through their involvement in the local rugby club, which had replaced the pit as the focus of community activity, and the preservation of 'traditional' gender divisions of labour (Jones, 1997). It seems that what acts as a spur to changing domestic divisions of labour is women's participation in and commitment to paid labour on a full-time basis. The motor of change is the nature of women's economic activity and, more importantly, their access to and control over resources. This is counter-intuitive because of the generally-held assumption that women's participation in paid employment is limited by their domestic responsibilities; it may in fact be the other way round.

The gendering of breadwinning

This brings me to the issue of the gendering of breadwinning, how the idea that the primary breadwinner is or ought to be male structures men's and women's participation in the labour market, domestic divisions of labour, and access to resources within the home. Thus responsibilities are allocated between heterosexual couples in the expectation that men will be the main providers once children arrive.

In the early days of marriage, often when both partners are in full-time employment, couples come to adopt a gendered notion of a primary breadwinner, which then plays a fundamental role in structuring both partners' future behaviour both in the labour market and in the home. Men's jobs come to be regarded as more fundamental in providing for basic family expenditure than women's jobs, which are regarded as temporary and potentially disposable . . . [This] plays a key role in structuring social relations within the household . . . [and is] . . . one of the main reasons why the increases in women's labour market participation have so far failed to challenge the traditionally gendered division of labour within the home. (Vogler and Pahl, 1993:91)

There are conflicting interpretations of this, with some arguing that it is the anticipation of parenthood which leads couples to adopt this division of labour while others argue that it is part and parcel of becoming a 'wife' (see e.g. VanEvery, 1995, 1997). Whatever the explanation, such divisions of labour have profound implications for men's and women's employment patterns, domestic divisions of labour, access to resources, and parenting. Patterns of money management are influenced by the extent to which the responsibility for ensuring that the family has an adequate income is gendered male. Those who disagree that the husband should be responsible for ensuring an adequate income for the family tend to adopt pooling systems, while those who think husbands should be breadwinners are likely to adopt an allowance system. Conversely joint-pool couples are most likely to agree that responsibility for breadwinning and housework should be shared and those adopting a house-keeping allowance system are least likely to agree. Indeed one study concluded that the most important variable affecting systems of money management was whether the husband occupied the status of primary breadwinner in the household (Vogler and Pahl, 1993).

The importance of the gendering of the breadwinner role was brought out in a study of newly-weds which found that most young women and men 'knew' how to behave once they were married (Mansfield and Collard, 1988). Thus a young newly married woman said:

I knew before I got married what I would have to do. I knew that by seeing other people being married—my sister has been married a long time before me. (Mansfield and Collard, 1988:127)

And a young man said:

I think it gets back to my image, I follow my dad—it was always the wife who cooked the meals and did the ironing and did the vacuum cleaning and washed the kitchen floor and I do all the decorating because they're the more masculine jobs. (Mansfield and Collard, 1988:127)

This knowledge affects young women's attitudes towards paid work and the amount of investment they are prepared or able to make in their careers. In fact it seems that very many young women put up with dull jobs because they see paid work as a temporary interlude between leaving full-time education and marriage and motherhood (cf. Pollert, 1981; Rees, 1992). Most of the young women in Mansfield and Collard's study were dissatisfied with their jobs, a view that was in marked contrast to their husbands' feelings about theirs, and most were taking on a greater share of domestic work in the home and lowering their commitment to paid work on the assumption that their jobs would take second place to their husband's. This was the case even when both partners were in full-time employment, and most newly-weds already prioritized the husband's career and his role as provider. This has led some to argue that becoming a wife is the root of women's subordination and that husbands appropriate their wives' labour, regarding the wife's employment as a temporary interlude before the arrival of children (Delphy and Leonard, 1992). As Mansfield and Collard note:

The unspoken rule in most couples is that the work of the wife outside the home should not dominate her life to such an extent that the spouse or the house 'suffer'. (Mansfield and Collard, 1988:145)

The gendering of the breadwinning role is associated with a particular domestic division of labour and reduces women's expectations of paid work. This partly explains why women are concentrated in low-paid, unskilled work—they do not expect that it will form their primary commitment once they are wives and mothers. By the time they realize that it is permanent it is often too late to do anything about it.

Institutionalized heterosexuality

The gendering of the breadwinning role can be seen as part of familial ideology (Barrett, 1980). It has also been theorized as part of institutionalized heterosexuality. This refers to the way heterosexual relations are institutionalized within marriage and the family, within education, social security, and, as we saw in the last chapter, within employment. In contrast, gay and lesbian partnerships are not seen as 'proper' families, homosexuality is not institutionalized and socially sanctioned, it is defined as deviant. There are signs that this is changing: towards the end of 1999 Judge Butler-Schloss said that gay couples should be able to adopt; a gay man established in law that 'a "stable and permanent" homosexual relationship confers the rights of being a member of a family' (*Guardian*, 29 October 1999) and a gay British couple had both their names on the birth certificate of their twins who were born to a surrogate mother in California (*Guardian*, 28 October 1999). However, although it is beginning to be recognized that heterosexual relationships are not the only ones to involve rights and responsibilities, heterosexuality remains institutionalized within British society and shapes the way we behave, the expectations we have about relationships (whether gay or heterosexual), and the division of responsibilities within marriage. There is evidence that moving beyond heterosexuality, by being or becoming lesbian for instance or through relationship breakdown, affects the importance women attach to their employment (Siltanen, 1994). This is because it is associated with the realization that they will have to be financially self-supporting and, if they have children, will have to be both provider and carer. As one woman in Gill Dunne's study put it, 'I know that I'm not actually going to have [a male breadwinner] to fall back on' (Dunne, 1997:121). Indeed, heterosexual marriage creates problems for women's commitment to paid work even when no children are present. As we have seen, the normative expectation is that a wife's primary commitment will be to her husband and her home. A career is acceptable for married women but, as one of the women in Dunne's study said: 'The male should be, in the world's opinion, a breadwinner; the woman can be successful provided the male is more successful' (Dunne, 1997: 218). Dunne theorizes this in terms of a gender script which differs for women and men and which is followed on entering a heterosexual marriage. To go against this script is difficult because it provides a 'framework of meaning, guiding how they felt they should act out their womanhood' (Dunne, 1997:116). One of the women in her study said: 'I felt I was acting, I was acting the way I had seen other people act . . . I did all the things that a good little wife does' (Dunne, 1997:115). Moving beyond heterosexual marriage, into lesbian relationships, meant that women were no longer in the straitjacket of the gender script and this often involved a major change in their employment status upwards.

Ethnicity also affects women's expectations of paid work. Thus Afro-Caribbean women expect to be emotionally and economically independent and able to support themselves (Mirza, 1992; Thorogood, 1987). Women's financial dependence is not assumed and does not structure their participation in the labour market and, as we have seen, Afro-Caribbean women are more likely than white women to be in full-time employment. Indeed, it may be very difficult for Afro-Caribbean women to rely on men for financial support because of the high levels of unemployment amongst Afro-Caribbean men (Bruegel, 1989). Asian households are different again and what little research there is suggests that there is considerable variation between them.

The gender ideology of the male breadwinner/female dependent, and the high degree of domesticity of women in some ethnic minority communities, constrain women's participation in the paid workforce. It is not simply the fact of having children that does this, indeed many Afro-Caribbean women with children are in full-time employment, but the whole set of expectations associated with institutionalized heterosexuality; and this is true across ethnic groups although the forms that it takes may differ. Thus it seems that institutionalized heterosexuality constrains women's access to resources and reproduces gender inequalities. It is only by moving beyond it that we can see precisely how institutionalized heterosexuality reproduces gender inequalities. Thus it is not gender alone that explains women's disadvantaged position in paid employment and within the domestic sphere. If women refuse, in some way, the relations of institutionalized heterosexuality and the gender hierarchy that it involves they are often able to improve their situation (VanEvery, 1995). It therefore appears that 'heterosexuality is an institution which is deeply implicated in the production of gender difference and gender hierarchies' (Dunne, 1997: 228).

This evidence shows that sexuality, ethnicity, class, and values/ideology affect the form taken by domestic divisions of labour and that gender inequalities within the home are structured by gendered divisions of paid work and men's generally greater access to resources. There is also evidence of attitudinal change in the direction of gender equality which is particularly apparent amongst younger generations; how far this will have an effect on gender divisions within households remains to be seen. There is some evidence that women's commitment to the workforce and particularly their participation in paid employment has a significant effect on domestic divisions of labour and this seems key to creating more egalitarian gender relations.

The way sociologists study domestic divisions of labour has also changed. During the 1950s a basic gender division of labour was taken for granted and was not problematized until feminist scholarship emerged with its focus on domestic divisions of labour and the distribution of resources within households. Subsequently there has been a move away from looking at the division of work within households to looking at gender identities and sexuality and theorizing domestic divisions of labour in terms of not only gender but also sexuality. However there are still relatively few studies of domestic divisions of labour in ethnic minority households and this lack becomes even clearer when we turn our attention to studies of parenting.

Chapter 4

Gendered Parenting

Parenting involves the provision of economic support and caring, both practically and emotionally, for a child. Within British society these aspects of parenting are gendered with fatherhood being associated with economic support and motherhood with caring. Indeed, so pervasive is the gendered division between economic support and caring that parenting is often interpreted as involving caring alone. We saw in the last chapter that young married couples tend to adopt a specific gender division of labour—women reduce their commitment to paid work and take on the main share of domestic labour while men prioritize their jobs and see themselves as the main providers. In this way they anticipate the gendering of parenting. In this chapter I focus on the relation of parenting to paid employment and care work, how this gendered division has been constructed, and how it is reinforced. I then look at the conflict that has arisen in the policy domain over motherhood and fatherhood and how parenting and the way it has been studied has changed since the 1950s.

Motherhood in post-war Britain

The 1942 Beveridge report assumed that women would become mothers within heterosexual marriage, they would withdraw from the paid workforce, and be supported by a male breadwinner. These assumptions were reinforced by the marriage bar, which prevented women from working once they were married, and the lack of childcare facilities, which was accentuated by the closure of wartime nurseries. In 1943, for instance, there were 59,000 places in 'residential or day nurseries' compared with 44,000 in 1948 and 22,000 in the early 1960s (Summerfield, 1989:191–2, n.4; Lewis, 1992:75). In the early 1990s there were less than half the number of day care places for pre-school age children than in 1945 'before the closure of the wartime nurseries' (Lewis, 1992:29). In the immediate post-war years maternal employment was not approved of, and more mothers tended to withdraw from the paid workforce for longer periods of time to care for dependent children than they do now; they 'were advised to work up to the birth of their first child and again after their children had left school' and seemed to do so (Lewis, 1992:24). Women having their first child between 1950 and 1954 spent almost ten years out of the labour market but by the 1970s half of first-time mothers returned to work within four years of the birth (Lewis, 1992:74). Indeed Seccombe suggests that it was in the 1950s that the male breadwinner family 'had its hey day . . . prevailing as an ideal without serious challenge, while possibly enjoying a higher level of conformity than any familial standard in history' (Seccombe, 1993:207).

Immediately after the war the gendering of parenthood and the idealization of home-based rather than public provision of childcare was reinforced by 'experts' such as Bowlby and Winnicott (Rapoport et al., 1977). Bowlby claimed that maternal care was as important to the development of mental health as vitamins were to physical development and that it should consist of 'a warm, intimate, and continuous relationship with his [sic] mother (or permanent mother substitute) in which both find satisfaction and enjoyment' (Bowlby, 1972:13, cited in Rapoport et al., 1977:37–8). If this sort of relationship did not happen then maternal deprivation resulted which could lead to crime and delinquency. While the mother-child relationship was crucial for normal development the father-child relationship was not important; a father's contribution to his child's development was through economic activity. Men's paid employment made it possible for women to devote themselves full time to childcare in order to maintain 'that harmonious contented mood in the atmosphere of which her infant thrives' (Bowlby 1972:15–16, cited in Rapoport et al., 1977:40). These theories were popularized through women's magazines and the idea of maternal deprivation became common currency.

Parenthood and paid work

Employment practices have changed considerably since the post-war period. There has been a move from marriage bars and the encouragement of part-time employment for women to the development of family-friendly policies and an expressed need to enable mothers as well as fathers to combine paid work with family life (Social Justice, 1994). These changing policies can be seen as a response to changing patterns of maternal employment. Thus in the early 1950s only 13 per cent of women returned to employment within 12 months of the birth of their first child. By the late 1970s this had increased to 25 per cent and by 1986 'a third of women with a child under 5 . . . were employed at any one time' (Brannen and Moss, 1991:28). By 1994, 59 per cent of mothers were in employment, usually part-time or temporary, which represents a 10 per cent increase since 1984. Moreover, between 1984 and 1994 maternal employment increased at twice the rate of employment for other women. Hours of paid work are also lengthening for mothers and higher-status jobs, into which women are increasingly moving, are associated with longer hours (Brannen et al., 1998).

Until the 1980s many women had balanced the demands of paid work and childcare by taking up part-time employment but the indications are that this may be changing, that the association of motherhood with withdrawal from paid employment is fast becoming outdated, and that motherhood is being 'modernised' (Leira, 1998). In any case, the association of motherhood with part-time employment did not reflect the experience of black mothers, who have always tended to work full time, or middle class, white mothers who could afford to pay for help with childcare. There is also evidence that the 1980s saw the end of the 'one-earner' family and the growth of no-earner and two-earner families. It is important to note, however, that, just as male unemployment does not necessarily lead to a more equitable domestic division of labour, a 'dual-earner family is not a dual-career family' (Leira, 1998:163).

As we have seen, there are also increasing numbers of women bringing up children on their own, either because they choose to have children outside a live-in heterosexual relationship or because of divorce. After the war women were much more likely to become lone mothers because of the death of their husbands (Kiernan et al., 1998:4). 'During the 1960s, divorce eclipsed death as the primary cause of lone motherhood and in the 1990s divorce may be set to be eclipsed by the growth in never-married lone motherhood' due to choice rather than mistake (Kiernan et al., 1998:8). After the war women bringing up children on their own were defined in policy terms as mothers therefore entitled to state support (albeit minimal) to enable them to care for their dependent children full time. Now they are expected to combine mothering and paid employment (Lewis, 1993). This reflects a shift in both practice and attitudes towards motherhood which is now seen as more compatible with employment than it was and does not necessarily involve dependence, either on a man or on the state. This shift is, however, problematic given the difficulties faced by lone mothers in combining paid work with mothering. Thus a majority of 'lone mothers were not in employment in the early 1990s and compared with the early 1970s the proportion of lone mothers in the labour force has declined' (Kiernan et al., 1998:127). Furthermore, although the employment trend amongst married mothers is upwards (between the early 1970s and early 1990s the proportion of married mothers with children under 5 who were in the workforce doubled from around 25 per cent to around 50 per cent) this is not reflected amongst lone mothers. Thus in the early 1990s, 39 per cent of lone mothers were either in employment or seeking work (compared with 62 per cent of married mothers) and those who were in employment were more likely to be in part-time than full-time employment (Kiernan et al., 1998: table 5.2, p. 128, table 5.3, p. 130).

Fatherhood in contrast is unproblematically associated with full-time paid employment. In the 1950s, full male employment meant that almost all fathers would have been in full-time paid employment. Despite a slight downward trend in fathers' employment (which fell by one percentage point between 1984 and 1994), at the end of the twentieth century employment amongst fathers is higher than for any other group. Thus, in 1994, 85 per cent of fathers were in paid employment compared with 70 per cent of other men, 70 per cent of other women, and 59 per cent of mothers. Employment rates are high for fathers throughout Europe and nine out of ten fathers who are in employment are in full-time employment (Burghes et al., 1997:43). Fatherhood is also related to the nature of men's work: fathers are more likely to be self-employed or working shifts and are likely to work longer hours than anyone else. Indeed hours of work for fathers are increasing (Brannen et al., 1998) and men in the UK have amongst the longest average weekly hours of all men in Europe. In the national Child Development Survey a fifth of fathers were (at 33 years of age in 1991) working 50–59 hours a week. Mothers work shorter hours. In fact during the early years of a child's life when their father is likely to be the sole earner (and this is still the case even if it is seen as a temporary phase) fathers' hours of work are usually around 55 a week. This leaves little time for routine involvement in childcare even if men want to be involved. Thus becoming a father is associated with an increase in men's hours of work while becoming a mother is associated with a decrease in women's hours of paid work. The resulting combination of parents' hours of work can be seen in Table 4.1.

Table 4.1 Economic activity of married couples with dependent children, 1995, Great Britain (per cent)

Two earners	62
—wife full-time	22
—wife part-time	40
Husband only working	26
Wife only working	4
No earner	9

Source: Office of Population Censuses and Surveys (1997), *General Household Survey*, taken from Burghes et al., 1997, table 4.3, p. 47. Reproduced with kind permission of the former Family Policy Studies Centre.

These figures show that role reversal is relatively uncommon and that if both partners are in paid employment it is more likely that the husband will be in full-time and the wife in part-time employment. Indeed, 66 per cent of families with dependent children can be said to conform to the male breadwinner family if those where the wife is working part time or is a full-time housewife are taken together. Figures such as these suggest that claims that the male breadwinner family is a thing of the past are premature. Indeed, in only 26 per cent of families with dependent children are women either the sole or full-time earners (these figures do not include cohabiting couples with dependent children). Nevertheless, the contribution of male earnings to family income is falling while women's is increasing. Thus between 1981 and 1991 men's contribution to household income fell from 73 per cent to 60 per cent while women's rose from 15 per cent to 29 per cent (Burghes et al., 1997:49).

Although employment among fathers is higher than amongst other men and women, this is not the case for young men; for them fatherhood is not associated with full-time employment. In 1992 almost 50 per cent of 20–24-year-old fathers were unemployed. Unemployment is one of the factors that increases the likelihood of fathers not living with their children and is much more likely to be a problem for young, working-class, and ethnic minority men. 'Young unemployed fathers lack the status that employment bestows and are unable to make financial provision for their children' (Burghes et al., 1997:52). So in an important sense, not being able to be a breadwinner reduces the likelihood of young men who are biological fathers being effective social fathers.

Parenthood and care work

Mothers are the primary carers of young children and although this may now be combined with paid employment it is caring for, nurturing, and feeding children which define motherhood. Fathers, on the other hand, are relatively absent from the care work associated with young children; they tend to care about their children while women care for them (Hester and Harne, 1999). (See Table 4.2.) Thus,

even in families with the most egalitarian child-care arrangements—those in which both parents work full-time—a quarter of the fathers report that mothers are still mainly responsible for childcare, while a third of the mothers report being mostly responsible for it. (Burghes et al., 1997:56)

Although approval for maternal employment has increased since the war, only 2 per cent of men and 3 per cent of women think that it is right for a

Table 4.2 'Who is normally responsible for generally being with and looking after children', NCDS 1991

	Cohort fathers			
	Dual-earner		Single-earner	
	Wife f/t	Wife p/t	Wife home	Wife works
Mostly father	2	1	<1	16
Mostly wife	24	42	68	21
Shared equally	72	57	32	61
Someone else	2	—	<1	2
Total	100	100	100	100
(N)	(397)	(993)	(1,008)	(44)

	Cohort mothers			
	Dual-earner		Single-earner	
	Mother f/t	Mother p/t	Mother home	Mother works
Mostly husband	1	<1	—	9
Mostly mother	32	52	72	26
Shared equally	66	48	28	64
Someone else	1	—	—	1
Total	100	100	100	100
(N)	(532)	(1,261)	(953)	(66)

Source: Ferri and Smith (1996), taken from Burghes et al., 1997: table 5.1, p. 57. Reproduced with kind permission of the former Family Policy Studies Centre.

woman with pre-school age children to have a full-time job. This compares with 23 per cent of men and 29 per cent of women who think it is right if the job is part time (Scott et al., 1993). Thus mothers' responsibility for caring, both practically and ideologically, circumscribes their participation in paid work (Burghes et al., 1997:63). However there is now strong support for fathers' involvement with their children, with 86 per cent of men and 87 per cent of women believing that it is better for fathers to be involved in bringing up their children from the earliest age (Eurobarometer, 1993, cited in Speak et al., 1997). These attitudes, however, are not translated into an equal sharing of the work of caring. This suggests that—at best—fathers' employment and the fulfilling of their provider role places structural constraints on their involvement in the day-to-day care of their children and—at worst—that most fathers do not want to take an equal share of childcare (Hester and Harne, 1999:151).

Conflict over 'the family'

At the beginning of the twenty-first century there is a moral panic about parenting—both mothering and fathering. Despite the increased acceptance of maternal employment there is still concern about the effect on children of mothers working, especially full time. In contrast, it is not paternal employment that is seen as a problem so much as paternal *un*employment which is associated with fathers' withdrawal from parenting. This concern centres on men's absence from families, on the one hand, and their lack of involvement in the caring dimension of parenting on the other (Williams, 1998). In recent years organizations such as Families Need Fathers have tried to reassert the importance of the male breadwinner role to families and to re-establish male authority and control over children. Rather than being more involved in caring, fathers in such organizations

want to play a role in their children's lives, but for most, that role is merely a continuation of their predivorce role of the traditional father who exercises his power and control. (Bertoia and Drakich, 1995:253)

It is also argued that now that women's equality in the public sphere has been achieved, men should have equality in the home in the form of equal rights to custody of their children after divorce. This argument ignores the fact that gender equality cannot be said to exist in public or in private. As we have seen, women are still disadvantaged in paid employment and still shoulder the main burden of care work when they live with the fathers of their children (Neale and Smart, 1997).

The argument for reinstating the male breadwinner family has been advanced by sociologists who, like the British prime minister Tony Blair, are ethical socialists (Dennis and Erdos, 1993). Changes in women's social position, they argue, are destroying the male breadwinner family. In particular they point to women's opting to have children on their own, women's increased ability to control their own fertility, their increased ability to support themselves, and their refusal any longer to tolerate abusive relationships. They argue that these developments make men redundant because women no longer need them for financial support. This is leading to the destruction of 'the family' and is having dire consequences for men, particularly young men, who grow up in fatherless families without any idea of what is involved in being a responsible adult male citizen. Furthermore men are 'barbarians' without the civilizing influence of responsibility for a wife and children (Murray, 1990). Consequently they father children with no recognition of their responsibilities, they resort to criminality, and they are a burden on the state, as are the children they father and the children's mothers. Another dimension of this crisis, one on which Dennis and Erdos are strangely silent, is the high levels of unemployment amongst young men and their lack of achievement in school. Unemployment, as we have seen, makes it less likely that men will operate as social fathers to their children. So what is to be done?

It is argued that the solution to this problem is to strengthen the 'traditional' family and reassert men's rights over women and children. This is because the so-called traditional family is

crucial for maintaining stability. Men are controlled by their familial responsibilities; women are controlled by husbands and children are controlled by parents. Women are to be full-time mothers socialising their children and caring for their husbands. The role of the state is to support this natural, God-given unit, not to undermine it with easy divorce, abortion, contraception for under-age girls and social security payments for single-parents. (Abbott and Wallace, 1992:12)

Indeed, Families Need Fathers argues that it is always better for children to see their fathers even when they have been violent towards them and their mothers. Thus they are on record as saying

We believe it is fair to see much of the physical violence . . . as a final response to violence inflicted in other forms, especially by women, verbal violence. (Cited in Segal, 1990:53)

This view is often upheld in the courts, with disastrous consequences for children and their mothers (Neale and Smart, 1997; Hester and Harne, 1999). In contrast the Child Support Agency, which is only interested in a father's financial responsibilities to his children, allows women whose partners have been violent towards them or their children to withhold the name of the child's father from the agency.

In the past fifty years attention has turned from the idea that maternal deprivation leads to delinquency to the idea that it is the absence of a father which leads to delinquency if not social breakdown. These concerns are reflected in the policy domain where attempts are being made to try and reinstate fathers within families, not only by ensuring that they meet their financial responsibilities for their children but also by addressing the responsibility to care. Thus the Child Support Act (1991) defines fatherhood in terms of economic responsibility whereas the 1989 Children Act enshrines a notion of parental responsibility and encourages 'the involvement of both parents in the care of their children after divorce or separation' (Speak et al., 1997:15;

Williams, 1998:72; Hester and Harne, 1999:154). One of the impacts of recent legislative changes has been 'to sustain the familial relations of the hetero-sexual nuclear family, even after separation and divorce' (Hester and Harne, 1999:155). This is despite that fact that 'the material and emotional resources for sustaining co-parenting are scarce and there is no real infrastructure avail-able properly to support co-parenting during marriage, let alone after divorce' (Neale and Smart, 1997:214). Attempts are also being made to reconstruct social fatherhood on a basis other than that of the sole breadwinner and to facilitate men's greater involvement with their children (Williams, 1998). However, there is scant evidence that fathers want equal responsibility for caring or that a move towards the de-gendering of parenting is driving such initiatives. Rather, in the absence of a commitment to creating the conditions on which gender parity in parenting depends, it can be seen as an attempt to increase fathers' rights (in a situation in which they are perceived to have become marginal to the family and, hence, discriminated against) without changing mothers' primary responsibility for care (Hester and Harne, 1999; Williams, 1998). Indeed,

the emphasis on fathering is also another way of asserting the importance of the trad-itional heterosexual nuclear family: 'good families' are male-headed nuclear families. (Segal, 1990: 53)

In addition to being silent on the way some men abuse women and children within traditional, nuclear families, the focus on fatherhood and a child's need for two biological parents to bring it up (which is asserted on the basis of dubious research) marginalizes other forms of child rearing such as collective forms of living, gay couples, and single parents (Segal, 1990).

Studying parenting

Sociological studies of parenting are scarce and those that exist owe more to social psychology than to sociology. They have shown 'very little interest in the social institution of fatherhood' and their theoretical concerns derive from attachment and object-relations theories (Richards, 1982; and cf. Cho-dorow, 1978). Studies carried out in the 1950s and 1960s did not problematize the gendering of parenting—it was too obvious to deserve comment. Thus the Newsons begin a chapter entitled 'Father's place is in the home' with the observation:

Obviously the care of infants is a predominantly female occupation, and in most normal families the mother is necessarily the central figure in the child's early life. (Newson and Newson, 1965:133)

This study of 'how infants are being reared in England' focused on 700 Nottingham *mothers*. Fathers were important in so far as their occupation provided the basis for assigning mothers and children to classes, identifying class-based differences in child rearing practices, and in assessing the 'extent to which fathers actually do participate in the care of one-year-olds' (ibid.: 134). This research took place in the same decade as studies which argued that families were becoming privatized and men were more focused on the home than they had been hitherto (see e.g. Goldthorpe et al., 1969). Indeed, Newson and Newson found that

At a time when he has more money in his pocket, and more leisure on which to spend it, than ever before, the head of the household chooses to sit at his own fireside, a baby on his knee and a feeding bottle in his hand: the modern father's place is in the home. (Newson and Newson, 1965:147)

They link the alleged increase in men's participation in infant care to, on the one hand, the disappearance of domestic servants and the resultant lack of domestic help available to middle-class women and, on the other hand, the 'isolation of the immediate family unit from the wider circle of the extended family and the close-knit neighbourhood unit' (Newson and Newson, 1965:141). This means that

Wives can no longer expect help from older women relatives living close by, upon which their mothers were able to call ... The husband thus becomes the wife's sole and indispensable source of companionship. (Newson and Newson, 1965:141–2)

These observations underline the point made in the last chapter about the changing nature of families' social networks and the effects this was having on the domestic support available to women and their perceptions of gender 'iniquities' within families. In Young and Wilmott's earlier study of Bethnal Green they found that, within an established working-class community, networks of female kin helped and supported each other with domestic work and childcare (Young and Wilmott, 1962). Indeed, the home was an exclusively female domain and close-knit networks of female kin were at its centre. Men were largely absent from the domestic sphere, their role as father being confined to the provision of a wage to support their wives and children (Dennis, Henriques, and Slaughter, 1956). Geographical mobility and slum clearance programmes were, however, breaking up these kin networks and isolating young wives in new ways; something which also attracted the Newsons' attention in Nottingham.

The Newsons noted a class difference in fathers' participation in housework and childcare. Thus men in social class 3 were more likely to help their partners with housework and childcare than those in social classes 1 and 2 or 4 and 5.

They suggested that this was because of the long hours worked by male, manual workers and young, professional, and managerial men which made them less available to share housework and childcare (Newson and Newson, 1965:226–7).

Many of these studies were marked by a conviction that contemporary fathers were more involved with their families than previous generations, much as they found evidence for the emergence of the symmetrical family (Young and Wilmott, 1962; Newson and Newson, 1963:140). It has been argued, however, that this assumption is not based on sound evidence and that fathers in the past were just as likely (or unlikely) to be domesticated and participative as fathers in the 1950s and 1960s (Lummis, 1982). What is missing from this period is detailed studies of men as fathers because of the (not unreasonable) assumption that women as mothers were responsible for childcare. Men were studied in the public world of work rather than the private world of home and family. Furthermore, this division of labour was assumed to be rooted in biology. Thus Parsons and Bales wrote:

In our opinion the fundamental explanation of the allocation of the roles between the biological sexes lies in the fact that the bearing and early nursing of children establish a strong presumptive primacy of the relation of mother to the small child and this in turn establishes a presumption that the man, who is exempted from these biological functions, should specialise in the alternative instrumental direction. (Parsons and Bales, 1955:23, cited in VanEvery, 1997:416)

The social construction of motherhood

This acceptance of biology as explanation of the inevitability of gendered parenting began to be questioned in the 1970s. Feminists focused their attention on motherhood, arguing that the form it takes is socially, historically, and culturally specific. In advanced, capitalist, industrial societies motherhood has been constructed as dependence on a male breadwinner and is associated with withdrawal from economic production. This is far from natural or biologically given. On the contrary it had to be constructed through legislation and 'teaching' working-class women about motherhood. Thus in the early stages of industrialization women and children as well as men were in the mines and factories. But legislation in the nineteenth century restricted the hours of work of women and children. At the end of the nineteenth century, the newly emergent profession of social work (lady visitors) instructed working-class women how to be 'good' mothers and one of the defining features of motherhood was that it should be a 24-hour-a-day occupation and should not be combined with paid employment (Wilson, 1977). So with the development of capitalist, industrial society and the withdrawal of children from the paid workforce, motherhood was also (ideally) divorced from paid work and economic activity. The burden of motherhood was to manage the home and feed the family— most importantly ensuring that the male breadwinner was fed sufficiently so that he could return to work and earn the family's wage. Women's manager- ial role in the home could be undermined by their employment. As Tilly and Scott note,

The centrality of food in the family budget and the mother's responsibility for providing food were dominant features of working class life. The married woman's control over family resources and her self-sacrifice for her family were two sides of the same coin. (Tilly and Scott, 1987:138–9)

Thus women's absence from the home jeopardized its smooth running and was actively discouraged by middle-class reformers in the nineteenth century.

The social construction of fatherhood

Attention was also turned to the association of fatherhood with notions of provider and breadwinner. Historically fatherhood has not always been associ- ated with paid work as opposed to care work (McKee and O'Brien, 1982). In early-modern Europe, for instance, fathers were seen as more important than mothers in caring for, bringing up, and educating their children; caring was not yet seen as something associated with women rather than with men. And fathers took primary responsibility for the moral and religious instruction of their older children (Lupton and Barclay, 1997). The emphasis on the father's role was related to assumptions about men's rationality and their association with culture, order, and civilization (an echo of this is to be found in the argu- ments that fathers are necessary to teach young boys about civic duty). They were seen as superior to mothers in providing guidance because of their greater reason and their ability to control their emotions (Lupton and Barclay, 1997:37). However with industrialization and urbanization, and the separation of paid employment from the domestic sphere, conditions were created which made possible the emergence of the idea that men should be the financial providers for women and children and women should look after children in the home. The idea that fatherhood is associated with breadwinning, with participation in paid employment, and that this is the main way that men can be social fathers, is therefore historically and culturally specific.

Feminist studies of motherhood

Feminists were concerned to deconstruct the 'myth of motherhood', arguing that it delegitimates mothers' participation in the workforce while legitimating their dependence on men within socially sanctioned heterosexual relationships (Comer, n.d.). Women's responsibility for child rearing within the nuclear family disadvantaged them relative to men at work and confined them to reproductive rather than productive activities. Women's experience of motherhood was shown to be contradictory, having negative as well as positive dimensions (Oakley, 1981). Moreover—in contrast with the myth—many women combined motherhood with paid work, in either the formal or the informal economy (see e.g. Westwood and Bhachu, 1988). Such analyses conceptualized the care work associated with motherhood in terms of social reproduction and focused on the way the law, the medical profession, and social policies, by defining motherhood and attempting to control women who chose to mother in other ways, reproduced gender divisions of labour which were oppressive to women. They operated on the boundaries of sociology and social policy and explored the gendering of care work in both the private and public domains (Graham, 1991).

The medicalization of motherhood

In the 1970s, and associated with the women's health movement, feminist sociologists began to study the way that motherhood was medicalized. They showed that the medical profession judges who is and is not fit to be a mother and controls the whole process of becoming a mother, from confirming pregnancy through access to many forms of contraception and abortion to childbirth itself (Oakley, 1981; Doyal, 1981). Studies of the medical control of contraception illustrated the strength of the association of acceptable motherhood with 'race' and class. Thus many of the most effective forms of contraception can only be obtained through a doctor; the medical profession has a monopoly of knowledge about them and the effects they have on women's bodies, and, through its control of access to them, can transform moral judgements about women's suitability for motherhood into practices which differentiate between groups of women. Thus the injectable contraceptive, Depo-Provera, is used widely by population planners in the third world and in working-class and ethnic minority communities in Britain: it is also prescribed for students (personal communication). Its efficiency as a contraceptive which does not rely on user compliance—it is an injection administered every three months by health care professionals—outweighs (for those administering it) its potentially harmful side effects (Richardson, 1993:67). In Britain the drug has been used primarily on black women, poor women with large families, and women with learning difficulties; women who, in the eyes of the medical profession, cannot be trusted to contracept effectively and whose motherhood is not desirable. There is evidence that black women particularly have been pressured into accepting it (or sterilization) as a condition of abortion (Bryan, Dadzie, and Scafe, 1985).

Most abortion legislation does not give women the right to choose and the British legislation is no exception. Two doctors must agree that continuing with the pregnancy is more dangerous for the woman's health than its being terminated. Various studies have shown that doctors make moral decisions about who can and cannot have access to an abortion. In general it is more difficult for married than unmarried women but it is relatively easy for women on low incomes with large families or women with a mental or physical disability (Morris, 1991). One study showed that few doctors allow 'normal' married women to have an abortion because they judge that she is doing it for convenience (MacIntyre, 1977). Such decisions are based on the idea that motherhood is normal and natural within marriage but that outside marriage and among poor and ethnic minority women it is less desirable.

Motherhood and institutionalized heterosexuality

Feminist sociologists also problematized the association of motherhood with institutionalized heterosexuality, arguing that it was socially constructed. This was done through an exploration of the experiences of lesbian mothers or of lesbians wishing to become mothers. In British society, as in the west as a whole, it is assumed that biological and social motherhood go together; social motherhood without biological motherhood (fostering or adoption for instance) is considered not quite 'real' motherhood. So motherhood is associated with becoming pregnant which is associated with heterosexual intercourse. These associations mean that by definition women who are not heterosexual cannot become pregnant and cannot become mothers. But these assumptions are not valid for a number of reasons (Richardson, 1993). Thus, women who identify as lesbians may have sexual relationships with men or may have had in the past. Moreover, it is not necessary to indulge in heterosexual sex to become pregnant, 'It is sperm which is necessary for fertilisation, not its ejaculation from a penis inserted into a woman's vagina' (Richardson, 1993:78). And the development of reproductive technology means that, for many women, becoming pregnant has nothing to do with heterosexual intercourse at all. However, artificial insemination techniques are not as available for women who are lesbians as they are for women who are in a heterosexual relationship with a man. This is because of normative assumptions that a child needs a father as well as a mother in order to grow and develop 'normally'. Thus the Human Fertilisation and Embryology Act (1990) which governs the use of reproductive technology in Britain, states that in giving or withholding fertility treatment account should be taken of the welfare of 'any child who may be born as a result of that treatment (including the need of that child for a father)' (Richardson, 1993:78).

The construction of motherhood within institutionalized heterosexuality is also evident in the way lesbian mothers were treated by the courts if they were involved in disputes over the custody of their children. Even though mothers were almost without exception awarded custody (Lowe, 1982:34–5), lesbian mothers often lost custody cases. In 70 to 80 per cent of custody cases custody was awarded to the child's mother (Lowe, 1982:34) but, in the 1980s, 'around 90% of lesbian mothers [were] losing their custody cases' (Segal, 1990:52). If lesbian mothers were awarded custody, stringent conditions were often attached in order to ensure that their children did not grow up gay. One woman said:

It's terrible really when I think about it. In order to keep my children I had to agree to bring them up to be heterosexual whatever that means, and I ask myself what does that say about being gay, which I am. And what happens if my kids do decide to have gay relationships? It's not on is it? Not seen as a viable option? (Richardson, 1993:81)

This happened despite the complete absence of evidence that having a lesbian mother inclines children to homosexuality or of how it is possible to ensure heterosexual development. Indeed, a recent article by a father in the *Guardian* newspaper underlines the ludicrousness of trying to legislate against homosexuality, recounting the experiences of his identical twin daughters, reared by heterosexual parents, one of whom has married a man and has a baby while the other is in a lesbian partnership (Preston, 2000). Although lesbianism is still seen as in contradiction with motherhood (Weston, 1991) the 1989 Children Act has enabled lesbian couples to have equal parental rights (Dean, 1994; Dyer, 1994).

Motherhood and caring

Feminists have also studied caring, analysing it as gendered, constructed as women's work, and as something which is overwhelmingly carried out by women (Graham, 1991; Finch and Groves, 1983). In the 1980s there were numerous studies of caring—of both children and other dependents—showing how women care for their families by feeding them (Charles and Kerr, 1988; DeVault, 1991), by looking after their health (Graham, 1984), and by carry-

ing out the daily tasks associated with 'looking after able-bodied and dependent people at home' (Graham, 1991). Mothers rather than fathers feed their
children; it is an important dimension of motherhood. Thus 'at the age of one
year solid feeding is labelled by many parents as the responsibility of the
mother' (Lewis, 1986:97). Charles and Kerr found that it was overwhelmingly
mothers who cooked for the family (in the form of a proper meal of meat and
two vegetables) and who fed their children (Charles and Kerr, 1988). DeVault
also explored the relationship between feeding, caring, and motherhood in a
qualitative study which demonstrates a strong, socially constructed and negotiated association between '"mothering" and the preparation of food'
(DeVault, 1991:104). Feeding is an important part of nurturing and caring for
children and it is constructed as part of mothering across all ethnic groups and
even globally (Dwyer and Bruce, 1988). It is also overwhelmingly women who
cook; men cook for special occasions or on Sundays, women are responsible for
ensuring and worrying about the daily nourishment of their children and partners (Charles and Kerr, 1988). Studies of caring for older dependants show that
this is also gendered. Women are more likely than men to provide informal
care for relatives or friends (22 per cent of women aged between 45 and 64
provide this sort of care compared with 17 per cent of men) and the type of care
that they provide also differs (Cabinet Office, 2000:45). Men are more likely to
provide financial support while women give practical caring help which takes
time. This mirrors the provider-carer division of labour which characterizes
parenting and does not seem to vary with ethnicity (Finch and Mason,
1993:165).

Attention was also drawn to men as carers (Arber and Gilbert, 1989) and,
later, to the way studies of caring focus on its gendering to the exclusion of its
'race' and class dimensions (Graham, 1991). Thus black and working-class wom-
en's care work in white, middle-class women's homes—including looking after
their children—has not been explored even in studies of domestic service
(Gregson and Lowe, 1994). This is particularly significant because of the way
black women's motherhood is problematized, yet black women are relied on to
mother other women's children and to care for their dependants, either in
other women's homes or in residential care settings, hospitals, etc. As we have
already seen white, middle-class couples are more likely than others to employ paid help in their homes, but little British research exists into caring and
ethnicity (Beishon et al., 1998:68).

Feminism and fatherhood

It was not until the 1980s that researchers began to pay attention to studying men as fathers. This attention was galvanized by the demands from feminists for men to share domestic work and childcare and the feminist critique of masculinity: gender was now seen as something which pertained to men as well as to women (Kimmel, 1990). One of the first comprehensive studies of fatherhood, which built on the earlier studies of the Newsons and was located in social psychology but which also modelled itself on feminist studies of motherhood, was Charlie Lewis's *Becoming a father* (1986). This study demonstrated the lack of change there had been in fathers' caring activities and revealed the persistence of gendered parenting, with mothers being the primary caretakers and fathers playing an ancillary—though not unimportant—role:

nobody really expects fathers to play a major role in childcare as long as their wives are capable of coping themselves. They simply accept the cultural prescription that the mother should take primary responsibility for the baby. (Lewis, 1986:82)

Thus in 1960 and in 1980 'roughly 40% of men changed less than 13 of the two thousand or so nappies that each child had worn over the first year!' and 'while there has been a slight increase during 20 years in their practical involvement, the figures show no evidence of any increase in men's ideological commitment to the daily care of their children' (Lewis, 1986:173, 175). In line with other studies Lewis finds that men have become more involved in some tasks, but that their main involvement with their young children is as playmate—responsibility for the routine, daily care remains with mothers even in the very few role reversal couples included in his study. He explains this as follows:

As lower-status, secondary care givers they are compensated in that to a certain extent they can choose the activities in which they become involved. As a result, fathers tend to participate in those tasks which might enhance their relationship with the child and which they can fit in at convenient times. (Lewis, 1986:99)

Thus mothers are felt to be necessary while fathers are 'a bit of a luxury' (Lewis, 1986:176). Lewis also notes that there is resistance to breaching these divisions of responsibility because of the way gender identities are tied up with caring and nurturing (for women) and providing (for men) (Lewis, 1986:184). The most important factors affecting involvement with childcare and housework were maternal and paternal employment (Lewis, 1986:104). He also found (in line with the Newsons' earlier findings) that fathers in social class 3—non-professional, white-collar workers—were more involved in childcare than other fathers (Lewis, 1986:109). More recent research confirms that shared childcare is less common amongst professional and managerial fathers than amongst fathers in other social classes (Williams, 1998:81 citing Ferri and Smith, 1996). Indeed, father participation is

clearly delimited within physiological and cultural guidelines, which are sanctioned by both parents. Fathers, as secondary care-givers, settle for an 'incompetent' role, and this of course enables them to evade certain tasks. As primary care-givers, mothers have to perform these chores, but by way of compensation they are conceded the role of 'experts' in the domestic sphere. (Lewis, 1986:111)

As McKee observed in an earlier study:

While fathers could opt into childcare and influence the sex-role division of childcare work, mothers did not feel that they had an equivalent facility for opting out of childcare or into full-time waged work. (McKee, 1982:134)

Thus fathers' increased involvement in childcare results from a positive choice by them whereas mothers have no choice in the matter; the primary caretaker role is theirs whether or not they choose it.

An important finding of these studies is that many young men experience becoming a father as a maturing process which makes them into responsible adults; they take their jobs more seriously as they no longer have only themselves to think about (Simms and Smith, 1982). This is true for young men who are not living with their children as well as for those who are and provides some support for the idea that marriage and children can be a civilizing influence on young 'barbaric' males. Thus fatherhood, like motherhood, is a gendered sign of adult status in British society.

Fatherhood and caring

Studies in the 1990s were mainly qualitative and explored men's involvement in childcare roles and the constraints under which they operate. They pinpoint a disjuncture between the level of involvement fathers would like to have with their young children and the level that is attainable, given the biological fact of breast feeding and the constraints imposed by the increased significance of men's paid employment once they become fathers and their partners withdraw (temporarily or permanently) from paid work (Lupton and Barclay, 1997). They have tended to focus on small samples of white, middle-class men and there has been a dearth of research on parenting among ethnic minorities.

Indeed, Lewis consciously chose not to include ethnic minority fathers in his study and was therefore unable to explore the effects of ethnicity on fathering (Lewis, 1986:21). Studies which take ethnicity into account are more evident in the USA than in Britain. They find that black fathers are more involved with childcare and housework than fathers from other ethnic groups and that, in contrast to Hispanic and white fathers, their involvement increases with their paid hours of work (Shelton and John, 1993:141). In addition, research suggests that black fathers, even when they do not live with their children and/or are unemployed, are more involved with them than fathers in other ethnic groups (Stier and Tienda, 1993). Contrary to this there is evidence, from Britain as well as the USA, that unemployment or insecure, low-paid employment reduces the likelihood of fathers' involvement with their children, and that, given the high rates of unemployment experienced by black men, these factors need to be disentangled from the effects of ethnicity in exploring ethnic and 'racial' variations in the construction of fatherhood. As two researchers in the USA comment, perhaps 'economic stress affects fathering behaviours more strongly than mothering behaviours because it challenges a central component of the fathering role, economic providing' (Mosley and Thomson, 1995:150). Indeed, it may be that there are more similarities than differences across different ethnic groups. American research suggests that it is employment status rather than cultural differences between ethnic groups that affects the nature of men's social fathering.

Recent studies of men as fathers have explored the experience of becoming a father and how macro-structures operate against fuller male involvement with children. They tend to operate within a theoretical perspective which explores fatherhood at the level of meaning and identity (see e.g. Lupton and Barclay, 1997). Despite this they almost universally show that the ability to provide for their children is a crucial part of being a father but that many men feel constrained by the structure of paid employment from being as involved as they would like in caring. And although fathers desire greater involvement, there is scant evidence of their wanting to share equally in caring for their children. Even men who take on the role of primary carer relinquish it when the child's mother is present (unless of course they are lone fathers). However, American research suggests that women's assumption of a co-provider role and the availability of workplace encouragement of caring fatherhood leads to a greater involvement of fathers in housework and childcare (Coltrane, 1995). Such findings reinforce those that link women's full-time employment to more egalitarian domestic divisions of labour.

De-gendering parenting

There are very few studies of gay and lesbian parenting which, if developed, have the potential to explore ways of parenting that are not necessarily gendered (Williams, 1998). In an American study of 'families we choose', Kath Weston points out that the de-gendering of parenting is difficult to imagine: if two women or two men are sharing parenting then it is often felt that one would 'have' to be the mother and the other would 'have' to be the father (Weston, 1991:172–3). There is suggestive evidence, however, that moving beyond institutionalized heterosexuality can lead to changes in the gendering of parenting. Thus mothers bringing up children on their own may identify themselves as providers as well as carers and give increased priority to their careers in order to improve their own and their children's standard of living (Blackaby et al., 1999; Siltanen, 1994). However many single mothers are unpartnered for a relatively short period of time and, in those circumstances, solve the problem of gendered parenting by finding a new partner; a solution which is even more likely to be the case for single fathers (Kiernan et al., 1998:53).

Evidence suggests that parenting, even at the beginning of the twenty-first century, remains fundamentally gendered with fatherhood being associated with providing and motherhood with caring. And despite the focus of research on whether or not fathers are becoming more involved with caring for their children, there is still relatively little British research that analyses the gendering of parenting and the way that this varies in relation to sexuality, class, and ethnicity. Rather than demonstrating any fundamental shift in the gendering of parenting, this chapter suggests that the association of motherhood with caring for young children and fatherhood with providing for them both structures and is structured by the labour market. It is now more acceptable to combine motherhood and paid employment but the association of fatherhood, paid employment, and the ability to provide remains strong. Similarly concern about maternal deprivation has been replaced by concern about paternal deprivation. Such concern suggests that the gendering of care work, like the gendering of paid work, is not as clear as it was fifty years ago.

Chapter 5

Schooling—it's a Girl's World

Having discussed the ways in which paid employment, domestic labour, family households, and parenting are structured by gender, I now turn my attention to the gender dynamics of schooling. I begin by looking at continuity and change in ideas about the curriculum, patterns of achievement, and the relation between examination success and the labour market since the 1950s. I then explore the way sociological studies of education have moved from a focus on class inequalities amongst boys in the 1950s and 1960s, through a concern with deviance, delinquency, and the reproduction of educational and class inequalities—again amongst boys—to a focus on boys' alleged under-achievement in relation to girls. In the 1970s and 1980s this focus on boys was interrupted by attention to girls and schooling, in particular the gendering of the curriculum and the ways in which education contributed to the reproduction of gender relations and specific gender divisions of paid work. These shifts are represented in Table 5.1.

The curriculum

The 1944 Education Act was based on the notion of equality of opportunity and provided, for the first time, free, compulsory schooling to the age of 14. However, the inequalities that education was supposed to counteract were those of class, particularly as they related to boys. The concern was that able working-class children should have the same opportunity as their middle-class counterparts to pursue a secondary education (Foster et al., 1996). Gender differences, in contrast, were an integral part of the curriculum. A series of reports, published during the 1940s, 1950s, and 1960s, stipulated that girls were to do

Table 5.1 Parallel educational discourses

Historical period	Prevalent discourses of education	Prevalent discourses of gender and education
1940s, 1950s	Equality of opportunity: IQ testing (focus on access)	Weak (emphasis on equality according to 'intelligence')
1960s, 1970s	Equality of opportunity: progressivism/mixed ability (focus on process)	Weak (emphasis on working-class, male disadvantages)
1970s to early 1980s	Equality of opportunity: gender, race, disability, sexuality, etc. (focus on outcome)	Equal opportunities/anti-sexism (emphasis on female disadvantage)
Late 1980s, early 1990s	Choice, vocationalism, and marketization (focus on competition)	Identity politics and feminism (emphasis on femininities and masculinities)
Mid-1990s	School effectiveness and improvement (focus on standards)	Performance and achievement (emphasis on male disadvantage)

Source: G. Weiner et al. (1997) 'Is the future female? Female success, male disadvantage, and changing gender patterns in education' in A. H. Halsey et al. (eds) *Education: culture, economy, society*, Oxford University Press, Oxford, table 41.4, p. 622. Reproduced by permission of Oxford University Press.

the 'domestic subjects' because 'knowledge of such subjects is a necessary equipment for all girls as potential makers of homes' as well as being useful for their future occupations (Norwood, 1943:127). There was a recognition that married women were a significant and indispensable part of the workforce and that, in order to facilitate their return to work after having children, 'girls should be encouraged to qualify before marriage in a greater number of professions or occupations which will provide opportunities for them in later years' (Crowther, 1959:33). Secondary education for those who left school at the earliest opportunity needed to be realistic and relevant to the adolescent and should reflect their current and future interests. For boys it was assumed that this would be 'the world of machines' and that 'many boys find technological subjects their easiest and most natural approach to science' (ibid.:111). In contrast,

The passionate interest that many girls feel in living things can be as strong an educational incentive as the love of machines. It is not for nothing that biology is the main science taught to girls, as physics and chemistry are to boys. (Crowther, 1959:112)

Girls were to be educated to become wives and mothers and to take up appropriately gendered paid employment once their children were old enough, boys to become husbands and fathers, providing for their dependants, and working full time in a man's job (Crowther, 1959). This need to prepare children for the gendered world of paid work and parenting did not, however, preclude concerns about some aspects of the gendering of the curriculum whereby, in the sixth form, girls were more likely to do arts subjects while boys were more likely to do sciences (Crowther, 1959:251–6).

The Newsom report, which was published in 1963, noted that the social position of women was changing and, because of this,

Girls themselves need to be made aware of the new opportunities which may be open to them, and both boys and girls will be faced with evolving a new concept of partnership in their personal relations, at work and in marriage. (Newsom, 1963:28)

As in the other reports, the domestic crafts were seen as particularly suitable for girls because 'they are likely to find themselves eventually making and running a home' (Newsom, 1963:135) although the relevance of such courses for boys was also recognized due to the fact that 'partnership in marriage, whether in household chores or in bringing up the children, is an important concept for our society' (Newsom, 1963:137). The curriculum was therefore gendered because it needed to fit children for a gendered society.

The gendering of the curriculum, with physics and maths being seen as boys' subjects and modern languages as girls', is also apparent in the pattern of subject choice reflected in examination passes. Thus in the 1970s there were 'broadly similar numbers of passes between boys and girls' in English and history, 'far more girls were successful in French than boys, whereas this pattern is slightly reversed for maths and to a much greater extent for physics' (Deem, 1978:66). This is shown in Table 5.2.

Although there are still gender differences in examination passes which reflect the gendering of modern languages as feminine and physics as masculine, there is now a gender parity in maths (Dennison and Coleman, 2000:104). Such changes have led to claims that there has been a significant reduction in the gendering of the curriculum and that there is a 'new gender symmetry' with 'roughly even proportions of boys and girls' attempting GCSE/SCE (S grade) in maths, English and modern languages (Walby, 1997:48).

There is, however, a continuing gender imbalance in physics, computing, and craft, design, and technology, which are taken by more boys, and home economics, which is taken by more girls. This can be seen in Table 5.3.

Much of the reduction in gender differences has come about since the introduction of the national curriculum in 1988 which was seen in some quarters as a means of lessening the gendered nature of subject choice in secondary school and a step forward for gender equality. This certainly seems to be the case for subjects that are obligatory; where choice *can* be exercised, however, gendered

Table 5.2 Examination passes, 1970 and 1974 (grade 5 or better), selected subjects, CSE

Subject	1970			1974		
	Boys	Girls	% Girls	Boys	Girls	% Girls
English	95, 855	84,551	47	185,562	191,275	51
History	36,281	32,954	48	59,328	60,562	50.5
French	20,790	30,587	59.5	37,127	59,492	62
Maths	89,582	76,294	46	152,672	142,801	48
Physics	46,180	4,181	8	76,074	10,221	12
Biology	14,558	36,576	71.5	35,261	78,465	59
Technical drawing	47,356	358	0.75	69,418	860	1
Metalwork and woodwork	52,027	96	0.2	92,015	533	0.6
Geography	49,165	33,303	40	80,043	58,980	42
Domestic subjects	1,111	54,653	98	5,524	109,787	95
Commercial	5,609	27,318	83	10,031	50,231	83
Social sciences and vocational	9,326	8,972	49	35,438	38,384	52

Source: Adapted from Deem, 1978: table 3.2, p. 67. Reproduced by permission of Routledge.

Table 5.3 GCSE/SCE (S grade) attempts and achievements in schools, by sex, 1993–1994 (thousands)

Selected subject group	No. of attempts			% grade A–C	
	Males	Females	% Female	Males	Females
Biology	33.7	34.8	51	73	72
Chemistry	37.9	26.4	41	78	81
Physics	42.1	20.7	33	80	82
Single Science	52.2	55.4	51	36	41
Double Science	213.7	212.0	50	49	49
Maths	315.0	311.7	50	46	45
Computing	44.3	25.4	36	49	55
Craft, Design, & Technology	162.4	49.1	23	38	52
Home Economics	15.2	88.1	85	21	44
Social Studies	11.3	21.5	66	37	51
English	306.4	296.5	49	49	66
English Literature	200.6	219.3	52	54	67
Modern Languages	265.9	315.5	54	43	57

Source: Walby, 1997: table 2.17, p. 48. Reproduced by permission of Routledge.

patterns are still evident (Paechter, 1998:27; O'Donnell and Sharpe, 2000). Nevertheless the fact that large numbers of girls are now taking science subjects and maths at GCSE whereas in the past only a small minority studied science is not insignificant.

Class as well as gender affects both the subjects pupils choose to study and their career aspirations. Thus research in the Grampian region of Scotland found that working-class girls were likely to aspire to jobs in 'nursing, secretarial and clerical jobs, hairdressing and childcare' while boys identified 'trades in skilled manual occupations' (Darling and Glendinning, 1996:98). Gender differences were also apparent amongst students from non-manual households where engineering (boys) and teaching (girls) were counterposed. In terms of subject choice, middle-class boys were likely to study physics, middle-class girls biology, and working-class girls and boys general science (ibid.:102). This related to their career aspirations: middle-class boys (and some girls) aspired to high-status jobs, middle-class girls (and some working-class girls and middle-class boys) 'occupy an intermediate position', while working-class girls 'aspire to either junior non-manual positions or to lower-status manual jobs' and working-class boys 'hope to enter skilled manual jobs or trades' (ibid.:107). Thus subject choice in secondary school has implications for future careers, with 'male-academic' subjects being seen as those which will enable you to attain high-status jobs; they are also taken by more boys than girls. This evidence suggests that in the early twenty-first century the curriculum is still gendered although there have been significant changes since the 1950s and 1960s.

Gender and achievement

Since the war the proportion of boys and girls staying on at school and taking public examinations at 16+ has increased. Thus in 1953, 11 per cent of boys and 10 per cent of girls passed five O levels but by 1973 this had risen to almost equal proportions of boys (22.7 per cent) and girls (23.3 per cent) (Byrne, 1978:129). By the end of the 1990s the 'gender gap' had been reversed, with 53 per cent of girls achieving five or more grades A to C at GCSE compared with 43 per cent of boys (Cabinet Office, 2000:21). Girls' performance at A level has also improved but more slowly. Thus although by 1973 a similar proportion of boys and girls were passing two A levels (4.1 per cent of boys and 4.4 per cent of girls), 9.2 per cent of boys passed three A levels compared with 6.6 per cent of girls (Byrne, 1978:129). This gap has now disappeared. Thus in 1985–6, 10 per cent of boys and 9 per cent of girls gained three or more A levels, in 1990–1 they were level pegging at 14 per cent, and in 1993–4 14 per cent of boys and 16 per cent of girls gained three or more A levels (Walby, 1997:44, table 2.12). Indeed, if the proportion of girls and boys gaining two or more A levels is considered girls have 'outperformed' boys since 1988/89 (ONS, 2001). It is figures such as these which support the idea of a widening gender gap and give rise to concerns about boys' 'under-achievement'. This concern needs to be set alongside the fact that 'similarities in males' and females' performance far outweigh any differences observed' (Murphy and Elwood, 1998:162–3) and that 'rates of achievement have been improving steadily for young people of both sexes' (Dennison and Coleman, 2000:103). This suggests that it may not be accurate to define what is happening in terms of boys' under-achievement when boys as well as girls are achieving more year on year.

Moreover there are serious problems with the way data on achievement are constructed (see e.g. Gorard et al., 1999) and there is ample evidence that the tendency for girls to outperform boys is not new (Cohen, 1998). Thus in the 1950s when children were selected for grammar schools by the 11+ exam, girls outperformed boys but, in order to maintain an equal gender balance in grammar schools, girls had to achieve better results than boys to gain a grammar school place (Epstein et al., 1998:5).

Class and achievement

The current focus on gender and achievement diverts attention from the way class continues to affect educational outcomes. For the most part, class inequalities in education have been represented in terms of boys' access and achievement. Thus in the 1970s Halsey et al. found that boys with service class fathers (professional/senior technical/managerial) were three times more likely than boys with fathers in manual occupations to go to grammar schools, four times more likely to be in full-time education at the age of 16 (the minimum school leaving age was 15 at the time of their study), ten times more likely to be in full-time education at the age of 18, and 11 times more likely to go to university (Halsey et al., 1980:202, 204). There is some evidence that class differences for girls are even sharper. A study published in 1971 found that middle-class girls were twice as likely as working-class girls to do O levels; 6.5 times as likely to do A levels and 13 times as likely to go to university. Class differences amongst boys were less marked, with middle-class boys being 1.4 times as likely as working-class boys to do O levels, three times as likely to do A levels, and six times as likely to go to university. The same study found that middle-class boys were 21 times more likely than working-class girls to do a full-time university degree.

At each level of education the sex-gap is bigger for the working class than the middle class and the class-gap is bigger for girls than for boys. As the level of education rises the sex-gap widens for both classes, but widens more for the working class. The class-gap also widens for both sexes, but more for girls than for boys. (King, 1971:171)

It is difficult to find more recent sources which deal systematically with class differences in educational outcomes but data relating to both girls and boys show that 'differences in educational performance still persist between social classes' (Foster et al., 1996:142).

Ethnicity and achievement

It is also difficult to find detailed data on achievement which combine the variables of class, ethnicity, and gender; most sources consider one or at best two but almost never all three (Foster et al., 1996:148; Raphael Reed, 1999:96). This difficulty is compounded by an unwillingness on the part of many schools to collect data on the basis of ethnicity (Dennison and Coleman, 2000:107). In addition, different studies use different classifications of ethnicity, so making comparison difficult. The Swann report, for instance, which was published in 1985, found that the academic achievement of South Asians was comparable to that of whites but that West Indians were under-achieving (Modood et al., 1997:63). This report, however, did not explore any potential link between gender and achievement and, according to Heidi Mirza, ignored the 'fact' that 'in all ethnic groups girls did better' (Mirza, 1992:28, citing ILEA, 1987). A survey in the mid-1970s, which looked at gender and ethnicity, found 'that Caribbean and Pakistani men were less qualified than their white peers, while Indians and African Asians were best qualified' and 'South Asian women, especially the Pakistanis, were much less qualified than the men' (Modood et al., 1997:63). These apparently conflicting statements about gender differences in achievement in different ethnic groups demonstrate the problems that arise from different definitions of ethnicity adopted in different studies. The most recent Policy Studies Institute (PSI) survey confirms that there are significant differences between ethnic groups in levels of attainment, that achievement outcomes vary with gender, and that the nature of the gender gap varies with ethnic group. Thus the lowest qualification levels for the 16–24 age group were found amongst young Pakistani and Bangladeshi women and men, with the situation being worst for Bangladeshi young women (Modood et al., 1997).

The same survey also found that young Caribbean men, while being out-performed by young Caribbean women, have higher qualification levels than young Pakistani and Bangladeshi men but lower levels than young white and

Indian men (ibid.). Despite this evidence, a recent research review states, in 'the *absence of statistical information*, concerns have particularly surrounded the performance of African Caribbean young men, *who have the lowest levels of attainment of all groups*' (Dennison and Coleman, 2000:107, my emphasis). This points up the confusion surrounding the way gender and ethnicity interact in influencing educational attainment and the danger of drawing firm conclusions on the basis of insufficient evidence. Moreover it is important that class, as well as gender and ethnicity, be taken into account because 'class and the associated level of education of parents (for both boys and girls) continue to be the most reliable predictors of a child's success in school examinations' (Epstein et al., 1998:11; Foster et al., 1996:160).

Educational achievement and occupation

The concern with boys' level of achievement is often linked to anxiety about their employment prospects; the gender gap in favour of girls is interpreted as advantaging girls in the labour market. However, the relation between educational achievement and jobs is far from straightforward, there is no simple equation between a good performance at GCSE and good employment prospects, and there is no evidence that girls' increasing success at GCSEs has yet had an impact on their occupational destinations. Thus 'there remains a very strong "bias" towards males entering skilled manual employment and females entering personal service occupations such as health care, childcare and hairdressing' (Dennison and Coleman, 2000:119). Whatever the level of performance, boys and girls whose highest qualifications are GCSEs are likely to find gendered jobs at the lower levels of the occupational hierarchy (Griffin, 1985; Walkerdine, 1989; Cockburn, 1987; Darling and Glendinning, 1996). And, as Foster et al. comment, 'working-class, female, and black people may find that their educational credentials do not always carry the same weight as similar ones held by middle-class, white males' (Foster et al., 1996:157). Indeed, this seems to be the case. Thus in the study by Marshall et al. of the class structure of modern Britain they found that at every level of the occupational hierarchy women had higher qualifications than men, suggesting that men can get further with fewer qualifications than can women (Marshall et al., 1989; see also Epstein et al., 1998:10). Seen in this light, girls' academic achievement could simply be necessary in order to give them the same chance as lesser qualified males rather than advantaging them in the competition for jobs. Indeed, Dennison and Coleman's (2000) report shows that while more young women stay on in education than young men (73% compared to 64%), and while girls out-perform boys at GCSE level (53% of young women achieved at least 5 A–C grades, compared to 43% of boys), occupational choice and career strategies remain in a gender rut. For example, 75% of year-11 students entering managerial and professional occupations are boys whereas 65% of those entering clerical and secretarial positions are girls, as are 75% of those entering personal services. Skilled construction and skilled engineering show the greatest disparity, with less than 5% of girls entering these occupations. (*Guardian*, 6 April 2000)

It seems then that girls' achievements fit them for gendered jobs rather than posing a threat to men's position in the labour market. Indeed there is evidence that academic achievement has historically 'been irrelevant to success for a particular social class', i.e. middle-class males and, until relatively recently, for working-class males who aspired to working-class jobs (Cohen, 1998:30; see also O'Donnell and Sharpe, 2000).

Studying schooling

The shift in focus from class- to gender-based inequalities which has characterized public debate about education since the 1950s (see Table 5.1 above) has also marked the way sociologists have studied education. Thus in the 1950s and 1960s most studies focused on boys and class inequalities, in the 1970s and 1980s attention shifted away from class, initially to culture, then to gender, and, to a lesser extent, ethnicity, and more recent studies explore masculinities, gender identities, sexuality, and ethnicity. In what follows, I consider these shifts.

Class and education

In the early post-war years sociologists of education were concerned to map the extent of educational inequalities which they saw in class terms: gender and ethnicity were not taken into consideration. Social class, i.e. the occupation of boys' fathers, was taken to be the cause of different educational outcomes for boys. Moreover it was the way class shaped family life that was seen as significant in determining whether or not boys stayed on at school, how well they did at school, and what sort of jobs they were fitted for on leaving school (Halsey et al., 1980). Thus working-class homes where the adult male was in a manual occupation did not provide an environment which was conducive to learning, both because of pressures to leave school at the earliest opportunity to contribute to household income and because there was no space or privacy to study at home. Middle-class homes, in contrast, where fathers were in non-manual occupations, provided an environment which was conducive to learning and children were encouraged to pursue education in order to get a good job. Furthermore in middle-class homes children were already immersed in the culture which was transmitted by the process of education while in working-class homes they were not (Halsey et al., 1980; Bernstein, 1977). Underpinning this sort of approach was an understanding of education as contributing to the reproduction of the class structure by fitting girls and boys for their places in society. Such an analysis can take either a functionalist or a Marxist form (Bowles and Gintis, 1976; Althusser, 1971); neither version problematizes gender, at best accepting that education fits girls of any class for their primarily domestic role (MacDonald, 1980; Wolpe, 1978). Both schools of thought theorize the education system as reproducing class relations by ejecting pupils at certain ages into the workforce and inculcating them with the values appropriate to a capitalist society—values which may be gendered. Those destined for working-class jobs leave at the minimum school leaving age and are absorbed into manual and low-skilled occupations; those destined for lower-level professional jobs will stay on until they are 18 while those destined for professional and managerial occupations will continue into higher education before entering the labour market. Schooling is organized hierarchically and treats children differently on the basis of ability. What is interesting sociologically is that, by and large, it is children from working-class homes who leave school to take up working-class jobs, while those from middle-class homes stay on in education and get middle-class jobs; the class structure is thereby reproduced by the education system.

School subcultures

In the 1960s and 1970s, with the influence of ethnomethodology and symbolic interactionism, attention was turned to the processes within schools which allegedly contributed to educational outcomes and the reproduction of class relations. Several studies focused on working-class boys who had no interest in being at school and who were involved in disruptive behaviour in school and delinquent behaviour outside it (Hargreaves, 1967; Lacey, 1970). A concern with boys' behaviour had also been expressed in the Crowther report (1959). Such studies argued that it was not the fault of the boys themselves that they became alienated from school, nor was it due to their home backgrounds, on the contrary it arose from the organization of the school and the way teachers treated them (Foster et al., 1996:68). Thus what goes on within schools was seen as contributing to the alienation of certain groups of boys from the whole process of education and as leading them to seek status in terms approved by their peers rather than their teachers. This was theorized by Hargreaves as the formation of delinquescent subcultures; conversely he also identified academic subcultures. Hargreaves conceptualized the school as a social system and the formation of delinquescent subcultures as the boys' solution to their inability to achieve status by legitimate means. It is the school's rather than the boys' failure that is critical as the school has neither integrated them nor developed their educational potential (Hargreaves, 1967:184).

This and other studies have been criticized for their failure adequately to link what goes on in the classroom to levels of achievement and by their tendency to treat schools in isolation from the rest of society (Foster et al., 1996). A later study, informed by a very different conceptual framework, which links detailed ethnographic data with a macro-level analysis of the education system and the state, is Paul Willis's *Learning to labour* (1977). In common with Hargreaves, he understands schools as embodying middle-class values, values which are rejected by the 'lads', a group of working-class boys who 'have a laff' and engage in delinquent behaviour. They value manual not mental labour and are contemptuous of the 'ear'oles' (also working class) who are sissy and who apply themselves in school. The class culture and values of the school are in conflict with the class culture and values of the 'lads'. Their resistance takes the form of an anti-school subculture which ensures that they fail at school but that they are thereby fitted for the manual, working-class jobs which await them: in fact they positively value them and choose them over and above success in middle-class terms. This process is theorized as the cultural reproduction of the working class and seen as essential for the continued existence of capitalism.

A major difference between Hargreaves and Willis is that Willis evaluates working-class culture in positive terms and does not see the 'lads' as victims; indeed, through their resistance they are acting on insights and understandings of the class nature of education in a capitalist society and positively valuing and reproducing working-class culture (Foster et al., 1996:15). Thus, while Hargreaves

sees the anti-school subculture of the lower-stream boys as a response to failure, for Willis it is a response to the attempt of the school to control 'the lads' and to impose middle-class culture and incorporate them into capitalist society. (Foster et al., 1996:14)

It is ironic that the lads' resistance to middle-class culture ensures that they are fitted for working-class jobs, thus obtaining their incorporation into a class-divided society. But the difference between Hargreaves and Willis has to be understood in terms of a theoretical shift. Hargreaves was trying to explain how the organization of schools created delinquency as a solution on the part of the boys to their inability to gain status in terms of the values of the school. His aim was to change what went on in schools so that working-class boys were able to succeed in educational terms. His theoretical understanding of schools and subcultures is functionalist. Willis, on the other hand, analyses cultural reproduction in class terms and defines the resistance of working-class boys to a system in which they cannot succeed as potentially revolutionary. That their resistance has the effect of reproducing working-class culture and creating a willing supply of (male) labour power for (male) working-class jobs is essential for the reproduction of capitalism and if it were not to happen would itself generate a crisis (Willis, 1977:178). Despite the attention Willis pays to the lads' masculinity and to their positive evaluation of manual, masculine labour and negative evaluation of mental, feminine labour, almost all these studies focused on boys and even those that included girls did not explore the significance of gender in the formation of subcultures; pro- and anti-school subcultures were understood solely in terms of class (see e.g. Ball, 1981).

Generalizations have been made on the basis of these studies about the nature of working-class culture and its relation to education. However the studies are located in a particular area, Birmingham, they are of boys rather than girls, and they are of white boys rather than ethnic minority boys. Thus the findings not only may not be applicable to all school children, they may not be generalizable to other areas of the UK such as Wales where the working class has traditionally had a more positive attitude towards education (see e.g. Reynolds and Sullivan, 1987). The other thing that is interesting is that the little research into girls undertaken at this time has sunk into oblivion whereas the research on boys is taken to be setting a trend (Llewellyn, 1980). Thus along with Hargreaves (1967) and Lacey (1970), who studied a boys' secondary modern school and a boys' grammar school respectively, Audrey Lambart studied a girls' grammar school (Foster et al., 1996:12; Lambart, 1976). Her study remains as a Ph.D. thesis while the other two are core texts for sociology of education courses.

Feminism and classroom interaction

With the advent of feminism and the influence of anti-racist critiques of education in the 1970s and 1980s the focus of attention changed. Studies of girls and ethnic minority pupils undermined the hypothesis that it was the formation of anti-school subcultures that led to failure at school (indeed it has been argued that the connection had never adequately been demonstrated anyway). Inequalities based on gender and ethnicity now claimed attention and it was suggested that girls and ethnic minority pupils were disadvantaged (Deem, 1978; Byrne, 1978).

Feminists initially took the same perspective as their male colleagues and explored what went on within school in relation to the curriculum and teacher-pupil interaction. They argued that within schools there was a hidden—or not so hidden—curriculum which directed girls towards 'feminine' subjects; this was more than apparent in the deliberations of the various government reports we have already considered, especially for working-class girls (Deem, 1978). Subject choices were made according to gendered expectations of life after school and gendered ways of behaving were reinforced by the way teachers reacted to pupils within the classroom (Rees, 1992; Sharpe, 1976). Studies investigated the gender dynamics of the classroom and found that boys took up an inordinate amount of teachers' attention, that girls were marginalized, and that if girls exhibited challenging and intellectually questioning behaviour it was regarded negatively in marked contrast to the same behaviour in boys (Stanworth, 1983; Walkerdine, 1989).

These studies showed that being noisy and demanding is perceived as inappropriate behaviour for girls but for boys it is a sign of intelligence. Thus a girl in Michelle Stanworth's study said:

They all make a lot of noise, all those boys. That's why I think they're more intelligent than us. (Stanworth, 1983:52)

Moreover when girls display 'confidence and *actively* [challenge] the teacher, they are met with resistance': this is because such behaviour is time consuming but also it does 'not accord with teachers' preconceptions of "correct" femininity' (Walkerdine, 1989:155; see also Younger and Warrington, 1996:307). In addition Valerie Walkerdine argues that,

whatever methods girls adopted in their pursuits of mathematical knowledge, none appears correct. If they are successful, their teachers consider that they produce this success in the wrong way: by being conscientious, motivated, ambitious and hard-working. Successful boys were credited with natural talent and flexibility, the ability to work hard and take risks. (Walkerdine, 1989:155)

Furthermore teachers recognize boys more readily than girls and this leads pupils to think that teachers have a higher regard for them. Stanworth comments:

both female and male pupils experience the classroom as a place where boys are the focus of activity and interest, while the girls are relegated to the sidelines. (Stanworth, 1983:50)

This marginalization of girls in the classroom did not, however, lead to the formation of anti-school subcultures nor was there any evidence that it was necessarily associated with a lack of achievement (Stanworth, 1983; Griffin, 1985; Mirza, 1992; Foster et al., 1996). Using a model that had been developed in studying boys was somewhat problematic when it was applied to girls—this of course questions the validity of the model in the first place.

Many of these studies, which provide detailed ethnographic material on the gendered nature of classroom interaction, set out to explore the extent to which classroom interaction reproduces gender divisions (Stanworth, 1983:23). They demonstrate how gender relations and gender identities are negotiated and how pupils learn to 'do' gender within the classroom. They have however been criticized for prioritizing gender over other social divisions and assuming that all girls were disadvantaged in relation to boys. This is clearly inaccurate and at the time it was pointed out that boys outnumbered girls amongst those who were most disadvantaged in the sense that they left school with no qualifi- ciations (Wolpe, 1988; Deem, 1978): something which is still the case (O'Donnell and Sharpe, 2000). Prioritizing gender, as with the earlier emphasis on class, makes it difficult to see that the form taken by gender divisions varies with class and ethnicity and that this affects the route taken through education. There is evidence, for instance, that white working-class girls as well as boys tend to consider school qualifications unimportant; an attitude that has been contrasted with that of Asian pupils (McRobbie, 1991:232). Assuming a dichot- omous model of gender difference does not capture the complexity of the social processes at work within schools. What these studies of pupil–teacher inter- action within the classroom succeeded in demonstrating, though, is that what- ever else schooling teaches girls and boys, it also teaches them about gender hierarchies, gendered power relations, and gender-appropriate behaviour.

These studies have also been criticized for failing to demonstrate the relation of within-classroom processes to educational outcomes (Foster et al., 1996). But rather than achievement *per se*, they were concerned with the way girls' achievement fell off in secondary school. This was often explained by girls' prioritizing attracting boys rather than being good at school: indeed the two were seen as being in contradiction with each other (Wolpe, 1988; Sharpe, 1976; Llewellyn, 1980:46). And many studies demonstrated that this was a realistic response to the opportunities available to young women, particularly young working-class women, and the relative significance of paid work, marriage, and motherhood in the lives of their mothers (Rees, 1992). Indeed, research, both at the time and later, indicates that the nature of the local labour market and the sorts of jobs available for young men and women affect assumptions about the destinations of children, assumptions held by teachers, parents, and chil- dren alike, and what they can realistically expect on leaving school (see e.g.

Clarricoates, 1980). Similarly it seems that changes over time in the opportunities available to young women and men in the labour market have affected their commitment to schooling and their motivation to 'achieve' (O'Donnell and Sharpe, 2000). Indeed there is some evidence to suggest that girls' achievement improves where more employment opportunities are available for women and that it is wider opportunities for women in the labour market that provide the incentive for mainly middle-class girls to choose high-status, 'male' subjects at school (Darling and Glendinning, 1996).

Sexuality

In the 1980s feminists took up the issue of sexuality, exploring girls' resistance to schooling and the ways in which their sexuality is controlled and constructed within as well as outside school. Girls' resistance was different from boys'. Whereas boys may be disruptive in class and adopt anti-school subcultures, girls' resistance 'is often seen in relation to their sexuality' and they do not form anti-school subcultures (Griffin, 1985:15; although see Mac an Ghaill's (1994) account of 'The Posse'). Thus they become more interested in boys than in school work, they subvert the school uniform to accentuate their sexuality, and they wear skirts that are 'too short' (Griffin, 1985:20). Indeed, teachers see female sexuality as incompatible with intelligence and achievement at school and if a girl has a stereotypically feminine appearance it is hard to take her ambitions seriously. A teacher in Stanworth's study said:

Susan is really rather hard and determined, but she's blonde. I've got nothing against that, poor girl, but she's got the superficial characteristic of being a rather dizzy blonde, and yet underneath it she's got this hard streak of wanting to get on. I can't reconcile the two. (Stanworth, 1983:18)

In response girls take pleasure in disrupting these stereotypes (Mirza, 1992:72). Thus a 'high-achieving' girl in Sheila Riddell's study 'talked about the way in which she deliberately wore make-up and short skirts because she resented the way in which teachers immediately assumed you were stupid if you dressed stylishly' (Riddell, 1992:158). On the other hand, girls had to be careful to maintain 'a good sexual reputation' and '"getting a bad name" as a slag, a slut, a whore or a pro was something to be avoided at all costs'. In addition it was essential to be heterosexual, alternatives to heterosexuality 'were seen as deviant, abnormal and pathological', and getting a boyfriend was proof of 'normal' heterosexuality (Griffin, 1985:59).

Sue Lees, in a study of 15–16 year old girls in three London comprehensives

(Lees, 1986), shows that girls' behaviour is controlled by the importance of avoiding the label 'slag' and that the only sure way of doing this is by having a steady boyfriend. If girls are outside the control of one boy they are controlled by the group and run the constant risk of being labelled as slags (by girls as well as boys) whatever their actual behaviour. The need to exhibit acceptable gender and sexual identities may also help to explain girls' reluctance to transgress gendered boundaries by choosing 'non-traditional' subjects (Riddell, 1992:108): thus studying physics or learning to be a motor mechanic might be construed as being lesbian (Cockburn, 1987:41; Lees, 1986:145; Rogers, 1994). Sue Lees also makes the important point that girls do not end up in marriage and domesticity because they have created an anti-school culture but because sexism and sexual harassment are present in the culture of the school and severely circumscribe girls' activities. In common with earlier studies she argues that despite the ambitions of many girls to have careers, after O levels 'they fall behind boys as they reconcile themselves to the reality of marriage and poor opportunities' (Lees, 1986:123). This is the outcome of a realistic assessment of the opportunities awaiting them and of the sexism evident not only in the informal culture of the school but also in the girls' homes and leisure activities. Indeed, many of the working-class schoolgirls in her study were already 'participating in their future roles of domestic labour— to the detriment of their schoolwork' (Lees, 1986:131). The middle-class girls in Lees's study were more likely than their working-class counterparts to have an academic orientation which relates to the ethos of their school and its valuing of girls' intellectual abilities. This study is important in alerting us to the social processes within schools that embody gendered power relations and the part played by boys, teachers, and other girls in controlling female sexuality and policing gendered boundaries.

Ethnicity

Just as most studies of class and education focused on white boys, most studies of ethnicity and education failed to take gender into account (Mirza, 1992). There are, however, some exceptions (see e.g. Mac an Ghaill, 1988). Thus Mary Fuller's research on young African Caribbean women shows that, despite the racism and sexism they encountered at school, they have high levels of achievement and work hard while creating the impression of not taking school seriously. The girls she studied were pro-education but not pro-school (cf. Lees, 1986). They positively identified as black and female, they were 'strongly committed to achievement through the job market', and wanted 'to be employed whatever their future domestic circumstances might be' (Fuller, 1980:57). Although she talks of these girls as forming a subculture, it is more fluid with less clearly demarcated boundaries than those identified amongst boys and it is not associated with failure. It is important for these black girls to maintain the support of their peer group and, because of this, they do not conform, but along with this resistance to schooling goes a commitment to achieve.

Fuller's findings question the model of pro- and anti-school subcultures developed by focusing solely on white boys. She has, however, been criticized for attempting to explain the achievement of black girls in terms of a subculture which is one 'neither ... of resistance nor of conformity' (Mirza, 1992:21). This contradictory attitude to schooling has also been found in other studies, particularly amongst young black women (Mac an Ghaill, 1988). Young black men, in contrast, respond to the racism they experience in schools by rejecting education and refusing work—which in any case is almost non-existent due to high rates of unemployment amongst black youth. There is evidence that the response of black students to schooling varies with class and, although there is a gendered patterning, their 'resistance to racism cuts across gender divisions, with girls ... totally rejecting school and boys sharing their pro-education/anti-school position' (Mac an Ghaill, 1988:36). Mac an Ghaill's study conceptualizes resistance to schooling amongst ethnic minority school students in terms of anti-school subcultures. Heidi Mirza, however, did not find any evidence of the formation of subcultures amongst young black women. Indeed it is ironic that while a culture of resistance condemns young, working-class men to working-class jobs (or to the dole), for young black women it is claimed to do the opposite. This could of course be conceptualized as these girls resisting the sexism and racism of school in the same way that some white, working-class boys reject its class culture, and aspiring to achieve in contradiction to the expectations that girls' primary role will be domestic (Foster et al., 1996:17). More importantly, though, the fact that black girls have 'not only ... high aspirations but also higher levels of academic attainment than their male peers' (Mirza, 1992:31) suggests that early theories about teachers' labelling of pupils being key to their school careers are inaccurate and that the processes leading to success or failure in educational terms are more complex (Mirza, 1992:54). On the other hand Mirza shows that teachers' negative evaluations of black girls could limit their opportunities and that, because of this, their career aspirations were often not realized. This was not because of their own lack of ability or aspiration but because the advice they were given directed them into a 'sexually and racially limiting labour market' (Mirza, 1992:121). She found that girls who wanted to pursue 'non-gendered' occupations were discouraged by being told that their aspirations were 'unrealistic' (Mirza, 1992:131). Similarly there was a lack of support for young black women who wished to go to university and eventually take up careers in 'masculine' professions; indeed Mirza notes that young black women are more likely than young white women to aspire to 'non-traditional' (in terms of gender) occupations and they also aspire to full-time work and economic independence. This is in contrast with the young white women who anticipated economic dependence and a job which fitted in with their prior domestic commitments. Thus, in contradistinction to Willis, who argues that his lads actively choose class exploitation and are not directed towards it by inadequate careers services or negative assessments by teachers, Mirza argues that young black women are deterred from realizing their ambitions and steered into jobs that are seen as appropriate in terms of 'race' and gender by the advice that they are given at school.

Masculinities at school

The subcultural paradigm remained influential in studying schooling until the late 1980s and 1990s when attention turned to the ways in which masculinities are constructed in schools and to considerations of the way heterosexuality is institutionalized and made compulsory for both girls and boys. Bob Connell's theorization of hegemonic and subordinated masculinities and his concept of the gender order have been very influential in studies of masculinities (this is explored further in Chapter 6). Like Willis, he conceptualizes schools as part of the state, arguing that they are hierarchical institutions which reproduce relations of domination and subordination (Connell, 1989). He suggests that masculinities are constructed in relation to the hierarchical organization of the school and to success and failure in academic terms. Willis's lads displayed a certain form of aggressive, macho, working-class masculinity, but he conceptualized their academic failure in terms of class resistance. Connell focuses on gender and sexuality rather than class and is concerned with the way schools deliver 'social power' to boys who are successful in academic terms.

Social power in terms of access to higher education, entry to professions, command of communication, is being delivered to the boys who are academic 'successes'. The reaction of the 'failed' is likely to be a claim to other sources of power, even other definitions of masculinity. Sporting prowess, physical aggression, sexual conquest may do. (Connell, 1989:295)

Or, we may add, delinquency. By distinguishing between success and failure schools force 'differentiation' on boys, and this differentiation is understood by Connell in terms of gender rather than class.

A considerable number of studies focus on this process of differentiation and the way boys collectively construct their gender and sexual identities. They conceptualize masculinities as operating through discourses and are interested in the ways in which gendered subjectivities are constructed in relation to different discourses of masculinity (see also Walkerdine, 1989). Thus the way pupils talk about their experiences becomes an important focus of study as it sheds light on the discourses (or ideologies) they are using to make sense of their social worlds. Discourses not only are forms of knowledge, but also involve power. For instance, the power to define girls as less mathematically able than boys is embedded in a particular discourse about the nature of maths and its rationality which, by definition, implies that women, because they are irrational, will have more difficulties apprehending it than boys who are by nature rational. Within this gendered discourse boys occupy the powerful position. However, there are competing discourses offering different subject positions involving different forms of power. Thus power is conceptualized as fluid rather than systemic and as something which individuals possess in some situations and not in others; thus in some contexts masculinity may be vested with power while in others it may not.

In a study of the cultural practices of various groups of boys in a Birmingham comprehensive, Mairtin Mac an Ghaill explores the way masculinities are constructed within discourses. He is interested in the way boys learn to be men 'while policing sex/gender boundaries' and in 'young heterosexual women's experiences of teacher and student school masculinities'. For him power is a central part of the analysis but he finds that it is the girls who are aware of and talk about power relations while the young men do not (Mac an Ghaill, 1994:13); a finding which supports the contention that power is only visible to subordinate groups (Griffin, 1996). In order to explore the range of masculinities in the school he develops a typology of pupil masculinities which he links to peer groups. These peer groups are 'more fluid and ill-defined' than earlier research on subcultures suggested, although there are strong echoes of subcultural styles in the different masculinities he identifies. There are four types of masculinity: the first three are the macho lads and the academic achievers (who are roughly equivalent to Willis's lads and 'ear'oles') and the new enterprisers; all of these are working class, ethnically mixed and heterosexual. The fourth is a middle-class peer group self-styled as the real Englishmen and they are all white. The macho lads and the real Englishmen share contempt for those who try hard at school, the former because they reject academic success and the latter because they have the class confidence and cultural capital to succeed without trying. The middle-class 'real Englishmen' were in rebellion against their liberal, and sometimes feminist, parents. One of them said:

We have been emasculated. Our feminist mothers have taken away our masculinity. When I was younger my mum would sit around with her friends and say bad things about men all the time. And then someone would say what about black men. And then they had to be anti-racist, so black men weren't included. (Mac an Ghaill, 1994:79)

In response to this they asserted their identity as 'real men'. Rather than feeling guilty about being white, middle-class, and male they celebrated it and the racism, misogyny, and homophobia it encompassed.

Mac an Ghaill also explores heterosexuality, arguing that even though the boys are constrained by compulsory heterosexuality it is a precarious identity for many of them. On the other hand it is very difficult for young men to claim a gay identity; this is also the case for young women (see Epstein, 1994). The young gay men in Mac an Ghaill's study, for instance, were not 'out' at school and 'poofter', like 'girl', was a term of abuse for boys who did not display suitably heterosexual forms of masculinity (Martino, 1999). Indeed, to be seen to be taking school work seriously was enough to call a boy's heterosexuality into question.

The association of femininity with studying and mental labour seems to be reversed once GCSE is past; studious males are then adopting a rational, intellectual form of masculinity which is acceptable (Epstein, 1998:104). This also has to do with class and the fact that the macho lads will have left school by this time. In Debbie Epstein's words:

The main demand on boys from within their peer culture (but also, sometimes, from teachers), up to the sixth form at least, is to appear to do little or no work, to be heavily competitive (but at sport and heterosex, not at school work), to be rough, tough and dangerous to know. But this is something that changes somewehere along the line, for among adult men, especially those of the professional middle classes, the harder a man appears to work within the public sphere of jobs and careers, the more 'masculine' he becomes. [In contrast] for adult women to appear to work compromises their femininity: to make home/family work visible is to become a 'drudge', while to become invested in a career and work hard at it is seen as masculinizing. (Epstein, 1998:106)

Other studies have confirmed that masculinities often involve being 'cool', i.e. not making an effort to achieve (Martino, 1999). Being seen as an achiever calls boys' heterosexuality into question and they are seen as effeminate. A study of young, Afro-Caribbean men, for instance, found that they, like their female counterparts, maintained a 'cool' front and thereby the support of their peers while, at the same time, pursuing success in academic terms (Sewell, 1998). Sporting masculinities (which are assumed to involve heterosexuality) have been identified as a legitimate and 'cool' alternative to academic success and have, in the past, been sufficient for middle-class boys to get places at Oxbridge (Skelton, 1997). Being good at sport can also override the negative connotations of being black or gay.

Many of the studies of masculinities and education show how boys control each other's behaviour and stress the interaction between them; girls are incidental to these social processes. This is in marked contrast to the studies of girls which show that girls' behaviour in schools is policed most forcibly by boys (e.g. Lees 1986). Thus an asymmetrical picture is constructed whereby boys (and teachers) occupy powerful positions in school in relation to girls and are involved in policing the boundaries of acceptable sexual and gendered behaviour for each other and for girls. The concern of most of the studies of boys and masculinities however is not with gender relations, but with relations between boys and the way they position themselves in the different discourses of masculinity available to them (an important exception is provided by O'Donnell and Sharpe, 2000).

Boys' 'under-achievement'

Mac an Ghaill's study and others do not concern themselves directly with academic achievement but focus on schools as a site of construction of gendered subjectivities. There is however an implicit assumption that certain masculinities are associated with failure and it is in response to academic success or failure that different masculine identities are adopted (Connell, 1989). As with earlier feminist studies, these studies also fail to demonstrate any empirical link between processes internal to the school and educational inequalities (however defined) (Foster et al., 1996). But like their feminist predecessors, they demonstrate that gender, class, ethnicity, and sexuality shape the experience of schooling and the subject choices that are made. Thus most pupils continue to opt for subjects which are defined as appropriate for their gender and class.

However, what goes on inside the school is shaped by opportunities in the labour market; increasing opportunities for women and skills shortages led to a concern in the 1970s with the wastage of talent represented by middle-class girls' refusal to take science and technology. In the 1990s decreasing employment opportunities for working-class boys led to their lack of achievement in school becoming a social issue. In either case the gendering of the curriculum relates to the gendering of jobs and the expectation that whatever else women do, they will also have domestic and childcare responsibilities. Thus even in the 1990s teachers were on record as saying that jobs were not as important for women as for men, hence their greater concern about the lack of job opportunities for boys (Mac an Ghaill, 1994:117).

Recent research reflects the popular concern with boys' under-achievement and much of it reverses the assumptions that underpinned earlier feminist studies. Researchers now argue that the type of attention teachers give to boys is detrimental to learning, that boys need remedial teaching in order to help them achieve (never mind that it is overwhelmingly boys who receive remedial teaching already), and that girls are privileged in the classroom. This view is shared by some boys who feel that they are regarded as potentially more disruptive than girls and that they are therefore treated more harshly. Conversely it is girls who get all the positive teacher attention (Younger, Warrington, and Williams, 1999). This gives rise to a view that girls get it all their own way and that the pendulum has swung too far in their favour (Riddell, 1998). In contrast, girls report that boys dominate all the new vocational courses, even those that have been introduced specifically to familiarize girls with technology (Mac an Ghaill, 1994:118), and boys confirm that they are, indeed, more troublesome than girls (O'Donnell and Sharpe, 2000). The debate continues to rage. Indeed recent analysis of exam results in Wales suggests that much research which attempts to account for the gender gap is ill conceived because the gender gap has been exaggerated and, contrary to media hype, has not increased in recent years (Gorard et al., 1999).

It seems then that with the changes in the labour market and the coming of the 'information society', working-class masculinities which emphasize manual over mental labour are becoming counter-productive—they no longer fit young working-class men for manual jobs because those jobs are ceasing to exist. Indeed, it is precisely working-class boys, not boys in general, who are the low achievers and this is not a new phenomenon (O'Donnell and Sharpe, 2000). What is new is that the white macho lads' mode of masculinity is 'outdated'. It centres round 'traditional manual waged labour, at a time when their traditional manual work destiny has disappeared' (Mac an Ghaill, 1994:71). The contraction of the manufacturing base has created a 'crisis in traditional white working-class forms of masculinity' (ibid.). It seems to me that this is the crux of the problem with boys' underachievement—that the lack of credentials of working-class boys means that they leave school unfit for the new world of work. In contrast, girls' increasing levels of educational achievement both fit them for and can be seen as a response to the growth in women's employment and the feminization of the workforce.

Boys have, in varying ways, been constructed as a social problem throughout the post-war period and schools' contribution to this has been theorized in different ways. Initially schools were seen as contributing to boys' failure through streaming and labelling; an outcome of the way schools are implicated in the reproduction of class divisions and inequalities. This then changed to a theorization of boys' resistance to schooling and rejection of academic work as a positive valuation of working-class culture and a positive choice of manual as opposed to mental labour. Latterly it has been understood in terms of masculinities and the decline of employment associated with the 'traditional' working class.

Despite this thread of concern with the effect of schooling on boys, sociological understandings of gender and education have changed significantly. While early post-war studies problematized the way the educational system reproduced the class structure, studies carried out in the 1970s shifted their attention to cultural reproduction and social interaction in the classroom. With the advent of feminist sociology attention was turned to gendered processes within schools, later encompassing ethnicity and sexuality as well as gender but moving away from attention to class. The 1990s were marked by the emergence of studies of masculinities in schools informed by concepts of discourses, subjectivities, and identities and reflecting popular concern with boys' alleged under-achievement. At the turn of the century some have blamed boys' 'under-achievement' on the influence of feminism and equal opportunities policies in schools which have favoured girls at the expense of boys and which have, allegedly, contributed to a crisis of masculinity (Epstein et al., 1998; Yates, 1997). This crisis is the focus of the next chapter.

Chapter 6

Young Men and the Crisis of Masculinity

I**N** recent years there have been claims that masculinity is in crisis, allegedly as a result of the feminist movement. As Julie Burchill wryly comments,

it's feminism that currently does scapegoat duty for all the social evils that the free market has inflicted upon us. Unemployment, the underclass, the unmarried mother who has nothing to gain from marrying a ManBoy on the dole—capitalism did all this but feminism carries the can. Yes, I admit it—it was me, Andrea Dworkin and Geri Spice who closed down the mines, shut down the steelworks and threw a generation of young urban men on the scrapheap. (*Guardian*, 26 February 2000)

Others suggest, however, that it is 'women's lives [that] have changed far more drastically than men's during the past few decades' and it is women, particularly black and working-class women, who 'suffer its effects at least as much as men do'. Thus journalists and academics share a recognition of a problem, a problem that is named not as a 'femininity crisis' but as a crisis in masculinity (Stacey, 1993:719). In this chapter I explore how it is that what is happening to men, particularly young men, in contemporary Britain has come to be understood in terms of masculinity.

Changing masculinities

Undoubtedly there have been changes in images of masculinity since the aftermath of the Second World War. Then there was a clearly defined model for respectable adult masculinity based on 'quite separate roles for husband and wife' with the husband being the provider (Segal, 1990:5). Adult masculinity of a particular class and status was symbolized by the suit—formal and casual—

and young men's transition to adult status was marked by its purchase (Mort, 1996:138). There were also angry young working-class men who were hostile to women and domesticity and were homophobic (Segal, 1990:15). But even in the 1950s—at least in the USA—sociologists observed that all was not well with men. Women were 'invading the strongholds of masculinity in work, play, sex, and the home. She seems to say ... "Everything you can do, I can do better".' This, together with the 'increasing social visibility of impotence and homosexuality', was taken as a measure of 'masculine role problems' (Hacker, 1957:228–9). At that time it was juvenile delinquency and 'latch-key kids' that drew the attention of policymakers and sociologists towards young people (mainly young men). In the late 1950s and 1960s, with full employment and affluence, a steady stream of youth subcultures emerged and 'youth' became a new consumer group with particular and idiosyncratic styles. The space they occupied was leisure, a space bounded by the institutional constraints of full-time education, domestic labour, and, later, by paid employment; their activities took place in public. While these young people may not have been delinquent (although they were often defined as such) they were seen as constituting a threat to the moral order of society; their leisure activities and styles created anxiety and envy (Cohen, 1980). In the 1970s unemployment, and particularly youth unemployment, began to increase and, in the 1980s, some young people (again largely young men) took to the streets; now, however, 'doing nothing' turned into riots (Corrigan, 1976; Campbell, 1993). Thus since the Second World War young men have been seen as constituting a problem for society, as juvenile delinquents, as members of deviant subcultures, or as the angry mob with no stake in society. In what follows I look at the gendering of juvenile crime and youth unemployment before considering how sociological studies of young people, particularly young men, have changed since the 1950s.

Boys as social problem—delinquency

Juvenile delinquency is overwhelmingly a male phenomenon although the 'gender gap' has narrowed since the 1950s. Thus the sex ratio has decreased from '11:1 in the late 1950s to approximately 6:1 in the early 1970s, and in 1995 it stood at 3.6:1' (Rutter et al., 1998:74). Moreover 'crimes by females have been increasing at a faster rate than crimes by males', albeit from a very low base (ibid.:261). The gendering of juvenile crime is reflected in official statistics which show that, in the 1990s, 'over 40% of all indictable crime appears to be committed by those under the age of 21' and 'approximately three quarters of these offenders are male'. Moreover, '18–20 year old males have the highest nationally recorded crime rate' (Muncie, 1999:14–15) and '80% of the total number of 18-year-olds found guilty or cautioned for an offence in 1998 were male' (Dennison and Coleman, 2000:136). The gender gap varies with age and ethnicity, being lowest for those aged between 10 and 14 and highest in 'early adulthood'. Amongst Afro-Caribbean young people rates of juvenile crime are higher and the gender gap is narrower than for whites, while for Asians crime rates are lower and the gender gap is wider (Rutter et al., 1998). The 'peak age' for offending is 15 for young women and 18 for young men (Dennison and Coleman, 2000:139). Self-report studies find a smaller gender gap especially amongst those aged 14 to 17. They also suggest that young women give up 'crime' earlier than young men and that those who engage in anti-social behaviour are more likely than others to become teenage mothers; this, in turn, makes it 'more difficult for them to be part of a delinquent peer group and to engage in criminal activities' (Rutter et al., 1998:275). Young men take longer to abandon their 'criminal career' and do not show a marked tendency to become teenage fathers (Rutter et al., 1998).

There is evidence that juvenile crime increased during the 1950s and 1960s but, since the end of the 1970s, it has levelled off and even decreased (although this may be a product of changes in how it is processed). By the 1990s,

the rate of male offending per 1,000,000 population had fallen since 1986 by 46% for those aged 10–13 and by 14% for those aged 14–17. For females there was a similar fall in the 10–13 age group, but a small rise for 14–17 year olds. The rate of offending for young male adults increased marginally; and fluctuated from a peak in 1993 for young adult women. (Muncie, 1999:15)

As we have already noted, from the 1950s to the 1970s there was 'an increase in the female crime rate' and, in the 1970s, 'the incidence of violence in girls' was '36 times as high as it was in 1955' (Campbell, 1981:24). Between 1984 and 1994 it more than doubled but, as Rutter et al. point out, 'the base rate is so low that a relatively small number of cases can make a great deal of difference' (Rutter et al., 1998: 75). It is also difficult to assess the extent to which this represents a real change in girls' behaviour rather than a change in the way their behaviour is labelled and processed (Shacklady Smith, 1978; Rutter et al., 1998). Similarly, while gangs are seen as a quintessentially male phenomenon, girl gangs have been observed since *at least* the 1960s (Campbell, 1981). Despite this there is regular comment in the media about girl gangs and how they are a new phenomenon indicative of girls taking on the negative attributes of masculinity.

Youth unemployment

If the gendering of juvenile crime remains overwhelmingly male, so too does youth unemployment. Thus the rate of unemployment for young men (under 18) increased from 0.33 per cent in 1951 to 2.02 per cent in 1970; comparable figures for young women were 0.29 per cent and 1.1 per cent (Social Trends, 1970). Given the changes in the way unemployment rates are calculated, direct comparisons are difficult. However it is clear that there has been a rising trend in youth unemployment since the 1950s (Hart, 1988) and figures for the 1990s show that between 1991 and 2000 unemployment was much higher than in the early post-war period, increasing for young men (16–17 year olds) from 15.4 per cent to 20.1 per cent and for young women from 14.3 per cent to 16.9 per cent. Unemployment rates are consistently higher for young men than for young women but decrease sharply for both genders after the age of 24 (ONS, 2001:table 4.21, p. 85). And, as we saw in Chapter 2, ethnic minority men experience higher rates of unemployment than either ethnic minority women or white men. It is often assumed that high rates of unemployment are associated with high crime rates; however, the trends in juvenile crime and youth unemployment since the war appear to question any direct or causal association (although there are links) and it has been suggested that factors such as failure at school and low parental supervision may predispose young people to become involved in crime (Rutter et al., 1998).

Unemployment is clearly a problem for significant numbers of young people and unemployed young people are seen as potential problems for society—young men because they are on the streets, unoccupied, and often indulging in violent behaviour, and young women because they become unmarried, teenage mothers (Campbell, 1993). Access to a wage is seen as critical for them. Thus, for young men,

work has great importance in structuring an adult identity. Despite its hardship and its sacrifices, going to work is an enfranchisement into a general political, social and cultural adulthood. (Willis, 1984a:476)

It is also associated with 'the traditional sense of working-class masculinity' and, without it, young men may adopt a more aggressive 'assertion of masculinity and masculine style'. Male power 'may throw off its respectable cloak of labour dignity' which may lead to increasing tension within families and violence (see also Segal, 1990). For young, working-class men the assumption of a 'respectable' adult identity depends on access to a wage which involves a distancing from the domestic sphere. For young women, in contrast, there is an adult female identity that does not depend on employment—motherhood.

This is, however, seen as problematic if it takes place outside marriage or without the support of a male wage which, in the latter part of the twentieth century, became increasingly likely (Willis, 1984b; McRae, 1999a).

For both young men and women, lack of a wage also means lack of access to the burgeoning consumer society and may mean that desired commodities can only be achieved through delinquency and criminality and, possibly, a rejection of work altogether if existence can be secured without it. Moreover young men attempt to differentiate themselves from young women and feminized domestic spaces and, in the absence of a wage, this differentiation may be achieved by becoming involved in criminal subcultures (Campbell, 1993). Thus rather than supporting women and children, men indulge in activities which take them away from the domestic sphere and reinforce a macho, irresponsible, and lawless masculinity. They play cops and robbers for real (Cohen, 1997). It is perverse to blame women for this problem. On the contrary it is social change and the resultant unemployment and poverty that have rendered young, working-class men redundant (Willis, 1984a, 1984b).

Youth culture

How have sociologists studied these changes and why, since the 1980s, have they homed in on masculinity? Why is it that what is happening to men is seen in terms of a crisis of gender identity in ways that it is not for women (Campbell, 1993:202)? And how is it that women are seen as responsible by many, both for the crisis and for its resolution?

In the early post-war years sociologists considered the youth question, along with juvenile delinquency and deviance, through a functionalist lens. Studies assumed that delinquency was a male way of growing up, a stage that young men went through which could lead to criminality but which, more often than not, ended with their twenties, marriage, and employment. It was seen as a working-class problem and often laid at the door of mothers who, instead of being at home to look after their teenage children, were out at work, leaving them to fend for themselves on the streets. Girls' delinquency in contrast was sexualized. Thus even when girls were involved in gangs and physical fighting these aspects of their delinquent behaviour remained invisible; it was their sexual behaviour that was policed (Campbell, 1981:esp. 89–91). These differences were understood in terms of gender in so far as criminal behaviour was seen as being in conformity with the male sex role and contradicting the female one. Being young and male was associated with risk taking and occupying public space where behaviour is subject to formal control (e.g. by the police), being young and female was more circumscribed, and young women's behaviour was more tightly controlled by parents (Downes, 1999:244). Thus gendered patterns of socialization and social control were linked to gendered patterns of deviance and delinquency. Questions of social control were uppermost and the concern was to provide more appropriate means of integrating young people into adult society. Deviancy had to be contained and strategies had to be developed to get young people to accept the work ethic and the values of mainstream society. Deviance and delinquency were explained as arising from 'anomie' and the adoption by some young people of illegitimate means to achieve legitimate ends. Thus failure at school can be compensated for by joining a 'gang' which provides criteria of status that can be met. Delinquency was theorized by some as a rejection and inversion of the middle-class values purveyed by the school and, by others, as a celebration of working-class values (Cohen, 1955; Miller, 1958).

With the advent of interactionism and labelling theory in the 1960s, attention turned to the importance of societal reaction in constructing deviant or delinquent acts. Thus being labelled as deviant can have the effect of intensifying a person's commitment to that social identity rather than controlling and eliminating it. An important study in this tradition is Stan Cohen's *Folk devils and moral panics* in which he explores the mods and rockers phenomenon of the early 1960s. He argues that societal reaction, via the media, the police, and the legal system, i.e. the control culture, created a moral panic about the mods and rockers. They were seen as posing a threat to the moral fabric of society because 'they had no real conviction about the rationality of the division between work and play, production and consumption' and, it might be added, they blurred gender boundaries. It was, however, the so-called vandalism on the beaches that attracted public attention through the media rather than the 'relative economic freedom' of teenage girls or the 'sexual confusion in clothing and hair-styles: the Mod boy with pastel-shaded trousers and the legendary make-up on his face, the girls with their short-cropped hair and sexless, flat appearance' (Cohen, 1980:193). And even though Cohen suggests that 'Mod was a more female than male phenomenon' (ibid.:186), he explores neither the gender relations that were embedded in it nor the forms of masculinity and femininity with which it was associated. This is despite his discussion of the effeminacy of the mods compared with the rockers who were more macho and into black leather, motor bikes, and metal studs (Cohen, 1980:185). He is attentive to the significance of style, arguing that Mary Quant, Twiggy, Carnaby Street, and mod magazines testify to the consumer power of young people and the diffusion of a particular mod style with its apparent gender ambiguity throughout society. However he theorizes the mods and rockers phenomenon in class terms, seeing it as a solution to the problems created by society 'for some of its members—like working-class adolescents' (Cohen, 1980:204). This approach also characterizes those who turned their attention to spectacular youth subcultures in the 1970s.

Subcultures

Under the influence of Marxism and developing an analysis of cultural resistance inspired by Gramsci's notion of hegemony, the 1970s saw the emergence of an analysis of spectacular youth cultures which understood them as a form of resistance to class exploitation. The problem was no longer how to control delinquent youth but how to transform symbolic resistance into real political resistance (Frith, 1984). Young working-class men became working-class heroes, challenging class domination by subcultural means. The focus was on spectacular youth subcultures and their emergence was linked to the culture of the working-class areas whence they came (the parent culture) and the dominant, middle-class culture which confronted them in the school and in wider society. They were conceptualized as an imaginary solution to the social problems faced by young, working-class men. They were a statement of working-class identity and a form of resistance to the hegemonic cultural values of the ruling class. The argument was that these subcultures, particularly through their style, challenged the cultural codes and values of the ruling class. And although recognition was given to the social context within which they emerged, the focus of analysis was public space and leisure activities (Cohen, 1980). Thus:

Members of a subculture may walk, talk, act, look 'different' from their parents and from some of their peers: but they belong to the same families, go to the same schools, work at much the same jobs, live down the same 'mean streets' as their peers and parents . . . Through dress, activities, leisure pursuits and life-style they project a different cultural response or 'solution' to the problems posed for them by their material and social class position and experience. (Clarke et al., 1976:14–15)

However distinctive youth subcultures were, they were bearers of working-class values found in the parent cultures such as collective forms of organization, territoriality, and 'particular conceptions of masculinity and male dominance' (Hall and Jefferson, 1976:53). But even though it was recognized that it was largely boys for whom subcultures provided a 'strategy for negotiating their collective existence' (ibid.: 47) and that they reproduced a working-class form of masculinity, it was the class rather than the gender dimensions of these subcultures which were deemed to be theoretically significant.

Working-class youth subcultures were theorized both as a means of reproducing class relations and class cultures and as a symbolic, but ultimately futile, challenge to the cultural hegemony of the ruling class. Thus Willis argued that resistance to the imposition of middle-class norms ultimately leads to conformity both to the manual, dead-end jobs which used to await young, working-class men and to racism and sexism. Moreover racism and sexism are the means by which the lads' capitulation to class exploitation is achieved. This is because, on the one hand, manual work is associated with masculinity and non-manual work with femininity, to be a 'real' man means doing manual work. And, on the other hand, manual, masculine work is not at the bottom of the heap: jobs which are taken by blacks being regarded as the most menial and degrading. So through racism the lads have a group to look down on even when they are engaged in manual labour. In this analysis a delinquent subculture is characterized as resistance to school and authority but as accommodation to manual labour and class exploitation through the ideologies of racism and sexism.

'Race' and racism

Although there were some exceptions (see e.g. Cashmore, 1979; Hall et al., 1978), most of these studies were of white, working-class boys. Neither girls nor young black people were given much attention and it was only after the 1981 riots that attention turned to 'black youth', which was defined as being 'in crisis'. This crisis was conceptualized in terms of racism, discrimination, and high levels of unemployment and, although it was seen as a crisis of 'black youth', it was young black men who were being talked about. It was not until later that this 'crisis of black social life [was] routinely represented as a crisis of masculinity' (Gilroy, 1993:7, cited in Alexander, 1996:158), indicating the way talk about masculinity can serve to mask and individualize problems which have structural and institutional roots. At the time predictions were made that public disorder was likely to get worse, that 'black youths do have a certain fascination for violence' and that black girls were forming gangs in emulation of their male peers (Cashmore and Troyna, 1982a:33).

Differences were noted between Asian and West Indian youth (i.e. young men). Young Asians were seen as caught between two cultures—home and host—and suffering similar crises of identity as educationally successful, white, working-class children (see Jackson and Marsden, 1986). Their home environments were, however, supportive of educational endeavour and this was reflected in the relative success of Asian children in educational terms (Rex, 1982; Cashmore and Troyna, 1982b). Young West Indians, in contrast, were seen as having had their culture destroyed by centuries of slavery and racism and therefore of adopting a similar response to that of some sections of white, working-class youth—rejecting the dominant values (work ethic/education) and 'affiliating to the marginal culture of the hustlers' or becoming involved in Rastafarianism (Rex, 1982:69; see also Allen, 1982; Pryce, 1986). Thus a distinction was made between Asians who have their own 'authentic' culture and West Indians/Afro-Caribbeans who are simply defined by 'race' (Alexander, 1996:11). The central dynamic explaining the behaviour of young West Indians was defined as class (overlaid by 'race') while for Asians it was culture. But as with the studies of white youth, young black women are absent, gender is taken for granted rather than problematized, and 'race' rather than class takes centre stage (Allen, 1982).

The racism of white, working-class subcultures was also explored but, as with sexism, it remains at best unproblematized and at worst almost revered because it is seen as an integral part of working-class culture.

These same values of racism, sexism, chauvinism, compulsive masculinity and anti-intellectualism, the slightest traces of which are condemned in bourgeois culture, are treated with a deferential care, an exaggerated contextualization, when they appear in the subculture. (Cohen, 1980:xxvii)

Although generally valid, this criticism is most apposite when aimed at analyses which focus on style, thereby moving away from analyses rooted in material conditions towards the more ephemeral realm of signs and symbols. Thus Dick Hebdige argues that the skinhead subculture developed in response to the mods phenomenon. Skinheads reasserted a lumpen identity rather than the mod option which was upwardly mobile (Hebdige, 1979: 55). In this process they appropriated elements of black (West Indian) youth subcultures and adopted and adapted not only reggae but also elements of their sartorial and linguistic style. Their racism, sexism, and homophobia is brought out in the following comment:

the alliance between white and black youth was an extremely precarious and provisional one: it was only by continually monitoring trouble spots (e.g. *the distribution of white girls*) and by scapegoating other alien groups ('*queers*', *hippies, and Asians*) that internal conflict could be avoided. Most notably, 'paki-bashing' can be read as a displacement manoeuvre whereby the fear and anxiety produced by limited identification with one black group was transformed into aggression and directed against another black community. (Hebdige, 1979:58, my emphasis)

It has been suggested that the different attitudes of young, white, working-class men towards West Indians and Asians noted here can be understood through a gendered grid (Cohen, 1997). Thus although young black men form rival gangs which have to be fought, their tough macho masculinity wins them respect from their white counterparts. Young Asian men, on the other hand, are regarded as effeminate and involved in jobs which are feminine, such as shop-keeping and office work. This suggests that the way these young men understand their world is sharply inflected by gender and partly explains why they are so reluctant to avail themselves of jobs in the highly feminized service sector.

Feminist critique

During the 1970s feminists began to point out that the study of subcultures left girls out and problematized neither gender nor sexuality. This despite the recognition that within subcultures different forms of working-class masculinity were displayed and, if only at the symbolic level, gender boundaries were breached and norms of sexual behaviour subverted (Hebdige, 1979). In spectacular subcultures girls were never the focus; the important social actors were male. Girls were, however, involved in these subcultures just as they were involved in delinquency, and although their presence had been noted in earlier studies, it was feminists who made visible the gendering of youth subcultures. They argued that studies of youth subcultures were primarily studies of masculinity, but masculinity as if it existed in isolation from gender relations and as if only one gender was significant. In addition, subcultures have gender relations inscribed in them and, in terms of style at least, may blur (or reinforce) gender boundaries.

Studies showed that girls were present in subcultures but that they were subordinate to their male peers and not so evident in the violent incidents which attracted public attention (McRobbie and Garber, 1991:6). Thus the style of mod boys was 'effeminate' and that of mod girls 'sexless'; both boys and girls tended to have office jobs and the subculture was 'feminised' (ibid.). This contrasted with the rockers where a macho masculinity was in evidence and girls were never at the handlebars, they were present as boys' partners rather than in their own right, and with punk girls who were masculinized, wearing a hyper-masculine uniform and indulging in masculine forms of behaviour such as attending football matches. Girls were obviously present in the more middle-class, hippie counterculture which was 'sexually ambiguous'. McRobbie and Garber comment:

As 1960s unisex gave way to hippie sexual ambiguity and then to mid-1970s high-camp glitter rock, we can see that both girls themselves and femininity as a representational form became more acceptable within the prevailing vocabulary of youth subcultures. However the feminising of the male image as seen in the iconography of Bowie or Jagger or even Gary Glitter, should not blind us to the asymmetry which remains in relation to the feminine image . . . The girl is by definition 'forever feminine'. (ibid.:7)

Thus representation of gender and sexual ambiguity are precisely that—representations—and do not necessarily affect gender relations. Moreover, as we have seen, the concept of subcultures developed to explain young, working-class men's behaviour cannot explain what happens to working-class girls nor, for that matter, to most working-class boys (see also Chapter 5). Thus, girls occupy a 'different leisure space' from boys and are partially integrated into adult female roles through their participation in domestic labour; they achieve 'feminine status through acquiring a "steady"' (McRobbie, 1991:33). In contrast boys' achievement of masculine status is not dependent on girls but on entering a world which is separate from the domestic sphere, whether that be the streets or work.

Masculinity and style

In the late 1980s and 1990s attention turned explicitly to masculinities. Those studying young people focused on the way that increasing unemployment problematized the transition to adulthood while others explored masculinities and style, particularly the different masculine identities associated with young men as a new and important consumer group. Thus, on the one hand, study of the material social relations within which gender identities are constructed remained important but, on the other, studies of consumption and masculine styles emerged. The new man, a media creation (Chapman, 1988), emerged in the 1980s as did magazines dealing with 'lifestyle' issues targeted at young men and modelling themselves on those aimed at the female teenage market. Young men could be 'liberated' from the constraints of their sex roles; they could wear perfume and make-up (and increasingly suffer from eating disorders) without immediately being labelled gay. Men were encouraged to get in touch with their emotions and heal the wounds inflicted on them by their fathers (Bly, 1990); all this without reference to women or to gender relations. Frank Mort argues that these styles were influenced by youth subcultures and gay politics, they stressed sexual ambiguity and homosociality. He also sees them as a response to feminism and, more centrally, to the culture of homosexuality (Segal, 1990; Mort, 1996: 145). He details how the consumption power of gay men and the cultural space occupied by gay cultures in Soho influenced the purveyors of style. Despite the influence of feminism, however, he argues that these developments involved relations between men and were predicated on the marginalization of women.

This shift to a concern with cultural representation has influenced the study of both youth and masculinity. Seeing masculinity as style creates the impression that gender (and sexual) identities can be freely chosen and are not inscribed within social relations of class, race, and age, as well as gender (see e.g. Giddens, 1992). The arrival of the new man provides (seemingly) another 'choice' for men. They can be sensitive and caring and more in tune with the feminine side of themselves. Similarly, studies of youth now argue that music and style are essentially eclectic and are chosen as a process of constructing identities and lifestyles from the almost infinite range of commodities offered to individuals by consumerism (Bennett, 1999:600 passim). The concept of sub-cultures, with its implication of bounded groups, has been jettisoned in favour of neo-tribes with fluid boundaries and shifting composition, thus completing the move away from material and structural constraints towards seeing consumerism as liberation. Consumerism allows the expression of lifestyles and identities which are no longer tied to class (or any other structural constraint) but are created in the process of consuming.

One of the issues ignored by analyses which focus on style, identities, and consumption is the class dimension of youth cultures and masculinities. The images of masculinity purveyed in the 1950s and analysed by Mort are associated with particular class positions and demonstrate, above all, respectability of a lower-middle/upper working-class variety. The 1980s styles to which he pays attention play with the borders between hetero- and homosexuality but again, I would suggest, are class and age specific. They are associated with mental not manual labour, with access to a wage (adopting a style costs money and is part of consumption), and with oppressive (for women) gender relations. They are also not accessible to a certain stratum of young, working-class men because they have no or low-waged work and because such 'effeminate' masculinities are precisely those that they hold in the deepest contempt because of their association with gay men, with women, with Asians, with mental labour, and with the middle class.

Masculinities in context

Many studies of masculinity (and youth cultures) also ignore gender relations and this contrasts profoundly with studies of girls and women where gender relations and divisions are always central. Indeed the problem with many such studies is that they ignore the material social relations, particularly relations of power, in which masculinities are embedded (Hearn, 1996). There are, of course, exceptions such as Claire Alexander's ethnographic study of young black men (Alexander, 1996) in which she argues that enacting being male and black is about asserting control: publicly in relation to women and other groups of young men, particularly white men, and in private over women. Central to asserting control is being able to attract women and to fight if necessary (Alexander, 1996:143). Thus heterosexuality and violence are critically important ingredients of black masculinity which is thereby located within gendered power relations. An association of violence with masculinity has also been found amongst groups of young, unemployed, working-class, mainly white men (Canaan, 1996). Alexander's analysis has much in common with the studies of subcultures in the 1970s although her central concern is how young black men negotiate their identities in the context of home, work, and community. She also deconstructs the folk devil image which young black men have attracted, showing them as 'belonging to the same families, working at much the same jobs and living down the same "mean streets" as their peers and parents' (to misquote Clarke et al., 1976).

Another study which conceptualizes masculinities in terms of gendered power and in relation to class is Bea Campbell's analysis of the riots that took place in the summer of 1991. In her analysis, class, gender, and race come together to provide an important way into the hopeless situation faced by many young men in contemporary Britain and its implications in terms of gender. She argues that, in the absence of a wage, young men are forced to differentiate themselves from women by creating a space for themselves outside the domestic sphere. With employment this was provided by paid work but in its absence it is the streets, delinquency, and criminality which provide the means of differentiation and which initiate young men into a violent, racist, and sexist masculinity. The riots have no purpose, she argues, they are directed against the communities in which the young men live, their targets are Asian shopkeepers in those communities, and they take the form of a battle between the young men and the police. Women's attempts to create solidary social relations within the communities also become the target of young men's rage. 'Crime and coercion are sustained by men. Solidarity and self-help are sustained by women' (Campbell, 1993:319). The forms of masculinity adopted involve control over technology (stolen cars) and over public space (the streets); violence (against the 'other'—Asian shopkeepers and women at home); and irresponsibility (being responsible is something associated with women). They are asserted in conflict with the police who embody a more legitimized macho and brutal masculinity (graphically represented in Kubrick's film, *A Clockwork Orange*). As Campbell points out:

Certainly, the economic crisis gendered an identity crisis—for men and boys. However, it was not that they *lost* their identity, but the way that they *asserted* it, that was the problem. (Campbell, 1993:322)

This problematic assertion of masculine identity and the fact that 'being male is one of the strongest predictors of crime' is neither a recent phenomenon nor one that is specific to Britain. There is however a 'paucity of empirical research' into gender and crime (Rutter et al., 1998:254) and, in its absence, it is tempting to explain young men's anti-social behaviour (as well as boys' under-achievement in schools) as caused by a 'crisis of masculinity'.

Theorizing masculinity

As we have seen, many studies of masculinity are marked by a lack of attention to material social relations, focusing instead on cultural representation, identities, and style. This emphasis arises from the influence of poststructuralism and, in particular, theorizations deriving from Foucault (see Chapter 1). Thus masculinities are conceptualized as existing within discourses, and young people construct gendered subjectivities within different discourses of masculinity (see e.g. Mac An Ghaill, 1994). For Foucault, however, discourse is about power and knowledge; discourses define the world and institutions are established which support specific forms of knowledge and power. This theorization of discourses has something in common with notions of hegemony in so far as it involves the power to define and to create meaning, but it is precisely this element of power that seems to have got lost in many analyses of masculinity (see Connell, 1993b). Masculinity has come to be understood in terms of adopting a particular gender and sexual identity and, although recognition is paid to the fact that controlling behaviour and defining what is and is not 'masculine' is a collective enterprise, the process of positioning the subject is inevitably an individual one. As we have seen, this type of study has dominated recent discussions of gender and schooling and has revealed much about how boys learn to 'do' gender in school. What is left out, however, is the relation between masculinities and power.

This is perhaps surprising given that these analyses owe much to Bob Connell's theory of hegemonic masculinity (Connell, 1995). He argues that it is important to theorize the relation between masculinities, sexual politics, and gendered power relations (see also Carrigan, Connell, and Lee, 1985) and that, at any one time and within specific societies, a particular form of masculinity—hegemonic masculinity—is culturally dominant. Hegemonic masculinity is part of a strategy of maintaining male dominance (Connell, 1993a:603). However, as many writers on masculinity have observed, neither masculinity nor hegemonic masculinity is defined (Donaldson, 1993). Indeed Connell himself argues that such a definition should not be attempted. Instead,

'Masculinity', to the extent the term can be briefly defined at all, is simultaneously a place in gender relations, the practices through which men and women engage that place in gender, and the effects of these practices in bodily experience, personality and culture. (Connell, 1995:71)

Notwithstanding the opacity of this non-definition, he goes on to argue that 'gender is a way in which social practice is ordered' (Connell, 1995:71). He thus points to the importance of processes and practices to understanding gender relations and the place of masculinities within them rather than seeing either gender or masculinities as attributes of persons. He therefore makes an important conceptual distinction between real men and masculinities. Furthermore, the concept of hegemonic masculinity directs attention towards

how particular groups of men inhabit positions of power and wealth, and how they legitimate and reproduce the social relationships that generate their dominance. (Carrigan, Connell, and Lee, 1985:92)

Thus the hegemony of a particular form of masculinity may support the class, gender, and sexual power of specific groups of men; it is a means of legitimizing the power of ruling-class men over younger men and all women (Donaldson, 1993:655), i.e. it legitimates patriarchy and the gender order. This echoes Susan Brownmiller's argument about the way that rape supports male dominance. Thus although most men do not rape women, the fact that some men do benefits all men because it keeps women in a state of fear and therefore dependent on men (Brownmiller, 1986). Similarly all men benefit from the existence of hegemonic masculinity without having to display it themselves; they do not all need to be violent towards or exhibit 'naked domination' over women but as long as some men display these characteristics, whether in films or in real life, and the culturally dominant definition of masculinity incorporates these features, women's position *vis-à-vis* men will remain relatively powerless (Connell, 1995:80). Here, however, the conceptual distinction between real men and hegemonic masculinity seems to be less clear.

It is perhaps more helpful to regard hegemonic masculinity as part of gender ideology (McMahon, 1993). Thus ideologies of masculinity which define men as naturally strong, aggressive, rational, technically minded, and competitive legitimate men's domination of the state, the military, bureaucracies, science, and technology: their power is defined as a function of their maleness. This idea is developed by MacInnes who argues that masculinity is an 'ideological construct' and it is misguided to try to make it the subject of empirical analysis . . . Just as there is no such thing as masculinity, neither are there any such things as masculinities—the increasing recourse to the plural is only a dim recognition of the insoluble theoretical problems offered by the singular term. We cannot understand gender identity to be something which produces or reproduces the sexual division of labour. Rather it is the ideological reflection, created through the fetishism of sexual difference, of men and women's attempts to explain that division of labour to themselves. (MacInnes, 1998:39–40)

Moreover it is more important to look at what men do in relation to women (and other men) than to explore the different masculine identities which are now available and, in any event, hegemonic masculinity cannot be challenged by individual men going on quests for a new identity or by a male identity crisis (Hearn, 1996; Segal, 1990, 1993). In MacInnes's words,

masculinity can be seen as the last ideological defence of male supremacy in a world that has already conceded that men and women are equal. Invented in order to argue that men's power is socially rather than naturally derived, the concept suffers from the patent flaw . . . that what is socially rather than naturally constructed can be socially challenged and changed. I think that we have reached the point where masculinity as a concept obscures the analysis of social relations between the sexes, especially when it is imagined to be something that empirically existing individuals possess, which they might reform. (MacInnes, 1998:59)

The strength of Connell's argument is that he tries to bring together analyses of cultural representation and identity with an understanding of gender relations and sexual politics. How the one relates to the other, however, is left unsatisfactorily vague because of the conceptual confusion at the heart of his analysis. As a result, and despite his attempts to avoid this, his work courts the danger of dissociating masculinities from the relations of power which they legitimate and seeing the flowering of many different masculinities both as a challenge to hegemonic masculinity and as something liberating in itself. Thus a change in masculinities can be read as representing a change in the material relations of gender. However,

The fact that men are rebelling against their role as breadwinners does not entail the undermining of their dominance in the political and economic spheres. Nor, for that matter, does it imply that they have surrendered authority in the family or household. What has changed is not male power as such, but its form, its presentation, its packaging. In other words, while it is apparent that styles of masculinity may alter in relatively short time spans, the substance of male power does not. (Brittan, 1989:2).

Thus for Brittan, unlike Connell, new styles of masculinity do not necessarily imply a crisis either in hegemonic masculinity or in the gender order and they leave male power untouched (see also Messner, 1993). What they do signify is an increased range of images of masculinity created largely by commercial pressures and deriving from the gender and sexual ambiguity of youth cultures. What this means is that men are less constrained by expectations about appropriate masculine behaviour; they are constructed as consumers in an analogous way to women and have been given permission to be interested in fashion, clothes, perfume, hair styles. However, these consumption-based identities are only available to young men who have access to a wage. For those who do not, delinquent and criminal forms of masculinity are all that they can aspire to.

What is confused in much of the literature is men and masculinities. It is men who occupy positions in hierarchical social relations, not masculinities. Masculinities can best be seen as cultural representations of different ways of being male which serve to define men and women as different and legitimate the existing gender order which privileges white, middle-class, heterosexual men. Connell includes in his analysis of gender relations relations between men, indeed he defines relations between men as gender relations. Although this courts the danger of once again making women invisible, it points to the importance of relations between men for understanding the gender order and highlights the role of institutionalized heterosexuality in structuring power relations, particularly men's power over women and the power of heterosexual over homosexual men.

Understanding the crisis

But what does all this tell us about the crisis in masculinity? Perhaps what is hailed as a crisis of masculinity is a moral panic over the undermining of the legitimacy of men's power over women. There is now hardly any sphere of activity legally barred to women and, in this sense, every male bastion has been stormed. The crisis in masculinity could signify a major shift in gender relations which has provoked not so much an identity crisis as a legitimation crisis. Old ways of being a man are no longer possible or acceptable and this gives rise to uncertainties and insecurity. These have not emerged from nowhere but are rooted in the economic and cultural changes of the last three decades of the twentieth century. In the post-war years boys grew up to be breadwinners, masculinity was not seen as an identity choice. Since then there has been a burgeoning of masculine identities. This has been associated with the targeting of men, especially young men, as consumers and, it has been argued, owes much to the emergence of gay styles and gay consumer power. It has also been suggested that the feminist critique of men's behaviour has resulted in a questioning of dominant forms of masculinity and experimentation with alternative ways of being a man (Segal, 1990). But alongside this new variety there has been a contraction in production-based forms of masculinity and, for young, working-class men, there is nothing to take their place. Both production and consumption-based forms of masculinity are closed to them because they depend on access to a wage. The real crisis of masculinity derives from the lack of a wage and the so-called compensatory and often violent forms of masculinity which are adopted in its absence (Segal, 1990; Campbell, 1993). This change can be summarized as a shift from the immediate post-war 'you've never had it so good' years which were characterized by the 'teenager', affluence, and spectacular youth cultures to the emergence of youth unemployment in the 1970s together with the end of youth cultures and affluence. It marks a structural and cultural shift in both class and gender relations which was pinpointed as happening during the 1970s and conceptualized as both an economic crisis and a crisis in hegemony. Before then sociologists studied youth in terms of class, subsequently they have recognized that it is young men they were studying and have begun to theorize what young men do in terms of gender.

Chapter 7

Sexuality, Power, and Gender

I N this chapter I explore the relation between gender and sexuality and suggest that, while there have been significant changes since the Second World War in terms of sexual behaviour, the extent to which this reflects a transformation in gendered power relations is debatable. Sexuality is an area which has been the subject of exhaustive exploration—mostly at a theoretical level and largely uninformed by what people actually do and feel and the meanings they attribute to sexual behaviour. It is something on which there are no official statistics and—until the advent of HIV/AIDS—there was a marked reluctance to sanction sex surveys. Thus a survey carried out by Mass Observation in 1949 was only published in 1995 (Stanley, 1995) and research council funding for a national survey (published in 1994) was blocked by the then Conservative government, only going ahead when the Wellcome Trust agreed to fund it (Wellings et al., 1994:11). I begin this chapter by outlining the findings of these two surveys separated by almost fifty years. I then look briefly at changes in the legislation relating to sexuality before exploring the way sexuality has been studied by sociologists.

Sex surveys

The survey carried out in 1949 attempted to explore people's attitudes towards sex. It aimed to show not only or even primarily what people did, but the significance and meaning they attributed to sex (Stanley, 1995). In contrast, the 1994 survey aimed to provide information such that the possible routes of HIV/ AIDS infection could be accurately predicted; it therefore focused on what people actually did rather than the meanings they attributed to sexuality and their feelings about it (Wellings et al., 1994:5; Stanley, 1995). Because of these different concerns the two surveys are not directly comparable, but taken together they show that while sexual behaviours have changed on some dimensions, on others there is considerable continuity. I look first at the main findings of the 1949 survey and then discuss the changes pinpointed in the one carried out in 1994.

Little Kinsey, 1949

The 1949 survey explored how people had found out about sex, what they thought of sex education and birth control, their experience and views of marriage and divorce, sex outside marriage, prostitution, the 'psychology of sex', and sexual morality. The report also included an appendix on the sex habits of a group (the panel members) and an observational account of a group of gay men. However the bulk of the report focuses unproblematically on heterosexual sex governed by the institution of marriage which presumably reflected the assumptions about sex made by the majority of their respondents.

In 1949 most people, women and men, simply picked up information about sex in a haphazard way with many remaining ignorant until their wedding night. Thus a working-class housewife said, 'I didn't know until I was married—all my mother said was "Behave yourself"—and none of the details' (Stanley, 1995:83). But there were gender differences in whether or not marital sex was enjoyable: thus women were more likely than men to find sex within marriage unsatisfactory and, amongst the panel sample, one in twenty was unsatisfied with their marriage, with 82 per cent of men being 'completely satisfied by marital intercourse' compared with 61 per cent of the women. In addition women were less likely to experience orgasm through penetrative sex. As the author comments, there is 'a striking difference between the sexes ... women are clearly much worse off than men in this respect' (Stanley, 1995:121).

The report also found gender differences in views on the relation between sex and happiness, with two men in every five compared to one woman in every five thinking that 'sex is indispensable to happiness' (ibid.:155). Sex was usually taken to mean heterosexual intercourse and was seen as natural—within marriage.

Sex is a natural function, common to all, universal and eternal, biologically essential to continuing human life—these are constantly recurring views. (ibid.:159)

Some women, however, voiced very strong reservations about sex. A middle-aged, working-class housewife said:

sex is very unpleasant. My husband says I'm not human. If I'd known what it was like before I got married, I never would have married at all. (op. cit.)

Women were less likely than men to have 'premarital relations' but the report infers from illegitimacy rates and conceptions 'out of wedlock' that 'at least one person in three, probably more, has intercourse either before or outside marriage' (ibid.:134). People's attitudes towards sex outside marriage depended on whether it was 'between two people who are in love, engaged, or somehow unable to marry', which tended to be condoned, or 'based largely on physical attraction', which was more likely to be frowned upon (ibid.:134–5). Higher levels of education were associated with greater tolerance of 'pre-marital sex' for women and men (ibid.:140) and there was a view that there was greater sexual freedom and openness than hitherto; something that was welcomed more by women than by men. Despite this there was a feeling that 'sex for its own sake must be wrong' and that 'marriage gives dignity to sex' (ibid.:137); views that were also apparent in the 1994 survey. Similarly, if sex was 'abnormal' or 'indulged in too much' it could be wrong or bad for you. Indeed there was a tension between an 'acceptance of the natural inevitability of sex' and the idea that 'sex for its own sake is lust and wrong' (ibid.:164).

In some of the men's accounts there was clear evidence of a double standard. Thus,

a 20 year old Londoner described to an observer how he had had intercourse with ten different girls (including a prostitute) but has not had intercourse with his fiancee: 'After I had been going with her for two months, I tried to go all the way with her, but it wouldn't work. She wants a white wedding and marriage in a church, and to be a virgin. I agree with her and I don't try any more. When I first tried and she refused I thought she was the right girl. If she had gone with me I don't think I would have gone out long with her because she would just have been another girl'. (ibid.:139)

Such views were more common amongst working-class than middle-class respondents and had repercussions for young women particularly. One young woman's account provides a moving description of the sorts of pressures that men can exert so that young women 'let them go all the way' even though they don't really want to, don't enjoy it and are scared of the consequences. The young woman reported that he had told her that she couldn't be in love with him if she refused to have sex and he punished her by not speaking to her when she refused on another occasion. She observes,

Men want to be intimate without any understanding. I couldn't be intimate with a man unless I was in love with him. (ibid.:185)

And she reported that he enjoyed it even though she didn't and that she had only done it because she was in love with him. As we shall see, young women of today report similar experiences of their first heterosexual sex.

The national survey

The 1994 survey found that gender differences in some areas of heterosexual activity had changed significantly since the immediate post-war years. For instance, young people engage in heterosexual activity at a much earlier age than was the case for preceding generations and this is true for women and men. Thus the median age for first heterosexual intercourse has fallen from 21 to 17 for women and from 20 to 17 for men (Wellings et al., 1994) and men are now 'only one-and-a-half times more likely [than women] to experience sexual intercourse before 16' (*Independent on Sunday*, 16 January 1994:6).

Class, ethnicity, and religion all affect when women and men have their first experience of heterosexual sex. Thus higher social class and educational levels are associated with later initiation into heterosexual intercourse for women and men; Asians (especially Asian women) are less likely than other groups to 'report early sexual intercourse' (before the age of 16) while black men are most likely to. And although gender differences are no longer apparent amongst whites they remain significant for ethnic minority groups (Wellings et al., 1994: 54). Similarly religious belief acts as a brake on first heterosexual intercourse. Furthermore, despite press coverage of stars like Britney Spears who is renowned for her virginity, 'saving yourself' is a thing of the past for most people (Wellings et al., 1994:6).

There is a gender difference in the factors leading women and men to engage in their first sexual activity. Thus 'being in love' and seeing sex as an expresssion of emotional intimacy are more significant for women while peer group pressure and simply wanting to 'lose their virginity' were more common amongst men. There have been generational changes in the importance of these factors. Thus the ideology of romance 'is in clear decline' with over half of the older women citing being in love compared to just over a third of the youngest. And the proportion of men saying that they simply wanted to lose their virginity has increased from the older to younger age groups (1 in 10 compared with 1 in 50) (Wellings et al., 1994). There are also gender differences in the number of heterosexual partners people report, with women being less likely than men to have multiple partners and, contrary to widespread stereotypes, there is no evidence of a (male) 'homosexual appetite for large numbers of partners, though this is undoubtedly the lifestyle chosen by a few' (Wellings et al., 1994:217).

There are gender and age differences in views towards sex outside marriage. Thus 8.2 per cent of men and 10.8 per cent of women believe 'sex before marriage' is wrong but only 5 per cent of the youngest age group (women and men) believe it is wrong while amongst the oldest age group one in seven men and one in five women disapprove. This suggests that attitudes have changed and, indeed, a repeat of a 1955 survey found that there has been a revolution in the last 50 years in attitudes to premarital sex. In the 1950s, two thirds thought it wrong for a girl to have some sexual experience before settling down and half the population thought a boy should not "sow his oats". There is still a gender gap but 66% think pre-marital sex acceptable for a young man and 62% for a young woman before settling down. (Travis, 1999)

There is now a much greater acceptance of heterosexual activity outside mar-riage but there is also a continuing gender gap, both in the behaviour thought acceptable for women and men and in their views. Thus 75 per cent of men compared with 66 per cent of women do not think sex before marriage is wrong, but women are less inclined than men to approve either of sexual activ-ity under the age of 16 or of casual sex and sex 'outside a regular relationship' (Wellings et al., 1994:249).

There is continuing evidence of a 'double standard', particularly amongst men, with 16.3 per cent of men thinking sex under 16 is acceptable for boys compared with 13.9 per cent who think it is acceptable for girls; the equivalent figures for women are 9.9 per cent and 8.7 per cent. This suggests that although fewer women than men think sex under 16 is acceptable for either sex, their views are less gender differentiated than men's (Wellings et al., 1994:234, 244). Furthermore, 'Ideals of monogamy seem to be more strongly held by women than men' (ibid.:252), which ties in with the greater likelihood that women link romantic love or emotional commitment with sex rather than seeing them as separate or as substitutes for each other.

Class and age as well as gender seem to be significant in affecting homo-sexual activity and non-penetrative heterosexual activity. Thus the survey found that 6.1 per cent of men and 3.4 per cent of women have had 'some kind of homosexual experience' and that this is higher amongst women and men who have been to boarding schools (Wellings et al., 1994:190, 206). Older women (over 45) were less likely than younger women to have had a 'homo-sexual experience'. Similarly, although a majority of women and men (two-thirds and three-quarters respectively) had experienced oral sex it was more common amongst younger age groups and amongst the higher social classes. In 1949 similar class differences in sexual experiences were noted (Stanley, 1995:194). The 1994 report's estimates of the prevalence of homosexuality have, however, given rise to considerable controversy and it has been claimed that it seriously underestimates its incidence in Britain (see e.g. Stanley, 1995).

The 1949 report was almost silent on homosexuality. In an article published in 1950, however, the report's author said that the survey had found 'a more genuine feeling of disgust towards homosexuality . . . than towards any other subject tackled' (England, 1950, cited in Weeks, 1989:241). This is an area where there has been significant change in the intervening period. The 1994 report shows a gender difference in attitudes towards homosexuality with women being more tolerant than men of male homosexuality, although levels of disapproval are still quite high. Thus 70.2 per cent of men compared with 57.9 per cent of women believed gay male sex to be always/mostly wrong. A lower proportion (64.5 per cent) of men disapproved of lesbian sex, which indicates that 'men, though not women, hold more negative attitudes towards male than towards female homosexuality' (Wellings et al., 1994:255). The authors construct a measure of permissiveness which shows that men generally have more liberal attitudes to heterosexual activity outside the confines of marriage but women are more tolerant of homosexuality (ibid.:260). There is also an age difference, with younger women and men being more tolerant than older people.

There is evidence in the survey that these age differences represent a generational shift in moral and cultural values which dates from the 1950s and 1960s. It also shows that the gender gap in heterosexual behaviour is narrowing, with women's behaviour coming to be more like men's. Thus women and men are having sex at much younger ages and gender differences in age of first heterosexual experience have almost disappeared. There is also more tolerance of sex outside marriage and of gay and lesbian sexualities. But there are also areas where there has been more continuity than change. Thus the 1949 report records women's experiences and clearly articulates their dissatisfactions with both the practice and the institutions of 'sex' (Stanley, 1995). What women voiced in the 1940s (and continue to voice now) is dissatisfaction with the emotional and sexual relationships they have with men, a dissatisfaction that has been given a voice by feminist researchers but which has hitherto remained unheard due to the predominance of men's voices and the presumption of penetrative heterosex as the norm.

Although useful, sex surveys are limited because they tend to focus on the white population and to say very little about lesbians and gay men or, indeed, about homosexual behaviour (Stanley, 1995:235). This is perhaps surprising given the significant changes there have been since the Second World War in state regulation of sexuality and the reduction in the stigma attached to so-called deviant sexualities.

Legislative change

In Britain during the 1960s and 1970s there were legislative changes relating to morality in general and sexuality in particular; this included the decriminalization of male homosexuality (female homosexuality had never been criminalized), divorce reform, the legalization of abortion, and state provision (through the NHS) of the means of fertility control to the unmarried as well as the married. According to Jeffrey Weeks, during the 1960s sexuality, in particular female sexuality, was being redefined 'in terms of its possibilities for pleasure, for enjoyment unbounded by the old exigencies of compulsory childbirth or endless domestic chores' (Weeks, 1989:258). This development was part and parcel of the rise of consumerism and the use of women's sexuality for selling commodities and was facilitated by the increased availability of woman-controlled contraception. It also allowed women to seek heterosexual pleasure without the fear of unwanted pregnancy but, as many feminists have pointed out, made them more vulnerable to men's sexual advances as fear of pregnancy was no longer an adequate reason not to indulge in heterosex. Indeed women's sexual freedom was defined in male terms and sexual liberation could simply mean 'greater access for men to women's bodies and the removal of [women's] right to say "No" to sex, lest they be damned as "unliberated"' (Jackson and Scott, 1996:4–5; Weeks, 1989:260). The counter-cultural movements of the 1960s and the New Left embraced ideas about sexual liberation which included 'the dissociation of sex from reproduction, the emphasis on sexual pleasure and freedom, the critique of marriage and monogamy' and, in the 1970s, the women's movement challenged 'the coercive and predatory aspects of male sexuality' (Jackson and Scott, 1996:5). The gay liberation movement facilitated the adoption of a gay identity and the celebration of 'sexual pleasure for its own sake' rather than as a means of procreation. Indeed during the 1970s sexuality assumed a central importance in definitions of identity and selfhood in ways in which it had not hitherto. The decades since the war have therefore been marked by significant changes in the legislative sphere which have facilitated women's access to the means of fertility control and have decriminalized male homosexuality. These changes have led to claims that sexuality is now divorced from reproduction, it is no longer governed by religious values, it is linked purely to pleasure, for women as well as men, and can be indulged in for its own sake without attracting moral opprobrium. As we shall see, however, such claims fail to take sufficient account of the ways in which sexuality is shaped by gender and the power relations which govern it.

Studying sexuality

For most of the twentieth century psychoanalysis and sexology dominated the way sexuality was studied. Psychoanalysis theorized male and female sexuality as different, although originating in a psychological bisexuality common to all infants, and understood normal sexual development as involving biological males becoming masculine and biological females becoming feminine; these categories being culturally specific (Mitchell, 1974; Millett, 1971). Sexology defined sexuality 'as a biological and psychological phenomenon' (Gagnon and Parker, 1995; Jackson and Scott, 1996; Jackson, 1987; Stanley, 1995). During the 1960s this paradigm was replaced by one that defines sexuality as socially constructed. Thus—in contrast to sexology and psychoanalysis—'the constructionist view was that sexuality was not based on internal drives, but was elicited in specific historical and social circumstances' (Gagnon and Parker, 1995:8). Arguably it was only with the ending of the 'sexological period' that sociologists became interested in studying sexuality.

Prior to the 1970s there were few sociologists who ventured into the realm of sexuality. Mary McIntosh, in an early article, theorized male homosexuality as a 'deviant social role' (McIntosh, 1968:182). She argues that in contemporary British society homosexuality is a social role whose existence is essential for the emergence of a homosexual identity. Without it, although people may engage in homosexual behaviours, they would neither adopt a homosexual identity nor be labelled as homosexual. At one and the same time this social role confirms them in a deviant sexual identity and is a means of controlling and segregating them. This is particularly the case for male homosexuals. A lesbian social role is 'much less well-developed' and women who engage in homosexual behaviour are therefore much less likely to be confirmed in (or to adopt) a deviant social role and identity. This is one of the earliest attempts to theorize sexuality sociologically and McIntosh's use of labelling theory and rejection of homosexuality as 'condition' is significant. She advances a sociological explanation for the emergence of a homosexual identity and distinguishes between a social role (or identity), which is only apparent in some societies, and homosexual behaviour which is apparent in many (see also Weeks, 1987).

Sociologists also developed social constructionist arguments, theorizing sexuality as learned behaviour which varied historically and cross-culturally. Simon and Gagnon (1969), for instance, argued that 'becoming sexual is a process of learning sexual meanings or "scripts" and locating oneself within them' (Jackson, 1999:9). They were critical of Freud's notion of repression, suggesting that there was no innate sexual drive which could be repressed and that what was defined as sexual was socially and culturally determined and therefore variable. Importantly they attributed significance to gender, arguing that at puberty boys and girls follow gender-specific sexual scripts and that

the ways in which these scripts are learnt is profoundly affected by the gender-role learning of childhood, so that girls and boys learn to be sexual in different ways. (Jackson, 1999:40)

Sexuality is 'built on an earlier foundation of gender role learning' and is therefore gendered (Jackson, 1999:37). Girls learn that heterosexual activity is appropriate in the context of a romantic love relationship while boys learn that sex is about achievement and conquest; unlike boys 'a girl has nothing to gain and her "reputation" to lose if she is too sexually active' (Jackson, 1999:41).

This symbolic interactionist approach relies on notions of sociosexual dramas that have appropriate scripts which are learned by social actors. However it locates sexuality at the level of individual social actors and does not conceptualize sexuality in terms of gender inequalities and/or power (Jackson, 1999:9). Conceptualizing sexuality in terms of power was something that emerged from radical feminism (Rich, 1980) and poststructuralism (Foucault, 1981) at a similar time (late 1970s) but in very different ways. Both have been highly influential on the way sexuality and its relation to gender is studied despite the fact that, for Foucault, gender is seemingly irrelevant. It is perhaps significant that it is a lesbian and a gay man who have developed critical analyses of sexuality as it has been theorized and institutionalized in western societies. For both theorization and institutionalization marginalize those who are not heterosexual and enable them to see as socially constructed what is taken to be 'natural' or 'normal' by those who are heterosexual.

Compulsory heterosexuality

It was the women's movement of the 1970s that identified men's control of women's sexuality and men's sexual violence towards women as important ways in which male power was maintained. Thus Susan Brownmiller identified rape as the means whereby all men kept all women in a state of fear and dependence (Brownmiller, 1986), Catherine Mackinnon defined a continuum of violence from rape to coercive and (more controversially) non-coercive heterosex, and the threat of male violence was seen as an important means of controlling women's behaviour whether in public or private (Hanmer and Maynard, 1987; Kelly, 1988). Thus the idea that heterosexuality was structured by gendered relations of power was a central dimension of feminist theory and practice. This presents problems for feminists who wish to contest male power but who are also sexually engaged with men (see e.g. Segal, 1997). If heterosexuality is defined as structured by male power and its very enactment as reinforcing male power then, for feminists, heterosex becomes consorting with the enemy and the only solution lies in lesbianism. This issue was explosive in the women's movement in Britain in the 1970s and served to silence any analysis of heterosexuality which heterosexual feminists might have been interested in developing (Jackson, 1999; Smart, 1996; Segal, 1987; Campbell, 1980). However, although certain sections of the feminist movement identified sleeping with men as sleeping with the enemy, the more considered analyses of heterosexuality as institution that emerged from radical feminism did not share this analysis.

Adrienne Rich was amongst the first to problematize heterosexuality and to question the assumption that women are 'naturally' sexually oriented towards men.

This assumption of female heterosexuality seems to me in itself remarkable: it is an enormous assumption to have glided so silently into the foundations of our thought . . . heterosexuality, like motherhood, needs to be recognised and studied as a *political institution*. (Rich, 1980:637)

She argues that heterosexuality, far from being natural, is a choice which women are compelled to make in societies which are male dominated and that those who resist compulsory heterosexuality are challenging one of the institutional bases of male power (see also Clarke, 1996:157; Tabet, 1996). Women's consent to the institutions of heterosexuality is maintained through violence and persuasion and, as men hold economic power and have greater access to resources than do women, there is also 'an economic imperative to heterosexuality and marriage' and there are 'sanctions imposed against single women and widows' (Rich, 1980:634). Her article is perhaps best known for her suggestion that there is a lesbian continuum which includes a 'range . . . of woman-identified experience' including but not confined to 'genital sexual experience with another woman' (Rich, 1980:648). She controversially widens the definition of lesbianism to embrace any woman who is woman centred (see e.g. Campbell, 1980), regarding this identification as a challenge to compulsory heterosexuality and a 'direct or indirect attack on male right of access to women' (Rich, 1980:649). What is less frequently discussed is her analysis of the institutions of heterosexuality as economic, political, and cultural. Women (or men for that matter) cannot simply choose to 'be' heterosexual as they might 'choose' one pair of jeans rather than another. There are economic, political, and cultural constraints on their choices and society punishes those who make the 'wrong' choice. Similarly, Rich distinguishes between being critical of institutional heterosexuality and condemning heterosexual relationships. What is important is that women are able to choose whether and with whom to engage in sexual relationships and that they should have the 'collective power to determine the meaning and place of sexuality in their lives' (Rich, 1980:659). As long as heterosexuality is compulsory and women are disadvantaged economically and politically they are unable to do this.

Rich's contention that heterosexuality has an economic basis is supported by evidence from a study of homosexuality in Mombasa where established same-sex partnerships exist and male and female homosexuality is accepted (Shepherd, 1987). Here homosexuality 'may be a rational decision, bringing fuller participation in and better benefits from the society of which the homosexual is a member' (Shepherd, 1987:240). Furthermore rank seems to be a more important social category than gender for understanding homosexuality. Thus for a low-ranking man or woman, choosing to become involved in a homosexual relationship with a higher-ranking person of the same sex is often a means of ensuring economic security. In other words, where homosexuality is economically advantageous, significant numbers of people choose to live in homosexual rather than heterosexual partnerships. Sexual behaviour is therefore shaped by economic constraints and, in some societies, there may be economic advantages attached to homosexuality rather than heterosexuality and heterosexuality may thereby lose its compulsory character (Shepherd, 1987).

Rich's analysis of compulsory heterosexuality sees it as intrinsically bound up with the maintenance and reproduction of gendered power relations in which men are dominant and women subordinate. Michel Foucault's analysis of sexuality, in contrast, concerns itself very little with gender although he regards sexuality as being fundamentally about power.

Foucault, sexuality, and gender

Foucault is primarily interested in sexuality as a mode of operation of power. He argues that the nature of power has changed from a legal power which prohibits certain actions and is repressive to one which operates strategically in order to produce a compliant population. The former operates by 'defining the permitted and the forbidden' while the latter operates through shaping people's desires in such a way that their behaviour is normalized and regulated. This is achieved not through prohibition but through the networks of power which enable us all to police our own and others' behaviour. Foucault is interested in discourses of sexuality as a means of control and his focus is on how definitions and classifications of sexual behaviours enmesh material bodies in relations of power. Within the discourse of sexuality the body and its pleasures are minutely investigated and described. What was secret is made available to all and although, ostensibly, the aim is to control through developing knowledge of sexual behaviour and particularly perversions, the effect is also to disperse knowledge of different sexual pleasures and bodily practices amongst the general population. Thus the deployment of sexuality (i.e. the generalization throughout society of the discourse within which sexuality comes into being) results in increasingly sophisticated forms of control over populations through 'penetrating bodies in an increasingly comprehensive way' (Foucault, 1981:107).

Foucault argues that historically discourses about sex have led to a multiplication of sexualities, rather than the repression of all forms of sexuality that are not directly tied to reproduction, and that within discourses of sexuality power, knowledge, and pleasure are linked in particular ways. Thus, once perversions were defined they had to be sought out in order to be controlled. The investigation of 'wayward or unproductive sexualities' was a source of pleasure both to the investigators and to those who were indulging in 'inappropriate' sexual behaviour; a pleasure which in both cases derives from the ability to exercise power, power of resistance and power of control.

These attractions, these evasions, these circular incitements have traced around bodies and sexes, not boundaries not to be crossed, but *perpetual spirals of power and pleasure*. (Foucault, 1981:45)

Foucault points out that one of the sites where this occurred was bourgeois households. Here power and pleasure were linked in the network of power relations between adults and children, the former seeking out infantile sexual pleasure in order to eradicate it, the latter evading discovery and thereby deriving pleasure from exercising a power of resistance. Similarly, although discourses on sexual 'perversions' such as homosexuality increased the exercise of social control, at the same time a 'reverse discourse' came into being,

homosexuality began to speak in its own behalf, to demand that its legitimacy or "naturality" be acknowledged, often in the same vocabulary, using the same categories by which it was medically disqualified. (Foucault, 1981:101; see also Rose, 1994)

The deployment of discourses on sexuality therefore works through power relations between those who are enforcing norms and regulating behaviour and those who are evading or resisting regulation and normalization. Thus, in Foucault's words, sexuality is

an especially dense transfer point for relations of power: between men and women, young people and old people, parents and offspring, teachers and students, priests and laity, an administration and a population. (Foucault, 1981:103)

The family and kinship relations are clearly significant for the way sexuality is deployed and bodies are controlled, although Foucault does not explore the implication of this in terms of gender. Thus he argues that the deployment of sexuality (involving normalizing power) was superimposed on a deployment of alliance (involving repressive power) (ibid.:106). The discourse of sexuality is about bodies and pleasures while the discourse of alliance is about how people are linked in kinship systems and involves prohibitions on sexual contact

between those related in particular ways, such as the incest taboo. Both discourses are linked to the economy, the discourse of alliance through the
'transmission or circulation of wealth', the discourse of sexuality through the
body which 'produces and consumes' (ibid.:107). Moreover the family, as part
of a system of alliances, 'anchors sexuality and provides it with a permanent
support'. It 'conveys the law and the juridical dimension in the deployment of
sexuality; and it conveys the economy of pleasure and the intensity of sensa-
tions in the regime of alliance' (ibid.:108). The deployment of sexuality is
therefore centred on the family which acts not as an 'agency of prohibition'
but as 'a major factor of sexualisation' (ibid.:114). This argument has been
taken up in recent studies of female sexualization (see e.g. Haug, 1983).

For Foucault the deployment of sexuality is a means of deploying power.
Sexuality is created within discourses which develop knowledge about sex as a
means of controlling the population. The strategies which are developed to
ensure this control involve categorizing forms of sexuality according to gender
(the 'hystericisation' of women but not men), age (children's sexuality is
problematized), and deviation from the heterosexual monogamous norm
(homosexuality), and normalizing reproduction within the heterosexual married couple in the interests of controlling the population. These strategies
involve developing knowledge about pathological forms of sexuality and
deploying this knowledge (power) throughout society so that those who are
able (such as the medical profession) can use it to define and contain others
within particular categories of sexuality; those so defined can resist their con-
tainment. In this sense the discourse of sexuality classifies and categorizes
behaviours thereby turning them into identities. This enables greater control
but also enables resistance to that control (control and resistance being two
sides of the same coin—cf. McIntosh's discussion of social role and identity
discussed earlier). And it is only with the emergence of a discourse of sexuality
and its deployment that sexuality can be seen as an essential dimension, if not
the essence of, identity.

Foucault has often been interpreted as arguing that there is no such thing as
the state or any organized power within society. It seems to me that he is in fact
centrally concerned with the way populations are controlled and that his analysis of the history of sexuality is a study of how discourses have developed which
subject populations to a power which is centrally institutionalized in the state.
The power that he discusses in *The history of sexuality* is a systemic power that
operates in the interstices of daily life but which is orchestrated within the
institutions of the state.

What is important about Foucault's theorization of sexuality is the connection between sexuality, pleasure, and power: thus pleasure is intimately connected to power, both in terms of pleasure derived from exercising power and

from resisting it and in terms of pleasure being defined within discourses which are techniques or technologies of power. Similarly, bodies are material and they are also normalized and sexualized within discourses of sexuality such that the pleasures they desire are those that are prescribed (or proscribed) within the discourse of sexuality. Finally he discusses the way that sexuality has come to be defined as the essence of identity within discourse and that in seeking a sexual identity we subjugate ourselves to power relations which control and regulate societies.

Although discourses of sexuality clearly distinguish between male and female sexuality and their deployment links them to gender and power relations through social institutions such as the family, gender is more or less absent from Foucault's analysis. Despite this his theorization of sexuality became increasingly influential within sociology during the 1980s and 1990s.

Normalizing power and the female body

One aspect of his analysis that has been taken up is the concept of normalizing power. Thus Frigga Haug and others explore the way girls learn to behave in feminine ways, focusing on the disciplining of the body and the way power operates through intimate social relations to ensure that girls embrace their own subjection and that this subjection is inscribed on their bodies. In this way of understanding the process of acculturation they are theoretically indebted to Foucault but, like other feminists who use Foucault to think with, are also very critical of him. They are interested in the way 'individuals orientate themselves around the same standards to produce themselves as individuals' and argue that there are gender-specific modes of individualization which, for women, involve the sexualization of their bodies (Haug, 1983:201).

The sexualization of a woman's body—a process equivalent to her individualization—represents an inclusion of the female subject in ordering of the sexual. (Haug, 1983:203)

This notion of sexualization also has similarities with Bourdieu's concept of habitus; that a particular orientation to oneself and to the social world becomes naturalized and normalized through everyday practices thus reproducing social relations of class (in the case of Bourdieu, 1977) and gender and sexuality in the case of Haug et al. Their critique of Foucault grounds this normalizing power in social relations which operate to reproduce the social order and are controlled by the state. They move beyond Foucault by defining sexuality as ideology, 'a complex system of norms and values, through which individuals socialize themselves from top to bottom' (Haug, 1983:207). Their central concern is with 'the question of how we have become women in the social sense' and, specifically, 'the way in which the female body is *made* as a socio-biological unity' (ibid.:30).

They study their own memories of childhood to explore the ways in which female bodies become sexualized and how different parts of the body become associated with sexuality. They also investigate the power relations within which this takes place and, in Foucault's terms, the micropolitics of power which ensures the normalization of female sexualization. They are concerned to

identify the ways in which human beings reproduce social structures by constructing themselves into those structures. (ibid.:43)

This process involves subjection to the dominant culture, its norms, and its values and, at the same time, they suggest 'it still contains an element of resistance' although precisely how is not made clear (ibid.:42). Through writing accounts of childhood events which concerned the body, they identified situations where they had 'voluntarily submitted to [their] own subordination' or 'had developed early forms of lived resistance' (ibid.:50). The object of the exercise was to deconstruct the 'normal' and to show how it has come to be lived and experienced as normality, thereby opening up the possibility of resisting the power of normalization. In the memory work accounts are provided of how girls' bodies are sexualized, through prescriptions not to sit with your legs apart, to hold your tummy in, to tie your hair back, not to bite your nails or 'you'll never find a husband', how these prescriptions emanate from parents, brothers, boyfriends, teachers and how girls learn to derive pleasure from their own subjection. In their words,

we saw ourselves taking pleasure in the very process of being trained into particular dominant structures rather than feeling tyrannized by them. (ibid.:81)

There were also prescriptions about conforming to cultural models of acceptable femininity—girls worried about growing too tall, being 'flat chested'— because of what others said to them. The upshot of this is that they internalize responsibility for their bodies' conformity to acceptable norms of feminine beauty and behaviour.

Disrupting gender

Judith Butler also develops a critique of Foucault in order to theorize gender and sexuality. She asks how the 'foundational categories of sex, gender, and desire as effects of a specific formation of power' can be exposed and thereby disrupted (Butler, 1990:x). As a feminist she is interested in how the oppression of gender and compulsory heterosexuality can be transformed, but because she accepts that gender, sexuality, and identity are all power effects which are discursively produced she has to identify a mode of resistance which operates within the power of the law (as she puts it) rather than being based on the possibility of a position outside it which is in any case impossible within the terms of her analysis. For her, in contrast with Haug et al., social reality is constructed within discourses and systems of power—she therefore adopts an idealist position and denies any material basis for power. She focuses on representation and meaning and conceptualizes gender as a system of signs which is infused with power. Power is not materially but discursively based. For her the crucial task of a feminist politics is to disrupt the binary definition of gender, thereby facilitating the end of gender (cf. MacInnes, 1998).

She takes seriously Foucault's argument that 'sexuality and power are coextensive'. Indeed it is not only sexuality and power which are coextensive but also gender, identity, and desire which are all part of the same discourse— they are therefore all categories with internal coherence in relation to each other. She suggests that what is necessary is not an overthrow of power or recourse to pre-discursive bodies and pleasures but a 'subversive and parodic redeployment of power' because power 'can neither be withdrawn [nor be] refused'. Parodying heterosexuality through the destabilization of the categories in relation to which it assumes coherence and 'univocity' 'robs compulsory heterosexuality of its claims to naturalness and originality' (Butler, 1990:124).

Butler's central argument is that gender is something we 'do' not something we 'are' or 'have'. In this sense our gender identity and sexuality are read off and constituted by the acts we perform and are assumed to be in conformity with our material bodies. In her view 'drag, cross-dressing, and the sexual stylization of butch/femme identities' disrupt this coherence and demonstrate the arbitrariness of the supposedly natural connections between the body, sexuality, and gender identity; they therefore show that sexuality and gender are not essential attributes but are constituted through endless repetition of a particular performance. Thus heterosexuality is performance and you learn how to perform gender according to a heterosexual script. Transgression jolts/disrupts the 'naturalness' of the performance. Putting it in these terms highlights the similarity of some of Butler's analysis with that developed earlier within symbolic interactionism. Then also performance and scripts were part of the understanding of how we 'do' gender.

This type of theory—queer theory—has come under severe criticism particularly from within feminism (see e.g. Jeffreys, 1996). It has been argued that cross-dressing, the adoption of butch/femme roles by lesbians and hyper-masculinity by gay men, transgenderism, and all the other forms of 'playing' with gender, simply serve to reinforce the power relations of heterosexuality. Indeed, transsexuals, rather than disrupting the categories of sex, are at pains to realign them through sex-change operations which bring biological sex into line with gender identity and reassert their unity. It is also problematic to assume that simply 'being' gay or lesbian in itself disrupts dominant discourses. Indeed, the establishment of oppositional gay and lesbian identities takes place within the discourse of compulsory heterosexuality, merely reversing the values attached to the categories. Furthermore, empirical research shows that although being gay/lesbian may theoretically disrupt the coherence of gender/sexuality/desire/identity, in practice attempts are made to minimize this disruption rather than to emphasize and revel in it. Thus the gay men studied by Connell were, as he puts it, 'very straight gays'. They were sexually attracted to other men but in all other respects adopted appropriate, and even heightened, masculine behaviour (Connell, 1995). Similarly, studies of masculinities in schools show that young gay men may be as macho, misogynist, and homophobic as any young 'straight' man, thus reinforcing dominant forms of masculinity and heterosexuality even while transgressing them (Mac an Ghaill, 1994). But perhaps, for Butler, this simply illustrates the performative nature of gender and emphasizes that coherence is not necessary for its successful performance. After all, this is what is being achieved when lesbians and gay men 'pass' as straight. For Jeffreys, this felt need to perform or 'pass' indicates the power of compulsory heterosexuality while, for Butler, it denaturalizes heterosexuality and reveals it also as performance; something that is constructed within discourse rather than being an essential and natural attribute of the masculine or feminine self.

The experience of heterosex

Much work on sexuality, both theoretical and empirical, is remarkably silent on gender (Allen and Leonard, 1994). Moreover much feminist research focuses on representation and is not centrally concerned with the way gendered social actors negotiate sexuality and sexual relations in their daily lives. There are important exceptions, some of which I have discussed in earlier chapters (especially Chapters 2 and 3). Here I focus on recent research on young people and on the emotional dynamics of intimate sexual relationships; the latter has emerged as part of the growing interest amongst sociologists in studying emotions.

This type of research shows that, contrary to the theorizings of postmodern feminists, gender and sexuality are not freely chosen and there are grounds for arguing that heterosexuality is indeed compulsory and organized in the interests of men within contemporary western societies. It shows that sexuality is organized around men's pleasure, is usually controlled by them, and is often experienced as coercive by women. Thus 35 of the 150 young women in one study had had 'unwanted sexual intercourse in response to pressure from men', a finding which echoes those of Little Kinsey almost half a century earlier (Holland et al., 1991:3).

Young people and heterosex

Despite the convergence in sexual behaviour noted in the 1994 national survey between young women and men, qualitative sociological research has revealed considerable differences. Thus young men usually find their first heterosexual intercourse enjoyable compared with young women whose 'accounts of their first sexual experiences are either negative or indicated limited satisfaction' (Holland et al., 1991:3). Young men are not usually aware of this, simply assuming that their partners are sexually satisfied (Holland et al., 1993:4). They may be aided in this interpretation by 'young women's efforts to conceal their lack of pleasure from their partners' (Holland et al., 1993:4). Young women still 'define sex in terms of love, romance and relationships with men' and this leads to

a widespread acceptance of sexual practices being defined in terms of men's needs. This gives men, whether wittingly or not, considerable power over young women's sexual practices. (Holland et al., 1991:2)

This study shows that there are significant gender differences, not only in how young women and men experience sex but also in the part they learn to play in heterosexual encounters. This leads to a situation whereby young men are in a position of power in relation to young women and makes it difficult for young women to exercise sexual autonomy. Thus,

(i) the male is regarded as the knowing sexual agent and the actor; the woman is unknowing and the acted upon; (ii) 'normal' heterosexual sex is defined by an act which is seen as meeting male need and desire, and providing pleasure and satisfaction for the male; women are seen as gaining satisfaction from meeting men's needs; (iii) women learn about sex through a 'protective discourse' which emphasises their reproductive capacity and danger, particularly of unwanted pregnancy, and in which images of positive female sexuality, desire and pleasure are largely absent. (Holland et al., 1993:8)

There is considerable evidence that, for boys, sexuality is about conquest and 'having something to tell your mates' rather than about developing intimacy;

their male peers are the audience for their first sexual experiences (Holland et al., 1996a: 240; Jamieson, 1998). This has led Holland et al. to suggest that young women and men construct their sexualities in response to the 'male in the head' (Holland et al., 1996a:242). By this they are referring to

constructions of bodies, sex and gender in which male needs, male bodies, and male desires were critically dominant. (Holland et al., 1996a:254)

They argue that heterosexuality is constructed around male domination and is about masculinity. Thus first intercourse turns boys into men whereas girls do not experience it as turning them into women; this is much more likely to be associated with menstruation (Holland et al., 1996b:153). Similarly sexual reputation has a different and opposite meaning for young women and young men; the former have to guard against sexual experience for fear of losing their reputation while for the latter sexual experience enhances theirs and leads to a double standard (Holland et al., 1996a; Wight, 1996). In addition it has been argued that young men view sexual intercourse as a performance of masculinity which they can control and in which they are the active partner (Holland et al., 1996b). This type of account is absent amongst young women. They have a negative power of resisting men's advances and controlling their bodies but it is difficult for them to assume an active and powerful female sexuality which is seemingly written out of the heterosexual encounters of young people (ibid.). It is also the case that for young women, allowing young men access to their bodies is risky not only because they might lose their reputation but also because they risk pregnancy or sexually transmitted disease. Thus the dangers of sex may far outweigh the pleasures which, in any case, young women are not very sure about. In the heterosexual encounter it is men's rather than women's pleasure that is paramount, women's pleasure is 'the icing on the cake' which confirms the man's performance (Holland et al., 1996b:148,118, 1994).

  This research is interesting for the way it brings together Foucaultian and feminist conceptions of power in order to understand the dynamics of power which construct heterosexual relations and how male dominance might be resisted. The authors are critical of Foucault's failure to theorize power as systematically wielded by certain groups over others. They take seriously Foucault's concern with the body as 'a site where the large-scale organisation of power is connected to the most minute and local practices' but are critical of his failure to specify 'the links between men's exercise of power in particular sexual encounters, and male power more generally' (Ramazanoglu and Holland, 1993:244). Thus while documenting the way young women subordinate themselves to male power within heterosexual relationships, they appear to conclude that, although power may be contested individually by young women 'asserting their pleasures in particular relationships' (ibid.:260) and the assertion of bodies and pleasures is a way of resisting the deployment of sexuality and, hence, male power, it is only by developing alternative discourses such as feminism, which assert women's power and autonomy and right to sexual pleasure, that male power within heterosexuality can be contested. They find evidence of this happening within particular relationships but not at the collective level where heterosex is still defined in male terms and in relation to men's pleasure. And, as Stevi Jackson points out, although we may be able to contest male power 'at the level of individual practice . . . this may have little effect elsewhere' particularly when we take into account the considerable amount of evidence that suggests that women

still discipline themselves to fit a model of sexuality which prioritises male desire and defines women's fulfilment in terms of 'love' and the giving of pleasure... This attribute of femininity is hardly confined to sexuality: the ethic of service to men is fundamental to other aspects of gender relations, to men's appropriation of women's labour as well as their bodies. (Jackson, 1996:35–6)

Intimate relationships

The other issue which has emerged and which echoes the findings of the 1949 survey is that women seek emotional intimacy and when emotional intimacy fades women's interest in sex declines. Indeed the withholding of 'emotional validation which [women] seek through intimacy may be a source of male power' within intimate sexual relationships (Duncombe and Marsden, 1993:236). Duncombe and Marsden suggest that there is a gender asymmetry in emotional behaviour within intimate heterosexual relationships, with women undertaking the emotion work to keep the relationship going and men withholding emotional intimacy from women and seeing intimacy in terms of sex. Furthermore, 'women's dissatisfaction with lack of emotional intimacy may . . . become manifest as sexual difficulties' (Duncombe and Marsden, 1995:163). Their research shows that with marriage women found it 'more difficult to refuse sex in case their husbands felt rejected' but, at the same time, husbands were 'less likely to express the emotional intimacy that wives felt they needed for sex to be fulfilling' (Duncombe and Marsden, 1996:225). It also suggests that married couples 'experience a long-term decline in sexual activity' (something recorded in the 1994 survey), usually reflecting women's dissatisfaction with marital sex (because of emotional distance or the waning of the insatiable desire of being in love) (Duncombe and Marsden, 1996; Jackson, 1993:210). A lack of emotional intimacy or betrayal through an affair could result in one or other partner, more usually the woman, building a 'brick wall' which prevented their wanting sex with their partners (Duncombe and

Marsden, 1996:231–2). Women's disappointment with lack of emotional closeness and intimacy with their male partners has also been recorded in other studies (see e.g. Mansfield and Collard, 1988).

A study of marital sexual pleasure amongst 60 women who were married to or cohabiting with men found that just over a third of them experienced high levels of 'marital pleasure' (which implies that two-thirds did not). It seems that this is associated not with intimacy in the sense of familiarity but with their partners' inaccessibility, something that Jackson also refers to when arguing that insecurity may be essential to being in love and desiring the other (Jackson, 1993:211). This suggests, contrary to Duncombe and Marsden, that sexual pleasure is not associated with any specific aspect of the marital relationship—such as lack of emotional closeness—but that 'continued sexual availability, anxieties about pregnancy, the "double shift" and feelings of powerlessness' contribute to a lessening of women's sexual pleasure (O'Connor, 1995:358). It also suggests that women's dissatisfaction with heterosex within marriage may be widespread and not simply a figment of feminists' imaginations.

Sexuality and ethnicity

There are very few studies that have focused on ethnicity or, indeed, on young people's assumption of gay or lesbian identities. Those that there are suggest that while young men may experiment with same-sex encounters at school and have acknowledged their gayness at a young age this is less likely for young women (see also Wellings et al., 1994). A recent study which focuses on sexuality and identity formation in the disciplinary context of schools reveals that so-called deviant sexual identities are often racialized. Thus a young Asian lesbian thought she was 'the only Asian lesbian in the world'; her image of a lesbian was a white woman with short hair and 'bovver boots'. Conversely, being gay can alienate young black men from the black community: like black lesbians they may be seen as traitors to a racialized community (Epstein and Johnson, 1998:159, 162; hooks, 1996; Clarke, 1996). Research on Irish gay masculinities has also shown that gay identities are nationally and racially (as well as class) specific and as such are often not available to lesbians or gay men from minority ethnic groups (Mac an Ghaill 1996). Such studies are thin on the ground and the relationship between ethnicity, gender, and sexuality has been explored more fully at the level of community, nation, and state than at an individual level (see Chapter 9).

The 'pure relationship'?

It is in the context of research such as this that arguments have been advanced about the 'pure relationship' and the democratization of intimate relationships (Giddens, 1992). Anthony Giddens argues that in modern societies sexuality is no longer tied to procreation but is solely about pleasure; it is plastic sexuality 'freed from the needs of reproduction' (ibid.:2).[1] Sexuality is now something we 'have', it is 'no longer a natural condition', it is part of our self-identity (ibid.:15). For Giddens sexuality has become part of the reflexive project of constructing the self which is characteristic of modern societies. He makes the extraordinary statement that 'reproduction was once part of nature' but that now 'sexuality has become an "integral" part of social relations ... heterosexuality is no longer a standard by which everything else is judged' (ibid.:34). It is hard to see how sexuality was ever not an 'integral part of social relations', particularly if it is accepted that it is socially and culturally constructed and varies between cultures and historically (see e.g. Caplan, 1987). As Jackson and Scott note, 'Human sexuality has always been a social product and will continue to be so, in whatever form of society comes into being in the future' (Jackson and Scott, 1996:11).

Giddens has come in for severe criticism from feminists and has been accused of ignoring feminist research into gender and sexuality, basing his thesis instead on therapeutic discourse (Jamieson, 1999:480). Feminist research shows that intimate relationships, particularly those between women and men, are structured by gender-based inequalities. Heterosex has been divorced neither from danger nor from reproduction, although the connections may be more directly relevant for women than for men and for younger rather than older women (Delphy, 1996). And sexual exchanges in heterosexual relationships are not based on the disclosure and autonomy which Giddens sees as characterizing the pure relationship. What these studies show is that sexuality is embedded in a matrix of social relations and that gender, race, class, and age are particularly important in organizing sexual relationships in contemporary British society (see also Caplan, 1987). Sexuality is therefore not disembedded nor does the evidence suggest that sexual relationships are becoming pure and democratic; on the contrary they develop in the context of major inequalities and differences of power. Furthermore, female sexuality is not freed from the

[1] Paola Tabet gives a different inflection to this shift by arguing that human sexuality is not and never has been 'naturally' tied to reproduction but that the confinement of women's sexuality to reproduction is something that has had to be achieved socially and often through violence and coercion. In her view human sexuality is 'naturally' separated from reproduction, polymorphous, and 'multiple in its forms as in its objects' (Tabet, 1996:133).

needs of reproduction, as Giddens would have us believe; contraception and the need to avoid pregnancy are very real factors in women's experiences and serve as constant reminders that pregnancy is always a possible outcome of penetrative heterosex.

The extent of change

There have clearly been substantial changes as well as continuities in both sexual behaviour and the way it has been studied since the 1950s. This is reflected in the findings of the national survey and the differences in attitudes and behaviour between pre-1960 and post-1960 cohorts. The equation of sex with sin unless it is within marriage and for purposes of procreation has loosened and it can now be indulged in for its own sake, by both women and men, purely for pleasure. This marks a decline in the hold of religious control over sexual morality which stems from the 1960s (Brown, 2001).

Although attitudes towards sexual behaviour may have become more liberal, there is evidence that the linkage of sex with male-dominated heterosexuality is as strong at the beginning of the twenty-first century as it was in the immediate post-war years and that changes in sexual behaviour have resulted in women being able to behave more like men but in male-defined ways. Thus they can engage in sexual activity and demand more and better orgasms, but the sexual activity they engage in is overwhelmingly on men's terms. Moreover sexuality is defined in instrumental terms: it is a means to an end (now pleasure, previously procreation), rather than an expression of emotional closeness, intimacy, or love, and thereby an end in itself. Arguably this way of defining sexuality is gendered and its predominance may help to explain many women's dissatisfaction with heterosexual relationships. In addition there has been an increasing commodification of sexuality since the 1960s, something that has gone along with the rise of consumer capitalism and the burgeoning of consumption-based identities noted in Chapter 6.

Sociological studies of sexuality have also proliferated, with many being heavily influenced by Foucault's analysis of sexuality and power. In the sociological study of sexuality there has been a shift from the social interactionist approaches of the 1960s to a concern with discourse and identity in the 1990s, a concern which has been associated with claims that intimate relationships are disembedded in high modernity and no longer structured by social relations which involve power and which are gendered. As seen in previous chapters, however, studying sexuality has also been integrated into research on work, families, and households where more materialist accounts predominate.

Chapter 8

Gendering Politics

IN the years since the Second World War there has been a significant change in politics, both in the way it is practised and in the way it is defined. In the immediate post-war years politics was defined as to do with political parties, trade unions, and government, something that took place in the public domain and was largely a male concern. As well as being masculine, politics was dominated by a class cleavage, with the two major parties representing opposing class interests and relating to class-based organizations such as the Trades Union Congress and the Confederation of British Industry. In the late 1960s and early 1970s this began to change. The so-called new social movements challenged the 'old' way of doing politics and in the process redefined it as something much broader than simply voting and/or entering the domain of party politics; they also disrupted class-based politics (see e.g. Dalton and Kuechler, 1990). Other bases of social differentiation besides class (such as gender, ethnicity, and generation) have emerged as significant to political processes and have provoked discussion about the dealignment of politics from class (Evans and Norris, 1999).

Narrow definitions of politics also circumscribed the focus of political sociology and political science (Bourque and Grossholtz, 1974). Studies of political elites and voting behaviour predominated and, until the emergence of the feminist critique in the 1970s, studies of men were taken to be representative of women (Goot and Reid, 1975). When gender was mentioned at all it was only as a way of explaining women's alleged lack of political activity and more conservative political views. These definitions and explanations have been challenged by feminist analysis which has sought to understand the way political processes are gendered and to transform the definitions of politics which associate political activity with men. In this chapter I look both at the gendering of politics and at the way gender and politics have been studied. I begin with an account of the gendered patterning of voting behaviour and participation in political elites since the Second World War, the traditional focus of political sociology and political science, showing how both have changed dramatically in the last decades of the twentieth century, before looking at the way gender and politics have been studied.

Voting behaviour

It has long been assumed that women are more likely than men to vote Conservative and, despite many disclaimers, there is evidence that there are significant gender differences in political support for the two main parties. Thus from 1945 to 1959 there was a gender gap between women and men such that the Conservatives did better amongst women and Labour did better amongst men; in 1964 a Labour government was elected due to a greater swing to Labour amongst women than amongst men while 'in 1970 men favoured Labour while women gave a greater lead to the Conservatives' leading to a Conservative victory (Norris, 1997:134). During the 1980s the gender gap all but disappeared, reappearing in the 1992 election but vanishing in 1997 when Labour won a landslide victory (Lovenduski, 1999:198). What is significant about these trends is that, as with sexual behaviour, there seems to be long-term convergence between women's and men's voting patterns. Further, there is a generational difference which almost completely explains the gender gap. Thus amongst older voters women are more conservative than men while amongst younger voters the pattern is reversed; indeed in the 1992 and 1997 elections younger women were more likely then their male peers to vote Labour (Norris, 1997:134; Lovenduski, 1999). In the 1997 election 55 per cent of younger women compared to 44 per cent of younger men voted Labour and 39 per cent of older women and 31 per cent of older men voted Conservative (Lovenduski, 1999). Thus 'younger women were more likely to vote Labour than younger men ... while older women were more likely to vote Conservative than older men' (Norris, 1999:159).

Norris argues that generational differences in the size and direction of the gender gap are due to a cohort rather than life-cycle effect and that it 'tends to be favourable to Labour' (Norris, 1997:137). There has been a change from a 'traditional' to a 'modern' gender gap, the former designating a greater tendencey to vote conservatively amongst women and the latter describing a greater tendency to vote Labour (Norris, 1999). Indeed amongst younger men Norris suggests that an anti-feminist backlash 'against changing sex roles' may be present (ibid.:161).

Voting patterns amongst ethnic minorities since 1974 when they first began to be measured show consistently high support for Labour (Saggar and Heath, 1999:109). There are class variations within the ethnic minority population as within the white population although at all levels of the class structure support for Labour is overwhelming. There are also variations between ethnic minority groups such that Asians are more likely to vote Conservative than are blacks. This partly reflects the greater likelihood of Asians being middle class but even amongst middle-class, highly educated, owner occupiers support for Labour remains very high and Saggar and Heath conclude that 'ethnicity clearly dominates class' (ibid.:113). There is therefore a significant 'ethnic gap' in voting patterns as well as a gender gap: what we do not have, however, is any systematic analysis of the way gender and ethnicity interact (although see Stephenson, 1998).

Political elites

The other dimension of political involvement that has been traditionally studied is participation in political elites and, until 1998 with the elections for the Welsh Assembly and the Scottish Parliament, this meant studying women's participation in the Westminster Parliament and local government. Such studies show that women's representation in Parliament has increased gradually since the war although, until the 1997 election, was still in single figures and considerably lower than in comparable western democracies (Lovenduski, 1996 and 1999). This can be seen in Table 8.1.

The figures in Table 8.1 show that the 1997 election represented something of a watershed with 18.2 per cent of MPs being women, double the proportion that were elected in 1992. This was largely due to Labour's fielding increased numbers of women candidates and being 'at the peak of its electoral success'. Some argue that this level of representation is unlikely to continue while others suggest that this marks a significant and not easily reversible change (Lovenduski, 1999:206; Norris, 1999:161). This latter view is supported by the fact that although the proportion of women elected in the 2001 election was slightly lower than in 1997, at 17.9 per cent it was still significantly higher than in 1992 (*Guardian*, 8 August 2001). The other important feature of the changing proportion of women MPs is the timing of the change. Thus from 1945 until 1983 there was virtually no variation in the gender composition of Parliament; this only began to change with the 1987 election and relates to the activities of women, particularly feminists, within the political parties subsequent to the 1979 Conservative victory (Perrigo, 1996) together with women's increasing levels of economic activity (Lovenduski and Hills, 1981:2). Interestingly, although the Labour Party has the highest number of women MPs it is the Liberals who fielded the largest number of women candidates in the 1997

Table 8.1 Women elected in British general elections, 1945–1997 (Northern Ireland excluded)

	Con.	Lab.	Lib.	Others	Total	% of MPs
1945	1	21	1	1	23	3.8
1950	6	14	1	0	21	3.4
1951	6	11	0	0	17	2.7
1955	10	14	0	0	24	3.8
1959	12	13	0	0	25	4.0
1964	11	18	0	0	29	4.6
1966	7	19	0	0	26	4.1
1970	15	10	0	1	26	4.1
1974*	9	13	0	1	23	3.6
1974**	7	18	0	2	27	4.3
1979	8	11	0	0	19	3.0
1983	13	10	0	0	23	3.5
1987	17	21	2	1	41	6.3
1992	20	37	2	1	60	9.2
1997	13	101	3	3	120	18.2

Source: J. Lovenduski (1996) 'Sex, gender and British politics' in J. Lovenduski and B. Norris (eds) *Women in politics*, Oxford University Press, Oxford, table 2, p. 9. Reproduced by permission of Oxford University Press. 'Sexing political behaviour in Britain' in S. Walby (ed.) *New agendas for women*, Macmillan, Basingstoke, table 11.1, p. 191. Reproduced by permission of Palgrave.
* February.
** October.

election, and all political parties have increased the proportion of women candidates fielded in general elections (Lovenduski, 1996).

Ethnic minorities are also significantly absent from political elites and it has been only recently that ethnic minority candidates have begun to stand for election to Parliament (Norris, 1997). Norris comments, 'If Parliament reflected the public, the Commons would include six times the number of black or Asian MPs' (Norris, 1997:184). Indeed, the overwhelming majority of Parliamentary candidates in the 1992 general election were white, male, and middle class for all parties; 99 per cent of Conservative candidates were middle class compared with 96 per cent of Labour Party candidates, 85 per cent of Conservative candidates were male compared with 74 per cent of Labour candidates, 99 per cent and 96 per cent respectively were white (Norris and Lovenduski, 1995:88, table 5.4). Clearly both women and ethnic minority candidates are under-represented in Parliament compared with their share of the electorate. This under-representation is also apparent in the hierarchies of the two main parties, where women's representation decreases the further up the hierarchy you go until at the top men are significantly over-represented. As far as I know no similar analysis of party organizations exists for ethnicity.

There is considerable debate about whether or not this matters and whether or not electing more women or ethnic minority MPs would make a difference in terms of practical politics. Evidence suggests that it would. There are significant differences between the attitudes of women and men MPs, with those of women being more left wing than those of men. Thus women are 'consistently more strongly in favour of women's rights' and on issues of domestic violence and abortion rights 'women Conservatives' are 'more strongly in favour of women's rights than male Liberal Democrats' (Norris, 1996:95). Thus although party is 'the best predictor of attitudes' there is a 'modest gender difference' on most issues, with women MPs tending to be more unilateralist than men and more left wing or liberal on almost all issues (ibid.:98).

Women are to be found in greater numbers in local than in national politics but it is difficult to find statistics on women's participation in local government (Randall, 1987; Stacey and Price, 1981; Norris and Lovenduski, 1993). The data that are available show that women have increased their representation as local councillors: thus in the 1960s 12 per cent of local councillors were women, in 1985 the figure had risen to 19 per cent, and by 1992 it was 25 per cent (Stacey and Price, 1981:141; Norris and Lovenduski, 1993:44). These figures mask differences between different parts of Britain. Thus in 1983

women were 14.4% of county councillors in England and Wales, 11.1% of regional councillors in Scotland and 7.9% of Northern Ireland district councillors. (Randall, 1987:105, citing Lovenduski, 1986)

A study published in 1980 showed that women were 'best represented in London councils and worst in Welsh councils' and that outside London women did better in rural than in urban areas (Randall, 1987:134, citing Bristow, 1980; Hills, 1981:20). In the mid-1990s 23 per cent of Labour councillors were women (Short, 1996:24) although in Wales in the 1999 local elections the proportion of women councillors remained around 20 per cent (Feld, 2000).

Quotas

Attempts to address the gender imbalance of political elites have been made, particularly by the Labour Party which, in the early 1990s, adopted a quota system to increase the number of women MPs.[1] Similar measures had been

[1] Accounts of the development, implementation, and demise of this policy can be found in Short (1996), Perrigo (1996), and Lovenduski (1999).

taken in other social democratic parties, significantly increasing women's representation in legislative assemblies, particularly in Scandinavia (Lovenduski, 1999; Short, 1996:20; Phillips, 1991). We have already seen that the adoption of quotas increased significantly the number of women elected as Labour MPs in 1997. In elections for the Welsh Assembly and the Scottish Parliament quotas were also used to ensure more equal representation of women and men. Thus in Wales and Scotland constituencies were 'twinned'[2] so that the Labour Party fielded an equal number of women and men candidates. This, together with a system of proportional representation (which is more favourable to the election of women and other minority groups than a first past the post system) led to a situation where in Wales 40 per cent of Assembly Members and in Scotland 37 per cent of Scottish MPs are women (Feld, 2000; Alexander, 2000). These proportions are comparable to those in the democratic legislatures of Scandinavia (Lovenduski, 1999) and contrast with representation of women at local level which in Wales continues to hover around the 20 per cent mark and in Scotland is 22 per cent. In neither body, however, are there any black representatives (Feld, 2000; Alexander, 2000).

Alternative politics

Clearly there have been significant changes in the gendering of politics since the war even if politics is defined as party politics. Most women, however, like most men, are not involved in party politics and there is evidence that this is affected by age and ethnicity. Thus, '76% of women are not involved in any form of party political activity' and those who are 'young, black and female are significantly less likely to be politically active than the middle-aged, the white and the male' (Squires, 1999:169). If politics is defined more broadly though, women's activism becomes much more apparent. Thus in the late 1960s and 1970s women were involved in alternative forms of politics such as the women's liberation movement and community action (Randall, 1987:59; Mayo, 1977; Lovenduski and Randall, 1993; Charles, 2000). The women's liberation movement was one of a wave of social movements that emerged in the 1960s and 1970s and in all of them women's participation was relatively high. This is reflected in the membership of social movement organizations such as Friends of the Earth which, in the mid-1990s, was 66 per cent women

[2] This involved constituencies being twinned in such a way that the selection committees in those constituencies form a single selection committee in order to select two candidates, a woman and a man, one of whom stands in one of the constituencies and the other in the other (Stephenson, 1998:58).

(Stephenson, 1998:102). In the 1980s women were instrumental in setting up and maintaining over a number of years the women's peace camp at Greenham and also in creating women's support groups during the miners' strike. Greenham involved 'hundreds of thousands of women' and

was the most visible form of women's activism (and together with the 1984-5 miners' strike of any form of oppositional politics) in Britain in the 1980s. (Roseneil, 1995a:3)

These movements, and women's involvement in them, suggest that women are politically engaged but because their engagement differs from that of men and is often outside conventional politics it is defined as social rather than political.

This brief overview demonstrates that the gendering of politics has altered since the Second World War. There has been a change from a traditional to a modern gender gap in voting patterns, an increase in women's participation in political elites and significant mobilization of women in social movements. In what follows I explore the way these changes have been studied by sociologists and, to a lesser extent, political scientists.

Studying gender and politics

Given these observations about gender and politics since the Second World War, it is ironic that until relatively recently studies of political behaviour stressed women's lack of political activity, their different political attitudes and values, and their failure to put themselves forward as candidates in the formal political process. During the 1960s these failures were explained in terms of gender socialization, women's confinement to the private sphere, and the burdens of domestic labour and childcare which left them with neither the time nor the experience to engage in autonomous political activity (Stacey and Price, 1981; Randall, 1987; Goot and Reid, 1975). Little attention was paid to the ways that political parties and structures operated to exclude women, the class basis of politics was taken for granted, and the gendering of parties and politics went largely unnoticed; studies of politics, like studies of work, focused almost exclusively on men (Siltanen and Stanworth, 1984).

One such study tested the hypothesis that with increasing affluence the working class was becoming more like the middle class in terms of political attitudes and behaviour, i.e. it was undergoing a process of embourgeoisement. Goldthorpe et al. found that affluent (male) workers saw the Labour Party as the party of the 'working man' or 'working class' and that their voting behaviour was influenced more by their membership of trade unions and 'white collar affiliations' than by affluence (Goldthorpe et al., 1968:17, 48). This led the authors to conclude that

The simple argument that working-class affluence leads to a 'middle-class' style of life, and that this in turn leads to a decrease in Labour voting, takes no account of the social structure in which class attitudes are formed and maintained. (ibid.:73)

Even though this study does not concern itself with women's votes and attempts to explain the trend in working-class support for Labour solely with reference to men's political behaviour, it suggests that different occupational locations and types of social network are associated with different political attitudes and (although the implications of this are not explored) that women's concentration in white collar occupations and their increasing levels of economic activity are likely to have an impact on the voting patterns of their menfolk by increasing men's 'white collar affiliations'. Thus trade union membership and manual work are associated with working-class consciousness and the Labour Party while white collar occupations and non-membership of trade unions are associated with a weakening of support for Labour. Despite this it is only *men's* political attitudes and behaviour that are seen as relevant to understanding changes in the political allegiances of the working class and the Labour Party is seen as the party of the working *man*, its image is gendered as well as classed.

Feminist critiques

During the 1970s feminists developed a critique of political science and political sociology (see e.g. Goot and Reid, 1975; Bourque and Grossholz, 1974). It was pointed out that much 'malestream' political sociology assumed an analytical separation between the public and the private which was gendered: men were in the public domain while women were in the private. It is women's role in the private domain of the family that is advanced to explain the nature of their political participation rather than their distinct work situations. This type of explanation can also be found in feminist accounts of women's lack of participation in politics (see e.g. Stacey and Price, 1981). Further, the private realm is by definition apolitical; thus women's association with it marginalizes them from politics and is used to explain gender differences in political behaviour. In addition, feminists pointed out that the boundaries of the public and private are themselves politically constructed and, hence, contested (Siltanen and Stanworth, 1984).

Since the 1970s, therefore, feminists have argued that not only should gender be problematized and the gendering of politics be recognized but politics should be defined differently. As well as being about class, politics is about gender, it is about the distribution of resources and power in society, not only about who people vote for in general elections. In this they were echoing Marxist analyses of class politics and class consciousness. Politics is also about meanings and definitions, and the feminist critique of how politics is defined can be seen as part of the epistemological challenge mounted by the new social movements which has led to new ways of defining political issues (Eyerman and Jamison, 1991). Thus the women's movement argued that domestic violence was a public rather than a private issue, in this sense the personal was most decidedly political. In contrast, they also argued that the decision to have an abortion rather than carry a pregnancy to term was something that was a woman's alone and should not be dictated by husbands, fathers, the church, or the state. Further, in order for women to live free of the fear of violence and to be able to control their own fertility, their rights to do so need to be respected by the men with whom they live, and in order to protect these rights there has to be political involvement in the private domain (Siltanen and Stanworth, 1984). The feminist movement contested the very definitions and boundaries of the political, a challenge which was epitomized in the slogan 'the personal is political'. Feminists also demonstrated that parties and Parliaments represent not only class interests but also those of gender and ethnicity (Walby, 1997:148). Politics is not therefore confined to the realm of party politics and is not only about class and what men do in the public sphere. Using this broader definition of politics women's and men's political activity can be seen in rather a different light and this is reflected in sociological studies of women's political activity.

Challenging 'politics-as-normal'

With the influence of feminism in sociology and political science which emerged during the 1970s, definitions of politics which confined it to what men did in the public sphere or to party politics were brushed aside and studies of voting behaviour and political elites came under attack for mobilizing sex-role theory and gender stereotypes as explanation for women's failure to behave politically in the same way as men. The thrust of these critiques was to demonstrate that gender differences were not as significant as they were being made out to be and that, where women did not have childcare and domestic responsibilities, they were just as involved politically as were men (Siltanen and Stanworth, 1984). They also showed that conventional politics, whether in the political parties or in trade unions, sidelined issues that were important to women and were organized in such a way as to make it difficult for women to participate. Trade unions defined their main concern as the wage packet, equal pay was a valid trade union issue but conditions at work and provision of facilities such as childcare were seen as outside their remit, and meetings were organized outside working hours in pubs which made it difficult for women with young children to attend (Charles, 1979 and 1983). Such studies began to highlight the fact that the problem lay not with women, but with the way organizations operated and the issues which they prioritized. There was also a concern with the way in which gender affected class consciousness, though this was problematized for women and not for men even by feminists. Such studies showed that women's consciousness was 'fragmented' and was shaped not only by work relations but also by their domestic and family situation (Pollert, 1981). The extent to which this was also true for men was not, however, examined (Charles, 1993:62).

As well as studying women's involvement in workplace politics and trade unions at the point of production, feminist sociologists explored women's involvement in community politics 'around issues of consumption and more particularly social reproduction' (Mayo, 1977:x). They argued that women were 'in the front line of interaction with the local state' because of having to deal with schools, social workers, and housing departments, and they were also

in the front line of interaction with capital in its distributive guise. They are the shoppers. Apart from beer and fags the household necessities in most families are bought by women. (Cockburn, 1977:63)

This analysis moves from what had been a predominant Marxist view of politics as class struggle taking place at the point of production to a view that class struggle also takes place in the sphere of reproduction, at the point of consumption. And because of the influence of feminism these struggles were beginning to be conceptualized in terms of gender as well as class.

Women's involvement and their militancy were influenced by several factors and here empirical observation replaces gender stereotypes and assumptions. In many community organizations such as tenants' associations women took on support roles—rather than chairing the organization they would be the secretary. Studies also showed that women who were elected to local councils often saw their role as one involving the welfare of their community and did not define it as political. The different contribution women could bring, to council work, to campaigns for better housing and childcare provision, was seen as relating to the sexual division of labour which allocated to women domestic labour and childcare and defined men as workers and providers. These structural constraints and the gendered life experiences that resulted led to a specifically female engagement with the political which reflected women's different interests. Such analyses emphasized women's difference from men rather than downplaying them, arguing that women could bring something to politics which men could not and that this was to be valued rather than dismissed as not political. But it was primarily the gender division of labour within the home which was identified as causing women's lesser and different participation in conventional politics (Stacey and Price, 1981). Such explanations, although couched in different language, had not moved all that far from those advanced by political sociologists.

Studies also showed that in some circumstances women took on leading roles and their activities outside the home had repercussions not only in the public but also in the private domain. Thus women take on leading roles which are usually gendered male when they are living in very straitened circumstances and, significantly, when they are not supported by a man (Gallagher, 1977:121). Community organizing and activity tended to be temporary, in the sense that the organizations disbanded when the immediate problem was sorted out, spontaneous, and dramatic, and those women with dependent children and without male support tended to be the most militant (Gallagher, 1977:131; Cockburn, 1977). Women also tend to be 'unexpected, to think up new ways of doing things' (Cockburn, 1977:63). Indeed, women tend to be less conservative than men according to this 82-year-old woman 'who had been active in struggles over pay and conditions as a hospital worker'. She said:

I think men are rather conservative. They meet people half way. We'd agitate. They'd put in a demand for us. Then they'd come back with a quarter of what we'd asked for and think they'd done all right. Women have got more go. We'll keep on rucking till we get what we want. (ibid.:63)

This view is ironic given the widespread assumptions about women's greater conservativeness in comparison with men and is perhaps a reflection of men's degree of integration into the system and the accepted way of doing things in comparison with women. Women are outsiders and may challenge the rules rather than simply abiding by them; in this sense their challenge is to the system itself rather than to the distribution of spoils within it and is therefore transgressive.

Women's political activities often have implications for their personal and domestic lives, thus illustrating another way in which the personal is political.

whatever the action women get involved in, it always modifies, sometimes transforms, personal relationships at home. (ibid.:64)

This suggests that women's politics cuts across the public-private divide in so far as women's activities in the public domain have an effect in the private realm of the family; there is no neat division between public and private.

Such studies showed that far from being apolitical and quiescent, women were involved in campaigning and organizing around issues such as housing and childcare provision, issues which could be described as welfare issues but which nonetheless involved confrontation with the local state in the form of the council, transformations of gender relations within the home (even if temporary), and alternative forms of activity and organization which challenged the politics-as-normal of the labour movement (Randall, 1987; Charles, 1995).

Political parties as organizations

During the 1980s attention turned to the culture and internal organization of political parties in an attempt to explain the under-representation of women in formal politics. The organizational culture of the Labour Party, with its roots in the trade union movement and its highly ritualized, formal, and masculine way of doing politics, was analysed in terms of gender (see e.g. Lovenduski, 1996). It is a culture 'rooted in the experience of male trade unionists' and 'extremely conservative in its attitudes towards women members' (Perrigo, 1996:120). In addition it

reflected a traditional, familial and paternalistic gender order in society in which men and women occupy different spheres. The model of the political activist, central to both party ideology and its ethos, was the male unionised worker. (ibid.:120)

Moreover the party 'was ruled by a coalition of Parliamentary and trade union elites' who were overwhelmingly male (ibid.). The existence of this masculine culture is used to explain resistance to moves towards greater gender parity, resistance which has been particularly strong in the old labour heartlands, 'the declining manufacturing and mining areas', where men's jobs in heavy industry were disappearing (Lovenduski, 1996:5, 14). There is a feeling in such areas that a woman's place is most definitely not in politics and most certainly not as a Parliamentary candidate instead of a man. In the words of an MP (gender not specified),

in a region like this there is a very substantial prejudice against women because it's a traditionally very heavy industry area and many people take the view that women have a place and it ain't at the meetings that men attend. (Lovenduski, 1996:14)

Unlike the Labour Party with its masculine image, the Tories' image is more feminine. Despite this their record on selecting women MPs lags far behind that of Labour (Lovenduski, 1996:15). Clare Short takes the view that at local level the Tory Party has a

women-friendly face and that Labour's local face is massively more male, bureaucratic and off-putting. This would help to explain how the Conservative Party has a smaller number of women MPs, has opposed social reforms that have benefitted women, and yet retains the women's vote . . . . at local level throughout the country older women, who are of the generation whose greatest pride is their achievements in bringing up a happy and successful family, see many women like themselves in positions of seniority and influence. (Short, 1996:26)

Despite the influx of women into Parliament in the 1997 election and attempts to modernize and 'feminize' the Labour Party, there is concern that cultural change within it has come to a grinding halt. In Anna Coote's words,

In Downing Street's inner sanctum, the occupants are predominantly *young, male, white graduates*: a generation who grew up feeling that the gender issue was sorted (perhaps by their own mothers) and are inclined to think feminism is yesterday's politics. They enjoy power and do not want to give it up. (Coote, 2000:3, my emphasis)

She suggests that although New Labour has been successful in capturing women's votes, it has marginalized 'feminist tendencies in its own ranks' (ibid.:4; Franklin, 2000).

The other way in which the masculine organizational bias of political parties is apparent is in the selection process, both in terms of the backgrounds of prospective Parliamentary candidates and in terms of the assumptions made by the selectorate. Thus,

To run for Parliament an individual must have financial security, public networks, social status, policy experience, technical and social skills. (Lovenduski, 1996:17)

Employment and political experience are both significant. Thus having experience in local government or trade unions qualifies you to be a Parliamentary candidate as does having a 'brokerage job' (Norris and Lovenduski, 1995:87; Randall, 1987). Brokerage jobs are 'complementary to politics' and include such things as being a barrister, journalist, lecturer, or trade union official (Lovenduski, 1996). These are, of course, all jobs and positions which are more likely to be filled by men than women and more likely to be monopolized by white, middle-class men than any others (ibid.). This is reflected in the fact that the typical Parliamentary candidate is 'a well-educated, professional, white male in early middle age' (Norris and Lovenduski, 1995:87). Coming from a political family is also an advantage in seeking selection and may be critical in making standing for election seem within the realm of possibility for women rather than being something that is unthinkable (Stacey and Price, 1981).

This has been theorized in terms of gender and class differences in cultural capital and habitus and Weberian notions of the legitimate exercise of power (Liddle and Michielsens, 2000). Liddle and Michielsens theorize the gendering of power in terms of both 'the recognition by others of a person's legitimacy to exercise power' and the 'self-confidence one feels in oneself to exercise power' (ibid.:129). Using these concepts, they provide an answer to the question of why it is that women in positions of power tend to come from more privileged backgrounds than their male peers. They suggest that elite women's higher class position is associated with greater access to symbolic capital and an 'entitlement to power' which together 'challenge the gendered power deficits attached to their femininity' (ibid.:127). Thus class position (and the cultural capital and habitus associated with it) provides upper-class women with a view of themselves as entitled to represent others and to exercise political power which is normally the preserve of men; in this way they can overcome the gender deficit they experience as women. This thesis is explored through a comparison of two Conservative MPs and provides an interesting contrast to the bulk of research that focuses on the Labour Party. What is most striking is that for the male MP his right to lead and exercise power is taken for granted, it appears to be 'natural' and has become part of his habitus. Because of this 'naturalness' he is 'unable to recognise that others without these social and cultural capitals might encounter difficulties in having their right to represent others acknowledged' (ibid.:134). In contrast the woman MP was all too aware of the 'authority deficits' she labours under and how she has managed to overcome them by constructing a 'narrative of entitlement' through emphasizing the specific contribution she could make to politics through her experience as a middle-class wife and mother. In her words,

I had to overcome the fact that I'm a woman in political life. There's no point in pretending there is no prejudice. And the biggest prejudice I had to overcome was in selection committees when I was asked questions like: Well Mrs Gray, do you believe there is prejudice against women being chosen as Parliamentary candidates, and what makes you think you can do better than a man? (ibid.:139)

Men assume they are entitled to exercise power and this entitlement is seen as legitimate by party selectors, women do not make this assumption but when they do it is not always seen as legitimate.

Recent explanations for the under-representation of women in Parliament have therefore tended to focus on cultural factors and gender identity, although sociological studies in this area are rather sparse. As Joni Lovenduski comments:

Analysts seeking to explore the components of the masculinity of public life must address both middle-class dominance and attitudes and working-class culture and attitudes. Such interdisciplinary research is at an early stage in Britain. (Lovenduski, 1996:16)

Studying 'alternative' politics

As well as there being few sociological studies of political parties there are also few of 'alternative' politics, the politics embedded in the 1984-5 miners' strike, or the politics of the women's movement in its widest sense. Here I focus on two studies of particular forms of 'alternative' politics involving women. One is a study of the aftermath of women's activism in support of the miners during the 1984-5 strike and the other explores the women's peace movement at Greenham. Although both were published in the 1990s they employ contrasting theoretical frameworks to understand the relation between gender and politics.

During the 1984-5 miners' strike women set up support groups which involved them in meeting the welfare needs of striking miners and their families. They spoke at demonstrations and were present on picket lines and, at the time, this was taken as evidence of the influence of feminism in working-class women's lives and a sign that things would never be the same again as far as gender relations in mining communities were concerned (see e.g. Stead, 1987). A study which explores the extent of social change in the aftermath of the strike was carried out in three mining communities in the Yorkshire, Derbyshire, and Nottinghamshire coalfields (Waddington et al., 1991). It takes as its starting point a definition of mining communities which includes a specific gender division of labour. Thus men are employed as miners and build up 'solidary social relations' which extend from their work underground to their leisure activities all of which are highly gender segregated. The 'miner's wife' services her husband and most of her social contact is based on social networks based on kinship and neighbourhood: 'Gender roles are highly differentiated' (ibid.:14). It provides empirical description rather than offering elaborate theoretical analysis and is underpinned by a somewhat 'old fashioned' structural functionalist approach. However it problematizes gender relations rather than seeing them as something rooted in essential differences between women and men and discusses, albeit briefly, women's involvement in politics in the broader context of the effect of the strike on gender relations and mining communities.

In contrast to the view that the strike had a significant impact on women's lives and wrought irreversible changes in gender relations, the researchers argue that while there had been significant changes for individual women which should not be underestimated, for most, whether or not they had been active during the strike, things reverted to normality once the strike was over. This was as much to do with the scarcity of jobs for women in the areas studied and the 'nature and ideology of male work' as anything else (ibid.:92); a finding which is supported by studies in mining communities in other parts of

Britain (see e.g. Jones, 1997). For some women, though, political involvement in the strike was transformative. One woman who worked in the pit canteen in the Yorkshire community told the researchers:

It's as much a woman's world as it is a man's. You can't go back because you think, 'What did I do before the strike . . . just bingo.' But now, there's so many things open to us women to get involved in. (Waddington et al., 1991:86)

Despite the researchers' concern with the effect of the strike on gender relations, they discuss party politics and the continuing and increasing support of these working-class communities for the Labour Party. Politics is defined narrowly. There is little consideration of the extent to which the strike might have led to a feminist political consciousness and no discussion of whether women's involvement could be understood in terms of gender politics.

In contrast, Sasha Roseneil's study of the women's peace camp at Greenham foregrounds gender politics, discussing the extent to which the politics of Greenham challenged gender relations and resulted in a feminist political consciousness (Roseneil, 1995a). She analyses Greenham as a social movement which is a response to the structures not of capitalism but of patriarchy; its conditions of emergence relate to its immediate political environment which include previously existing social movements and political processes as well as political developments on a global scale, and it led not only to outcomes which related directly to the deployment of cruise missiles but also to women's political consciousness, their identity, and their subsequent political involvement. Thus it brings together analysis of the state and individual women's transformations in consciousness, showing how social movements challenge conventional definitions of politics as well as (in the case of feminist social movements) transgressing gender boundaries. In Roseneil's words:

Greenham was not a pressure group, concerned to be integrated into the political process, but rather sought to undermine from outside the legitimacy of a political order which promoted militarism and excluded women. (ibid.:170)

It was a movement which profoundly challenged politics as normal and confronted, with unconventional forms of direct action, the armed might of the state. It also challenged patriarchy by operating at a symbolic level and 'conveying messages about women's independence, autonomy and agency'. It challenged and transformed gender relations by refusing 'men's power to control women's actions' and 'women's confinement by domestic responsibilities' (ibid.:171) even when those men were armed by the state and were acting in its name.

Greenham women refused to perform gender as they should, above all resisting the heterorelational imperative of patriarchy which demands that women exist first and foremost for men. Many challenged this as lesbians ... But, lesbian or heterosexual, Greenham women in their thousands symbolically and practically put women first in their political and daily lives. (ibid.:171)

Theoretically this analysis questions the characterization of 'new' social movements as cultural or social rather than political. The division that is made within new social movement theory between cultural movements concerned with meaning and identity and political movements concerned with issues of distribution and justice is shown to be inapplicable to a movement such as Greenham.

This sort of approach, which develops a critique of social movement theory and of class-based analyses of the state, has also been used to analyse the emergence of second-wave feminism and its impact on the state and social policies. Thus feminist social movements cannot be characterized as either cultural or political but their cultural and political practices cut across these boundaries (Charles, 2000). Along with others (see e.g. Tilly, 1984) it is argued that social movements are an intrinsic part of politics in liberal democratic nation states and that social movements have an impact on political parties, organizations of the state, and social policy development (Jenkins, 1995; Charles, 2000). In the case of second-wave feminism the political challenge of the movement involves a challenge to the gender order, an order which is evident in the political sphere as well as at the economic and cultural levels of society. Challenging this order is part of the dynamic of gender politics and has resulted in significant changes, one of which is women's increased representation amongst political elites. Such social movements demonstrate not 'the routine actions by which women contribute to the reproduction of patriarchy' but the 'non-routine, extraordinary political action, through which women seek social change' (Roseneil, 1995a:2).

Women are also involved in social movements which resist change and strive to ensure that the reproduction of patriarchy continues. Thus the New Right and the anti-feminist countermovement that was one of the reactions to second-wave feminism are supported by women as well as by men. It is around reproductive issues and the family that the anti-abortion and pro-family countermovements have been most active, particularly in the USA, and their influence in Britain is apparent in the continuing controversy over the acceptability of gay and lesbian relationships and particularly debates over 'the family' and parenthood (Charles, 2000).

Whether gender politics are conceptualized as being based in changing relations of patriarchy (Roseneil, 1995a) or as constituting 'struggles over the distribution of the tasks of social reproduction and over the control of reproduction' (Charles, 2000), what these analyses of feminist social movements suggest is that politics is about gender as well as about class, about meaning and identity as well as about distribution. These insights have not yet been incorporated into mainstream (malestream) analyses of politics and the state where the political is divided off from the cultural, the public and the private remain separate and gendered, and politics is what we engage in when we vote. Feminist political scientists have begun to study the gender culture of political parties and representative bodies such as Parliament, but the focus remains largely on voting and representation by formal means and it is still the class cleavage that is seen as important for British politics.

Changes in the gendering of politics

There is evidence that there has been significant change in women's political participation since the war both in conventional politics and in social movements such as the women's movement. There is also evidence that amongst younger women and men political attitudes are converging and even that younger women are to the left of their male peers. The impact of social movements on the political order has also meant that gender is now seen as relevant to politics in ways that it was not previously and class is no longer the only basis of interest formation. Indeed feminists argue that representative politics as it has been practised in Britain has actually represented the interests of men, and a small segment of the male population at that, men who are white, middle class, and heterosexual, and that the state and political parties represent these interests over and above those of ethnic minorities, women, gay men, and lesbians. The importance of gender for politics is demonstrated by current political concern

about young men not taking responsibility for their children, about boys under-achieving at school, about the rising tide of young offenders, who are almost all male, about the failure of young men to get jobs, about older men disabled by work-related illnesses, and about the fact that men suffer disproportionately from heart disease, suicide and premature death. All these factors are rooted—partly or wholly—in the ways in which time, power and responsibility are distributed between women and men, and the subsequent impact on male identities, lifestyles and opportunities. (Coote, 2000:11)

Gendering politics and redistributing resources and the tasks of production and reproduction between women and men are therefore in the interests of men as well as women. This is something that is still not included in mainstream politics except in the form of an anti-feminist backlash that argues that women, family, and community are one and the same and that there is no conflict of interests between women and men. This is something that is part of New

Labour's communitarianism and represents a particular form of gender politics that has more in common with the social conservatism of the New Right
than the politics of second-wave feminism (Franklin, 2000). Finally there is a
scarcity of sociological studies of gender and politics and the few that there are
have emerged from different theoretical and even disciplinary traditions. The
contrast between studies which prioritize class and class-based politics and
those which occupy the theoretical ground on the other side of the epistemological shift resulting from the social movements of the 1960s and 1970s could
not be clearer. As with real-life politics, there is still resistance in 'malestream' political sociology to incorporating the reconceptualization of politics
which has emerged from second-wave feminism and to recognizing the centrality of gender to both the theory and the practice of politics.

Chapter 9

Britain in International Context

I N previous chapters I have focused on gender relations at the societal level. In this chapter I turn my attention to 'what is "going on" in the world as a whole' (Robertson, 1992:10) and discuss gender in modern Britain in the context of globalization. In order to do this I provide a brief overview of changes in gender relations worldwide since the middle of the twentieth century and then discuss various explanations for these changes. Inevitably I simplify a complex and diverse set of phenomena, but what I want to highlight is that processes of change which are evident in Britain neither are peculiar to Britain nor capable of being understood without an appreciation of the global organization of capitalism and its cultural ramifications. I look first at changes in gendered patterns of paid employment and domestic divisions of labour in the second half of the twentieth century.

Patterns of paid employment

Since the end of the Second World War, women's participation in paid employment has been increasing worldwide while men's has been decreasing (UN, 1999:8; UN 1995). In advanced industrial societies, this has been associated with a change in the technological base from manufacturing and heavy industry to information technology. These changes have been understood as a consequence of the emergence of a 'global assembly line' whereby research and management are located in developed nations and labour-intensive parts of the manufacturing production process are located in developing countries (Moghadam, 1995). In developed countries there has been a shift from manufacturing to services and an associated increase in women's employment, while manufacturing and heavy industry have been declining with a loss of tradition-ally 'male' jobs. In contrast, in developing societies there has been a shift from agriculture to manufacturing and services and, in many third world countries, the preferred workforce for the labour-intensive, export-oriented, manufactur-ing processes in the garment, electronics, and pharmaceutical industries are young women (Pearson, 2000; Moghadam, 1996). The jobs that women in the textile industries of Britain, the USA, and the former GDR have lost are now being done by women in third world export processing zones (EPZs).

There has also been a 'flexibilization' of labour; insecure and/or non-standard forms of working, such as homeworking, petty-commodity produc-tion, part-time employment, self-employment, and contract labour, have increased (Felstead and Jewson, 1999; UN 1999:xvii). Women are over-represented in flexible forms of employment in both advanced industrial soci-eties and the developing world (UN, 1999; Dex and McCulloch, 1997). Similarly they are over-represented in low-paid occupations while men are over-represented at the top of the occupational hierarchy and in the most powerful positions in business (Vaiou, 1996:63; UN, 1995:153; UN, 1999).

In the last decades of the twentieth century, flexibilization was associated with ethnic minorities and increasing reliance on immigrant labour. This is in the context of a decrease in labour migration and the tightening of immigra-tion controls which worsens the situation of migrant workers (UN, 1999:35). Migrant women often find employment in domestic service, which is growing in significance. It is one of the ways that women in developed societies can reconcile full-time paid employment and childcare or (increasingly) care of older dependants; indeed in the USA in the 1980s domestic service was the 'fastest-growing employment sector for immigrant women' (Pettman, 1996:195; Westwood and Phizacklea, 2000).

It is ironic that in the latter part of the twentieth century working-class women in the industrialized world are losing their jobs, particularly in the textile and chemical industries, and that now, rather than encouraging foreign workers to migrate to developed countries as happened in Britain in the immediate post-war period, a reverse process is in train whereby labour-intensive parts of many manufacturing production processes are being exported to the third world. Those labour-intensive processes that remain in advanced capitalist countries, such as those associated with the garment indus-try in Britain, often provide a source of employment for ethnic minority and immigrant women (UN, 1999:33). Thus a consideration of the globalization of production processes can help us develop an explanation for changing patterns of gendered and racialized employment in Britain.

The state and patterns of employment

There is considerable variation in gendered employment patterns within the developed world which relates both to the structure of the economy and to the nature of the state (Moghadam, 1996; Monk and Garcia-Ramon, 1996). Thus although women's formal economic activity rates are relatively low in parts of Europe such as Spain, Ireland, and Greece, these figures underestimate women's paid work because it is often 'atypical' and 'informal' therefore 'unrecorded and without contract' (Vaiou, 1996:65). This sort of activity may include

farming for part of the year, tourism during the season, [working] in a family shop for some hours every day, or in industrial home-working. (Vaiou, 1996:65).

Furthermore, family enterprises 'depend on informal practices and low wages' (ibid.:66).

Men engage in family activities as employers or heads of micro-firms, while women (and children or youngsters) are 'family workers', more often than not unregistered and unpaid, but whose labour is a condition of existence of family businesses. (ibid.:68)

This situation is akin to that experienced by women working in so-called ethnic enterprises or homework in Britain and maintains the authority of the male head of household over the labour of other household members, an authority that is more difficult to maintain when women are in paid employment outside the home and their contribution to the financial well-being of the household is visible rather than invisible. The over-representation of women in informal and atypical jobs is due to a lack of alternatives coupled with their responsibility for domestic labour and caring for children and other dependants (Vaiou, 1996).

In northern Europe, in contrast, state provision has, for most of the post-war period, been more facilitative of women's participation in the workforce through the provision of maternity benefits and childcare (although this varies considerably and shapes women's participation in the workforce). Where there is such state provision women are able to participate more fully in the workforce and to have attachments to the labour market which approximate to those of men; furthermore the wage gap between women and men is smaller although gender segregation remains high (Duncan, 1996). Where there is little state provision, families are the main providers of welfare and it is women within families who are involved in domestic and care work; this affects their labour-force participation.

Although women's movement into paid work has been facilitated, to a greater or lesser extent, by welfare states, men's movement into unpaid work within the home and shared parenting has not. Indeed, at the beginning of the twenty-first century most societies are characterized by men's lack of involvement in unpaid domestic work, childcare, and care for other dependants (UN, 2000). Comparative studies of domestic labour in advanced industrial societies have shown some increase in men's participation in unpaid work within the home with women's increasing participation in paid labour, although the increase is not enough to reverse the situation whereby women undertake the bulk of unpaid domestic work. There is therefore some convergence in the time married women and men spend on paid and unpaid work and 'through successive decades, men do more unpaid work and less paid, women, less unpaid and more paid' (Gershuny et al., 1994:182). Overall however women's workload increases with their entry into paid employment and this is only partially offset by men's increasing involvement in unpaid work. Despite this 'lagged adaptation' (ibid.:185), women do more unpaid domestic work than men in advanced capitalist societies and, as we shall see, they do considerably more than men in the former socialist societies. Indeed, time allocation studies from a diverse group of countries around the world suggest that, 'in general, women's burden of household work and primary responsibility for childcare do not diminish with increased participation in paid work' (UN, 1999:13). There is some evidence that the 'inequitable sharing of responsibilities' for childcare and domestic work within the home, and the slow pace of change in response to women's increased participation in paid labour, has contributed to the low levels of fertility characteristic of advanced industrial societies (UN, 1995:18).

Patterns of paid work in former socialist societies

Although women's economic activity rates were high in state socialist societies after the Second World War and women were expected to participate in production on the same basis as men, employment was marked by gender segregation and women experienced a glass ceiling in much the same way as they do in Britain. In the USSR and the GDR women's economic activity rates equalled those of men and, at the end of the 1980s, were higher than in any capitalist industrial society (Schmude, 1996). In the USSR in 1991 women constituted 51 per cent of the workforce and this had been the case for the entire postwar period. There was very little part-time employment so this figure, unlike the figures for Britain, implies that women actually constituted half the workforce when counted in terms of full-time jobs (Charles, 1993; Rudolph et al., 1994; McMahon, 1994). Despite these high rates of economic activity and the significance of women to the labour force there was no attempt to challenge domestic divisions of labour and the family retained its importance as the basic social unit of society; indeed in rural areas family households were important units of production. Significantly in the USSR and the GDR marriage was not regarded as a source of economic support for women whereas employment was; women, like men, had a right and a duty to participate in full-time paid employment. That they had to combine this with very onerous domestic and care work was not seen as a problem and motherhood continued to be defined differently from fatherhood, albeit paid employment was part of it. In order to facilitate this, childcare facilities were widely available; in the 1980s, for instance, they were available for more than 80 per cent of children below school age in the GDR (Rudolph et al., 1994:17).

Since the fall of the wall in 1989 and the transition from centrally planned to market economies there have been huge changes in gender divisions of paid work. Unemployment has soared, particularly in the former GDR and USSR where women's economic activity rates were highest, and women have been hardest hit (Rudolph et al., 1994; McMahon, 1994). It is more difficult for women to find employment and in the former GDR—in contrast with Britain—unemployment is now higher amongst young women than young men. State provision of welfare, particularly childcare, has been reduced and state subsidies removed (Moghadam, 1995). In both the GDR and the USSR, despite very high economic activity rates for women, women were under-represented in senior managerial and other powerful positions within the workforce. Significantly this was not a reflection of their lesser educational attainment, indeed in the USSR in 1991, 'of men with higher education or specialised secondary studies, 48 per cent were engaged in managerial duties compared with 7 per cent of women with similar skills' (McMahon, 1994:65). This suggests that educational attainment is not directly translated into positions in the occupational hierarchy, at least as far as women are concerned, and puts a different light on the alleged educational under-achievement of boys in the advanced capitalist world. It is not necessarily the case that girls' increasing success in exams will be translated directly into a job. Indeed there is some evidence that higher education throughout the developed world is becoming feminized but at the same time it no longer holds the key to the top-paying jobs.

Even though women's economic activity rates were high, occupations remained segregated along lines of gender, women were concentrated in low-paid and less powerful positions in the occupational structure, and they retained responsibility for domestic and care work which was particularly onerous in face of a lack of consumer goods and the need to spend a consider-able amount of time queuing to buy basic foodstuffs. Indeed, it has been esti-mated that in 1990 'the average Russian woman spent approximately 35 hours per week on housework and childcare and 38 hours in paid employment; throughout the week, women spent nearly 48 hours more than men on house-work and childcare' (McMahon, 1994:66). Women's domestic burden was therefore heavy, much heavier than that of their western sisters, as was their burden of paid employment. And although there was extensive state provision of social facilities to ease this dual burden, no serious attempt was made to alter domestic divisions of labour. Thus in former socialist societies, as in Western Europe, North America, and Australia, women's increased participation in paid work has not been associated with a significant increase in men's participation in unpaid, domestic work.

It seems clear that despite variations within advanced industrial societies and the former socialist societies of the Soviet bloc there are some similarities in terms of gender relations. These are that the provision of social facilities such as childcare by the state reduces gender inequalities by facilitating women's par-ticipation in paid employment. Those societies where women's economic activity rates are or have been most similar to men's have been those with the highest levels of state provision and these are also where the 'traditional' family is less strong and women's dependence on men within family house-holds has been reduced. In Britain, as in most of these societies, the family household has ceased to be a unit of production and most of the population is engaged in wage labour outside the household. There are important exceptions to this such as family farms and small-scale commodity production which takes place in family enterprises. So-called ethnic enterprises in Britain, where family labour is important and remains under the control of the—usually—male household head, is an example of the continuing vitality of family-based pro-duction. In European countries where a higher proportion of the population is engaged in agricultural production family-based production is more signifi-cant, as it is in rural areas of the former USSR and Poland. Indeed, it has been argued that globalization and economic restructuring involve, among other things, 'the revival of homework and of domestic and family labor systems' rather than, or as well as, an increase in women's participation in wage labour (Moghadam, 1995:18).

Developing societies

In much of the third world, in contrast, where a much larger proportion of the population is rural, the family household retains its significance as a unit of production. Thus while in Britain the proportion of the population engaged in agriculture is 2.4 per cent, in Bolivia the figure is 46.9 per cent, in China it is 71 per cent, in Bangladesh it is 73.8 per cent, and in Kenya it is 78 per cent (Nelson and Chowdhury, 1994:780–1). Generally, the more industrialized and urbanized a country is the lower the proportion of the population engaged in agricultural production. Much of this production is household based and involves many different tasks during the day. It may consist of growing crops or tending livestock, either for subsistence or for the market (or both), or it may involve trading or household-based commodity production. In family-based production male control over female and child labour is marked and women's (as well as children's) contribution to the household economy is usually unpaid and therefore invisible. This sort of work does not fit into the categories for measuring economic activity that have been developed in the context of formal-sector employment and leads to an under-enumeration of women's economic activity (Charles, 1993). Nevertheless, women's official economic activity rates have increased in most regions of the third world since the middle of the twentieth century with the important exception of sub-Saharan Africa. Here, in contrast with all the other regions of the world, there is evidence that women's economic activity rates decreased between 1970 and 1990 and women are much less likely than men to be involved in wage labour (Bujra, 1986; UN, 1999:8). The lowest economic activity rates for women are recorded for the Arab countries of the Middle East although women's economic activity rates increased significantly and, in some countries, faster than men's in the last decades of the twentieth century (Moghadam, 1995).

In the third world the informal economy is significant and women are involved in trading, very often taking to market the produce of their agricultural labour. Women traders are common in Africa, South-east Asia, and Latin America; they tend to trade items to meet family needs and dominate the market place while men are involved in retail trade. Women are also located in home-based industries or petty commodity production and, as we have already seen, this type of household production is controlled by the male head of household. The informal sector in third world countries also includes domestic service and prostitution – the latter has grown considerably in recent years, particularly in parts of Asia, and women migrants from rural areas are often involved in both prostitution and domestic service, not only at home but also abroad (Westwood and Phizacklea, 2000:132). The increase in sex tourism and trafficking in women is another dimension of globalization and provides extremely dangerous and insecure work for many young women in third world countries who migrate to the towns for work (Pettman, 1996; Kempadoo and Doezema, 1998). They have become a focus of concern because of the creation of international and urban-rural conduits for the spread of HIV/AIDs.

Men tend to predominate in employment in the formal sector of the economy in capital-intensive industry although where EPZs have been established with labour-intensive production processes young, female labour is preferred (Elson and Pearson, 1981). However at the beginning of the twenty-first century there is a tendency for previously labour-intensive processes to become less labour intensive, involving more sophisticated technology, and for male labour to be supplanting female labour (Runyan, 1996:240). Whatever form women's paid work takes they are concentrated in labour-intensive sectors of agriculture and industry where technology is least developed while men are in the more capital-intensive, technologically advanced sectors (Croll, 1981). This gender division is also reflected in access to information technology (UN, 2000). Women's wages are lower than men's and there is no convincing evidence that women's increasing economic activity rates are leading to a reduction in the gender wage gap in the third world; men are over-represented in the formal sector of the economy where wages are higher than in the informal sector where women are over-represented. It is also women who undertake the bulk of unpaid work, whether this be agricultural work in the subsistence sector or domestic work in the home, whether it be caring for children, husbands, or other relatives. Indeed, there are significant commonalities in the experiences of women around the world despite their very different socio-economic circumstances. Divisions of household labour assign to women in countries as diverse as Wales and Ghana responsibility for feeding and caring for dependants in whatever way they are able (Avotri, Walters, and Charles, 1999). Globally, whatever women's participation in the paid workforce, they carry the main responsibilities for unpaid domestic and care work.

In households in the third world it is often difficult to disentangle domestic labour from other forms of work and, in many regions, households remain important units of production. As we have seen, gender relations within households in Britain are structured by women's and men's differential access to resources (mainly in the form of wages) and women shoulder the main burden of domestic and care work. This is true worldwide and has important implications, not only in terms of gender relations and women's and men's differential access to resources but also in terms of the well-being of children. Thus, increases in women's access to resources are reflected directly in improvements in children's well-being while increases in men's resources are not (Bruce and Dwyer, 1988:5; Mencher, 1988). In rural areas, the income from cash crops, which men customarily control, is not generally pooled in the household, while women's income is mainly used for food and other basic necessities. That explains why an increase in cash income controlled by men does not necessarily translate into improved household nutritional intake and food security. (UN, 1999:40)

Women's mothering role in many societies therefore includes nurturing and caring for their children by ensuring that they have the resources with which to provide them with food and shelter; getting a living is an important part of being a mother (Bruce and Dwyer, 1988:6). And in much of Africa where women's and men's responsibilities are separate and clearly demarcated and where the economic dependence of women and children is not a feature of marriage, 'almost universally, women . . . are viewed as ultimately responsible for fulfilling children's food needs' (ibid.:5). Similarly, 'becoming a parent has a significant effect on women's time use and very little on men's'. Thus it is mothers who balance 'the conflict between market work and childcare by reducing sleep and leisure' the world over (ibid.:7).

Changing gender ideologies

Since the Second World War there have been significant changes in attitudes towards gender, sexuality, the family, and women's participation in paid employment in Britain. Such changes are widespread in advanced capitalist societies and can be seen as reflecting the 'death of the male breadwinner ideology' (MacInnes, 1998:53). Thus in those countries where women's labour market participation is highest, men's agreement with the statement 'A husband's job is to earn money; a wife's is to look after the home and family' is lowest (ibid.:55). There is a generational difference, with older women and men being more likely to agree with the statement while younger women and men are less likely to (Scott et al., 1996). There is still, however, considerable (though declining) opposition in both the USA and Britain to mothers of young children working, particularly if their employment is full time (Stockman et al., 1995). This generational change in values has been linked to the declining power of religion and conceptualized as a shift from material to postmaterial values (Inglehart, 1990) and/or from modernity to postmodernity (Brown, 2001). Inglehart argues that material values have a strong hold in conditions of material insecurity but that since the Second World War and the development of welfare states material security has been experienced by most of the populations of the developed world. This has been accompanied by a secularization of values and a change in morality which is reflected in many of the changes in gender relations, sexuality, and families that we explored in earlier chapters. Postmaterial values are most common amongst younger generations and include liberal views on abortion, divorce, illegitimacy, fertility levels, women's employment, and an emphasis on quality of life. This ties in with the tendencies noted in Britain for sexuality to be seen as a dimension of individual identity rather than in terms of reproduction and the increasing tolerance of a diversity of sexual orientations interpreted as lifestyle choices. Indeed, with regard to homosexuality, Britain, along with the Netherlands, Sweden, Denmark, and west Germany is one of the most tolerant. This tolerance does not, however, mean that homosexual relationships enjoy the same status as heterosexual relationships. Within the EU for instance, despite homosexual unions being recognized in some member states, partners of gay men and lesbians who migrate from one member state to another for work are not granted the same immigration status as those in legally sanctioned heterosexual partnerships (Valentine, 1996).

Some sectors of the population, however, experience less material security and can feel threatened by what they see as increased instability in society. In such circumstances they are inclined to resist change, thus giving rise to support for the male-breadwinner family, opposition to abortion, and concern about maternal employment. Indeed those who experience the least economic and physical security have the most need for 'familiar cultural norms and absolute religious beliefs' (Inglehart, 1990:185). Religious values are associated with beliefs about the sanctity of marriage and the inseparability of sexuality and reproduction and societies where religion remains important are less tolerant of homosexuality (here are included Mexico and North America but not most of Western Europe). Indeed Mexico is taken as an example of a society where there is an ideology of machismo which rests on homophobia (cf. Lancaster, 1995): to be a 'real' man is defined in opposition to being gay.

One of the responses to the fact that 'norms linked with religion and the inviolability of the family have been growing weaker' has been 'a renewed emphasis on religious issues—in particular. . . a heated antiabortion movement' which has been interpreted by some as a swing to the right. In Inglehart's view this interpretation is at odds with the overall trend towards secularization and such movements should be seen as 'a reaction among a dwindling traditionalist sector' who feel their values and way of life to be under threat (Inglehart, 1990:201, 205).

No comparable attitude surveys exist globally but there is considerable social and political conflict over gender relations and particularly women's reproductive rights and sexuality. Before discussing this I focus on masculinity and consider the ways that sexuality, particularly women's sexuality, relates to group identity.

Masculinity

There are few comparative studies of masculinity and/or sexuality although there are studies which document the wide variety of sexual practices and gender roles in different types of society, showing that the meanings and behaviours associated with gender and sexuality vary considerably cross-culturally (see e.g. Caplan, 1987; Cornwall and Lindisfarne, 1994; Gilmore, 1990; Harvey and Gow, 1994). There are, however, some similarities. In a comparative ethnographic study of masculinity, for instance, Gilmore argues that almost universally boys have to achieve manhood by undergoing a highly stressful initiation process, often involving severe and violent treatment by older men. In almost all societies masculinity involves a denigration of homosexuality and a distinction between a 'real' man and someone who is not quite a man. Heterosexual exploits are therefore part of the masculine performance in many societies while homosexuality is frowned upon and used as a means of forcing young men to conform to what is expected of them, such as fighting for their country (Lancaster, 1995). Fighting and drinking are commonly engaged in by young men and masculinity is spoken of 'in terms of risk-taking, gambling, self-assertion, and violence' (ibid.:142). It also involves policing and defending group boundaries and controlling women's behaviour (Gilmore, 1990:224). Gilmore suggests that men in some cultures display protective and nurturing behaviour but this is contested by other students of masculinity who allege that 'the underlying theme is irresponsibility not nurture' (Lancaster, 1995:142).

Women's sexuality

Many social groups regard women as crucial for the preservation and transmission of their cultural identity. In order to maintain their identity they attempt to control women's sexuality and harness it to the reproductive needs of the group (Tabet, 1996). Controlling women's sexuality is an important way in which group boundaries are maintained; by ensuring that women only have sexual relations within the group its cultural identity is preserved. Women's significance as carriers of group identity and as boundary markers means that their adultery is far more dangerous than a man's because it pollutes the group: they may become pregnant thereby bearing a child that does not belong to the group but to another man's lineage. Men's sexual straying is not so critical because they cannot become pregnant. Moreover women represent 'the privacy and intimacy of the group' (Goddard, 1987:181). They are the bearers of values 'based on generalized reciprocity, generosity, self-sacrifice and devotion' in opposition to 'the impersonal, profit-orientated relations of capitalist production' (ibid.:185–6). Men have to operate in this impersonal world but the group's identity can be maintained by ensuring that women are contained within it and that, as mothers, they transmit the cultural identity of the group to their children. In many societies this is achieved by the application of religious law to issues pertaining to marriage, fertility, and reproduction (Yuval-Davis, 1995). In Israel, for instance, religious laws govern the private sphere; similarly Muslim Personal Laws or Family Codes affect 'about 450 million women who live in Muslim countries and communities' (Bryson, 1998:140; Helie-Lucas, 1994:394). Thus, 'In many countries the state delegates control of the family and women's sexuality to communal or religious authorities and/or to male heads of household' (Charles and Hintjens, 1998:9). Moreover, men of one collectivity can bring shame on those of another by gaining sexual access to 'their' women. Thus 'rape and impregnation of enemy women is often part of war and has been a mark of the so-called ethnic cleansing in former Yugoslavia' (ibid.:11).

This role of women [as transmitters of cultural identity] becomes particularly important in historical situations of actual or threatened destruction of socio-cultural groups in the face of religion, the state, and/or capitalism. (Goddard, 1987:190)

The control of women's sexuality by the group is evident in industrial settings and in many Mediterranean and Middle Eastern societies where women are charged with maintaining the honour of the family or group; conversely they can bring shame on their menfolk by indulging in culturally inappropriate behaviour (Goddard, 1987). This throws light on the preference amongst certain social groups (such as Bangladeshi women in London's East End) for women to work 'in small sweatshops or in their own homes, with far lower rates of pay and bad working conditions' than to work in factories (Goddard, 1987:166; Kabeer, 2000). It also illuminates the way young men attempt to control the behaviour of young women by labelling them as 'slags' and the significance of women's sexuality for the maintenance of group identity and respectability. This gives women power: they are dangerous if their sexuality is out of control and there is always this potential. It also underlines the way the domestic sphere, and women within it, can represent the maintenance of tradition and cultural identity in the face of a state which is perceived as acting against its citizens or in response to the dislocations and insecurity brought about by globalization and structural adjustment programmes (Charles and Hintjens, 1998; Moghadam, 1995).

Citizens . . . turn to their primary solidarities both to protect themselves from potentially repressive states and to compensate for inefficient representation. This reinforces the stranglehold of communities over their women, whose roles as boundary markers become heightened. (Kandiyoti, 1991:14)

The significance of women as 'boundary markers' helps to explain the political significance of women's role as mothers and the attempts to control their sexuality which emerged in the last decades of the twentieth century.

Political conflicts

Conflicts over gender and the organization of 'reproductive, domestic, productive, communal and political activities' are apparent throughout the world (Nelson and Chowdhury, 1994:11). These surface in the violent inter-ethnic and communal conflicts that ravaged many parts of the world in the second half of the twentieth century, in the rise of Islamist movements in the Middle East, and a more general resurgence of fundamentalism worldwide (Nelson and Chowdhury, 1994; Moghadam, 1996). They are also apparent in the rising divorce rates of most industrialized countries and in the conflicts over reproductive and parental rights that have marked the last quarter century (see Charles, 2000). In the developed world this has been particularly apparent in the conflict over abortion while, elsewhere, there is opposition to women's sexual and reproductive behaviour being the subject of strict family and communal control. In both the anti-abortion (pro-life) movement and fundamentalist movements, women's role in the family is emphasized and their employment and reproductive rights are 'downgraded' (Moghadam, 1995:18). International organizations such as the United Nations and, in many countries, a modernizing and emancipating state, are associated with a move towards gender equality worldwide, while opposition to modernization and, latterly, globalization, reasserts 'traditional' values which tend to prioritize the group over the individual and valorize women's familial and reproductive role. This type of conflict is represented politically in social movements such as second-wave feminism and the countermovement that it spawned (Staggenborg, 1991; Charles, 2000), in movements for socialism and democracy which tend to enhance women's rights, and in communal and fundamentalist movements which attempt to restrict them.

Women's liberation movements developed in most western societies in the 1960s and 1970s and feminism now has an international or global presence (Charles, 2000; Pearson, 2000). Women are involved in community politics worldwide and in nationalist and revolutionary movements, ecology movements, and peace movements (Jayawardena, 1986; Peterson and Runyan, 1993; Blumberg, 1995). In many parts of the third world there have been national liberation movements that have been socialist, e.g. Nicaragua, Cuba, China, and where women's emancipation has been high on the political agenda. In contrast, in the last decades of the twentieth century fundamentalist movements became more powerful and a core part of their agenda is reaffirming women's central role as reproducers. Along with this goes a validation of cultural practices which control women's sexuality and often involve violence. Thus Hindu and Muslim communal movements in India are calling for the reintroduction of *sati* (widow burning) and dowry payments respectively; there were 4,952 dowry murders in India in 1990 (Swarup et al., 1994:375). Many women support these movements because of the high value placed on motherhood even though they attempt to confine women within the family at the expense of their employment and reproductive rights (Benton, 1998). However, many also resist their confinement to the domestic sphere and continue to participate in the public domain (Moghadam, 1995; Kofman, 1998).

Political representation

Even though women are actively involved in social and political movements their representation in the formal political process is negligible and, with few exceptions, it is men who occupy positions of political power. Thus although women constitute half the world's population they occupy 'only 5–10 per cent of the formal positions of political leadership' (Nelson and Chowdhury, 1994:15). Between 1987 and 1994 women's representation in Parliamentary assemblies decreased in Eastern Europe and increased in Western Europe and other western democracies. In Africa and Latin America there were small increases but in Asia and the Pacific, with the exception of Oceania, women's representation stayed the same or decreased. In 2000 there were 26 countries worldwide, 13 of which were in the developed world, where women's Parliamentary representation was 20 per cent or over (UN, 2000:77).

It is in Scandinavia and, prior to the fall of the wall, Eastern Europe and the USSR that levels of representation of women in the formal political process are highest. Significantly, much of the increase in women's formal representation has come about by means of quotas (UN, 2000:76). Joni Lovenduski (1999) suggests that there is a rising trend in women's representation in most western democracies. This was first apparent in the Scandinavian countries in the 1970s and in other countries, including Britain, during the 1980s. The increases in representation have mostly been a result of women's organizing to increase their representation through working within political parties and by putting pressure on them externally through, for instance, the feminist movement and organizations such as the 300 group in Britain set up precisely to further women's political careers.

As we saw in Chapter 8, since the 1950s there has been a gender gap in voting patterns, with women more inclined to vote conservatively than men but, since the 1980s, although there is still a gender gap, in many countries it has been reversed. For instance in the USA women are more likely to vote Democrat than are men and there is a similar gender gap in Scandinavia; this tendency is therefore not peculiar to Britain but can be observed as a trend in most advanced industrial societies. This shift has been attributed to the cultural changes noted by Inglehart and the emergence of postmaterial values in younger generations (Norris, 1997; Lovenduski, 1999). These changes have to be seen in the context of different political systems which provide different possibilities for women's representation. Thus in a comparison of Britain and Norway Lovenduski points out that conditions are more favourable to women's representation in Norway because as well as women's having organized early to increase their representation, 'the electoral system is based on proportional representation and party lists' which mean that 'elections may be won and lost at the margins'. This leads political parties to attend to 'new political groups' (Lovenduski, 1999:196). In contrast Britain has a first past the post electoral system which, other things being equal, militates against the representation of women.

In former socialist societies women's representation was similar to that in Western Europe and better than in Britain. Since the fall of Communism, however, there has been a reduction in women's representation in all countries of the Soviet bloc. Thus in the first post-Communist elections women's representation fell from 21 per cent to 3.5 per cent in Bulgaria, 21 per cent to 7 per cent in Hungary, 29 per cent to 3.6 per cent in Czechoslovakia, 20 per cent to 13 per cent in Poland, and 34 per cent to 4 per cent in Romania (McMahon, 1994:73, n.7). In the rest of the world women's representation in formal politics is significantly less—with the exception of Cuba which is still ruled by a Communist Party committed to gender equality and where, unusually, reforms have been introduced to challenge domestic divisions of labour (Charles, 1993).

Understanding gender relations in a global context

Until the emergence of feminism and its growing impact in development agencies and international organizations such as the UN, gender was not a focus of concern in any of the disciplines concerned with comparative study or global social processes and it was only after the publication of Boserup's book on women and development in 1970 that gender began to be integrated into analyses of development (Boserup, 1989; Charles, 1993). In her analysis Boserup distinguishes between modern and traditional sectors of the economy, arguing that women's participation in the modern sector is an indicator of a society's economic development. Modernization (and industrialization) is conceptualized as the goal of development with tradition being seen as something to move away from. In the wake of this analysis, feminists researching gender and development focused on two significant issues: the first was the effect of industrialization and wage labour on gender relations and the second was the nature of gender divisions within households. Questions were asked about the extent to which women's participation in wage labour contributed to the weakening of male authority and control over them, both in terms of allowing them to escape the confines of rural, patriarchal households and in enabling them to exercise some control over decision making in households in urban areas. Questions were also asked about the distribution of resources in households and gendered power relations and inequalities. As we have seen, households vary considerably around the world, particularly in the extent to which they are units of production, and there is evidence that male control over women's labour and sexuality is more likely to be strong where production remains household based. Where women and men are involved in wage labour outside the home women's contribution to the household economy is visible and where women retain control over resources their power within households and in relation to their menfolk increases (Safa, 1990; Blumberg, 1991). In the workplace, although women are likely to be under the control of male superiors, they are able to exercise more autonomy and experience at least a 'partial liberation' from 'traditional patriarchal social relations' (Lim, 1983:83; Ong, 1990). Thus feminists concerned with the impact of women's participation in industrial wage labour in the third world have concluded that its effects are contradictory; as some gender relations are dissolved, others which may also involve women's subordination are constructed (Elson and Pearson, 1984). Despite this, a recent study of Bangladeshi garment workers in Bangladesh and the East End of London takes the view that working outside the home creates the possibility of change. Thus women working in garment factories in Dakha, through their exercise of individual choice in particular socio-economic and cultural circumstances, are challenging what Naila Kabeer calls the 'patriarchal bargain'. In Kabeer's view 'women's entry into factory work can be seen as both a response to past changes as well as a vehicle for future transformation' (Kabeer, 2000:362).

Underpinning much of this discussion is the notion that women's participation in wage labour is crucial for their ability to challenge inequitable gender relations. This has been particularly influential for feminists working within a Marxist framework and there has sometimes been a simplistic equation of increases in women's participation in the global workforce with a reduction in gender inequalities (Blumberg, 1995; for a critique see Walby 1996). However, research on households in Africa has shown that, although this might be true where it is the agrarian patriarchal household that is being undermined by capitalist development, in cultures where women and men have been regarded as independent and autonomous, with access to and control over their own resources, whether these be in the form of land or cash, then the introduction of a cash economy has undermined these much more egalitarian gender relations and reduced women's independent access to resources (for a more detailed discussion see Charles, 1993).

Patriarchy undermined?

Such research and its theoretical underpinnings has raised the question of the direction of change in gender relations. Some have argued that the emergence of modernity spells the beginning of the end of gender and that in advanced capitalist countries we are witnessing significant changes which will ultimately make gender irrelevant. Thus there are

strong material and ideological pressures in modern western societies which appear to work against patriarchy. They are forcing or encouraging men to become more involved in childcare and domestic labour and to accept a steadily greater role for women in the public sphere. (MacInnes, 1998:49)

In MacInnes's view, which on the basis of evidence considered in earlier chapters we might wish to contest, men are no longer able 'to define childcare and domestic labour exclusively as a woman's job' (ibid.:53). He explains the dynamic behind these changes as arising from the fact that modern capitalism is not patriarchal. On the contrary,

it systematically undermines patriarchy and creates the conditions for feminist struggle in much the same way as it has created the conditions for class struggle. (ibid.:55)

A similar argument is advanced by Lie but this time in the context of capitalist industrialization in the third world, specifically Korea. He argues that

industrialisation contributes to the dissolution of agrarian patriarchal households and to a gendered division of labour in the economy and within the household. Paradoxically, the same dynamic creates the conditions for gender emancipation, providing both social and epistemological bases for gender-based politics and consciousness. (Lie, 1996:34)

It provides the social base because women, when they participate in wage labour, are taken out of the agrarian, patriarchal household where they are embedded in family and community. Women's participation in wage labour is interpreted as representing a liberation from patriarchal control within the household and providing the basis for women (and men) to organize on the basis of gender as they are employed in factories where they are with other women and are paid less than men, often for doing the same work. Thus gender becomes a salient category both for organizing to improve conditions and for understanding why women's conditions are worse than men's. The conditions in world-market factories may be bad but, according to Lie's argument, they create the potential for gender-based organization. The significance of this is that gender is no longer embedded in other, prior social relations and thus becomes a relevant social category for organizing and understanding the world.

This contrasts with others who theorize the same phenomena in terms of a move from private to public patriarchy, thus seeing it primarily as a transformation of gender relations (Walby, 1996). This shift happened in Britain at the beginning of the twentieth century and, it could be argued, is now happening in countries which are experiencing industrialization and modernization. Women's political mobilization is an important element of this change, together with the recognition that they have a rightful place in the public domain. However, this right is contested in many parts of the world and significant political and social forces exist which wish to confine women to the private domain, thereby resisting the shift from private to public patriarchy.

Globalization

Many of the changes I have discussed in this chapter can also be conceptualized in terms of globalization. There are various theories of globalization, some of which emphasize its economic aspects while others focus on its cultural dimensions. Economically globalization consists of the development of capitalism into a global system whereby trans-national corporations (TNCs) are economically dominant, finance capital moves around the world freely, trade barriers have been removed, and the ability of nation states to control economic processes has been undermined (Runyan, 1996:238). This global development of capitalism is made possible by information technology and rapid communications systems which enable various parts of the same production process to take place in different parts of the world. Associated with this is the increased production of consumer goods and the opening up of global markets. Culturally the universal availability of the same consumer goods is leading to a homogenization of culture to which the mass media, controlled by a few powerful media moguls in the west, contributes. However, at the same time as having tendencies to uniformity, globalization leads to a reverse process of assertion of difference and identity and a tighter drawing of cultural boundaries (Featherstone, 1995). This is associated with the emergence of identity politics and movements for national autonomy as well as a resurgence of fundamentalism. Indeed, Robertson suggests that

Global capitalism both promotes and is conditioned by cultural homogeneity *and* cultural heterogeneity. The production and consolidation of difference and variety is an essential ingredient of contemporary capitalism, which is, in any case, increasingly involved with a growing variety of *micro*-markets. (Robertson, 1992:173)

Thus homogenization, arising from the expansion of consumer capitalism around the globe, goes hand in hand with cultural and political heterogeneity and an assertion of the importance of the local. Indeed it has been suggested that globalization is taking place 'in the absence of either a cultural or an economic "hegemon"' and that this explains the simultaneous occurrence of 'standardization and diversification, and unification and fragmentation' (Scott, 1997:7).

As we have seen, there are several ways in which the processes associated with globalization have affected gender relations in Britain: the relocation of labour-intensive production processes from high-wage to low-wage economies is linked to the loss of women's jobs in manufacturing in Britain and their increase in the third world. It is women in EPZs who are making the consumer goods, such as sportswear and clothing, which contribute to the burgeoning of consumer-based identities and style associated with the multiplication of masculinities we discussed in Chapter 6. The expansion of flexible forms of employment in which women predominate and which enable many of them to combine paid and domestic work and to renegotiate domestic divisions of labour is another dimension of globalization, as is the increasing involvement of women migrants in domestic and care work—particularly care of the elderly—in advanced industrial societies (Anderson, 2000).

The 'cultural turn' revisited

There is clearly considerable ferment and change on a global scale, gender relations are a site of intense conflict at both an individual and collective level, and changes in Britain can only be fully understood when they are seen as part of a global process. The direction of change is difficult to assess although in Britain and the developed world there is evidence that the trend is towards greater gender equality in the context of converging economic activity rates for women and men, low fertility rates, and the adoption by women of behaviours previously associated with men. The adoption by men of behaviours previously associated with women is slower but there is some evidence that this is taking place. What is also apparent is that although there was significant change in the second half of the twentieth century, power globally remains in the hands of men, and unless and until that is transformed it is unlikely that the socio-economic and political significance of gender will disappear altogether.

In this book, as well as considering changes in gender relations, I have been concerned to discuss changes in the way that sociologists have studied gender. In Chapter 1 I pointed to the 'cultural turn' that has characterized sociological research and theorizing since the 1970s and the move away from structural analyses which it implied. What is interesting about theorizations of globalization is that they bring together economic and cultural analyses. As we have seen, this is also true of some more recent studies of gender which explore not only structural inequalities but also cultural processes and the way social actors engage with them. Robertson points out that the

decline in sociological interest in culture after the period of classical sociology . . . needs as much attention as the recent increase in such interest, a major possibility in that connection being that mature modernity was unfavourable to concern with culture, whereas what is often diagnosed as postmodernity—or postmodernism—encourages it. (Robertson, 1992:42)

There is therefore a sense in which the 'cultural turn' can itself be seen as a product of globalization and a response to the increasing significance of 'culture' in everyday life. This also implies that the attention now paid by many sociologists of gender to the cultural dimensions of economic structures and the material embeddedness of cultural practices is both a product of societal change and an important means of understanding the changes and continuities in gender relations that have been the focus of this book.

Bibliography

Abbot, Elizabeth and Bompas, Katherine (1943) *The woman citizen and social security*, Katherine Bompas: London.

Abbott, Pam and Wallace, Claire (1992) *The family and the new right*, Pluto perspectives: London/Boulder, Col.

Adkins, Lisa (1995) *Gendered work: sexuality, family and the labour market*, Open University Press: Buckingham.

—— and Leonard, Diana (1996) 'Reconstructing French feminism: commodification, materialism and sex' in D. Leonard and L. Adkins (eds) *Sex in question: French materialist feminism*, Taylor & Francis: London, pp. 1–23.

—— and Lury, Celia (1994) 'The cultural, the sexual, and the gendering of the labour market' in L. Adkins and C. Lury (eds) *Sexualizing the social: power and the organization of sexuality*, Macmillan: Basingstoke, pp. 204–23.

Alexander, Claire (1996) *The art of being black: the creation of black British youth identities*, Clarendon Press: Oxford.

Alexander, Wendy (2000) 'Women and the Scottish Parliament' in A. Coote (ed.) *New gender agenda*, Institute for Public Policy Research: London, pp. 81–8.

Allen, Sheila (1982) 'Confusing categories and neglecting contradictions' in E. Cashmore and B. Troyna (eds) *Black youth in crisis*, George Allen & Unwin: London, pp. 143–58.

—— and Leonard, Diana (1994) 'From sexual divisions to sexualities: changing sociological agendas' in J. Weeks and J. Holland (eds) *Sexual cultures: communities, values and intimacy*, Macmillan: Basingstoke, pp. 17–33.

Althusser, Louis (1971) 'Ideology and ideological state apparatuses' in *Lenin and philosophy and other essays*, New Left Books: London, pp. 121–73.

Amin, Kaushika and Oppenheim, Carey (1992) *Poverty in black and white*, Child Poverty Action Group and Runnymead Trust: London.

Anderson, Bridget (2000) *Doing the dirty work?*, Zed Press: London.

Arber, Sara (1999) 'Unequal partners: Inequality in earnings and independent income within marriage' in L. McKie, S. Bowlby and S. Gregory (eds) *Gender, power and the household*, Macmillan: Basingstoke.

—— and Gilbert, Nigel (1989) 'Men: the forgotten carers', *Sociology*, 23:111–18.

Ardener, Edwin (1981) 'Belief and the problem of women' and 'The "problem" revisited' in S. Ardener (ed.) *Perceiving women*, J. M. Dent & Sons Ltd: London, pp. 1–27.

Avotri, Joyce, Walters, Vivienne, and Charles, Nickie (1999) '"Your heart is never free": women talking about depression and "thinking too much"', *Journal of Canadian Psychology*, 40(2):331–50.

Ball, Stephen (1981) *Beachside comprehensive: a case-study of comprehensive schooling*, Cambridge University Press: Cambridge.

Barrett, Michele (1980) *Women's oppression today*, Verso: London.

—— (1991) *The politics of truth: from Marx to Foucault*, Polity Press: Cambridge.

—— (1992) 'Words and things: materialism and method in contemporary feminist analysis' in M. Barrett and A. Phillips (eds) *Destabilizing theory: contemporary feminist debates*, Polity Press: Cambridge, pp. 201–19.

—— (1994) 'Destabilising sociology: changing disciplines in a changing world', presidential address to the British Sociological Association annual conference.

—— and Phillips, Anne (1992) 'Introduction' in M. Barrett and A. Phillips (eds) *Destabilizing theory: contemporary feminist debates*, Polity Press: Cambridge, pp. 1–9.

Beishon, Sharon, Modood, Tariq, and Virdee, Satnam (1998) *Ethnic minority families*, Policy Studies Institute: London.

Bennett, Andy (1999) 'Sub-cultures or neo-tribes? Rethinking the relationship between youth, style and musical taste', *Sociology*, 33(3): 599–617.

Benton, Sarah (1998) 'Founding fathers and earth mothers: women's place at the birth of nations' in N. Charles and H. Hintjens (eds) *Gender, ethnicity and political ideologies*, Routledge: London, pp. 27–45.

Bernstein, Basil (1977) *Class, codes and control*, vol. 3, 2nd edn., Routledge and Kegan Paul: London.

Bertoia, Carl E. and Drakich, Janice (1995) 'The fathers' rights movement: contradictions in rhetoric and practice' in W. Marsiglio (ed.) *Fatherhood: contemporary theory, research, and social policy*, Sage: Thousand Oaks, Calif. pp. 230–54.

Beynon, Huw (1975) *Working for Ford*, E. P. Publishing: Wakefield.

Bhachu, Parminder (1988) '*Apni Marzi Kardhi*. Home and work: Sikh women in Britain' in S. Westwood and Parminder Bhachu (eds) *Enterprising women: ethnicity, economy and gender*, Routledge: London and New York, pp. 76–102.

Bhavnani, Reena (1994) *Black women in the labour market: a research review*, Equal Opportunities Commission: Manchester.

Bhopal, Kalwant (1999) 'South Asian women and arranged marriages in East London' in R. Barot, H. Bradley and S. Fenton (eds) *Ethnicity, gender and social change*, Macmillan: Basingstoke, pp. 117–34.

Blackaby, David, Charles, Nickie, Davies, Charlotte, Murphy, Phil, O'Leary, Nigel, Ransome, Paul (1999) *Women in senior management in Wales*, Equal Opportunities Commission: Cardiff.

Blumberg, Rae Lesser (1991) 'Income under female versus male control: hypotheses from the theory of gender stratification and data from the Third World' in R. L. Blumberg (ed) *Gender, family and economy: the triple overlap*, Sage: London, pp. 97–127.

—— (1995) 'Introduction: engendering wealth and well-being in an era of economic transformation' in R. L. Blumberg, C. A. Rakowski, I. Tinker and

M. Monteon (eds) *Engendering wealth and well-being*, Westview Press: Boulder, Col., pp. 1–14.

Bly, Robert (1990) *Iron John: a book about men*, Addison Wesley: Reading, Mass.

Bott, Elizabeth ([1957] 1971) *Family and social network*, 2nd edn., Tavistock Publications: London.

Bourdieu, Pierre (1977) *Outline of a theory of practice*, Cambridge University Press: Cambridge.

Bourque, Susan and Grossholz, Jean (1974) 'Politics an unnatural practice: political science looks at female participation', *Politics and society*, 4(2):225–66.

Boserup, Ester (1989) *Woman's role in economic development*, Earthscan: London.

Bowlby, John (1972 edn.) *Child care and the growth of love*, Penguin: Harmondsworth.

Bowles, Samuel and Gintis, Herbert (1976) *Schooling in capitalist America*, Routledge and Kegan Paul: London.

Bradby, Hannah (1999) 'Negotiating marriage: young Punjabi women's assessment of their individual and family interests' in R. Barot, H. Bradley and S. Fenton (eds) *Ethnicity, gender and social change*, Macmillan: Basingstoke, pp. 135–51.

Bradley, Harriet (1999) *Gender and power in the workplace*, Macmillan: Basingstoke.

Brannen, Julia and Moss, Peter (1991) *Managing mothers: dual earner households after maternity leave*, Unwin Hyman: London.

—— and Wilson, Gail (eds) (1987) *Give and take in families*, Allen & Unwin: London.

—— Moss, Peter, Owen, Charlie, and Wale, Chris (1998) *Mothers, fathers and employment*, Department for Education and Employment: London.

Brenner, Johanna and Ramas, Maria (1984) 'Rethinking women's oppression', *New Left Review*, 144:33–71.

Bristow, Stephen L. (1980) 'Women councillors—an explanation of the under-representation of women in local government', *Local government studies*, 6(3):73–90.

Brittan, Arthur (1989) *Masculinity and power*, Basil Blackwell: Oxford.

Brooks, Dennis (1975) *Black employment in the black country: a study of Walsall*, Runnymede Trust: London.

Brown, Callum G. (2001) *The death of Christian Britain*, Routledge: London.

Brown, Marie (1974) *Sweated labour: a study of homework*, Low Pay Unit: London.

Brownmiller, Susan (1986) *Against our will: men, women and rape*, Penguin: Harmondsworth.

Bruce, Judith and Dwyer, Daisy (1988) 'Introduction' in D. Dwyer and J. Bruce (eds) *A home divided: women and income in the third world*, Stanford University Press: Stanford, Calif., pp. 1–19.

Bruegel, Irene (1989) 'Sex and race in the labour market', *Feminist Review*, 32:49–68.

—— (1996) 'Whose myths are they anyway?: a comment', *British Journal of Sociology*, 47(1):175–7.

Bryan, Beverley, Dadzie, Stella, and Scafe, Suzanne (1985) *The heart of the race*, Virago: London.

Bryson, Valerie (1998) 'Citizen warriors, worker and mothers: women and democracy in Israel' in N. Charles and H. Hintjens (eds) *Gender, ethnicity and political ideologies*, Routledge: London, pp. 127–45.

Bujra, Janet (1986) ' "Urging women to redouble their efforts . . .": class, gender and capitalist transformation in Africa' in C. Robertson and I. Berger (eds) *Women and class in Africa*, Africana Publishing Company: New York, pp. 117–40.

Burghes, Louie, Clarke, Linda, and Cronin, Natalie (1997) *Fathers and fatherhood in Britain*, Family Policy Studies Centre: London.

Butler, Charlotte (1999) 'Cultural diversity and religious conformity: dimensions of social change among second-generation Muslim women' in R. Barot, H. Bradley, and S. Fenton (eds) *Ethnicity, gender and social change*, Macmillan: Basingstoke, pp. 135–51.

Butler, Judith (1990) *Gender trouble: feminism and the subversion of identity*, Routledge: New York.

Byrne, Eileen (1978) *Women and education*, Tavistock: London.

Cabinet Office (2000) *Women and men in the UK: facts and figures 2000*, The women's unit, Cabinet Office: London.

Campbell, Anne (1981) *Girl delinquents*, Basil Blackwell: Oxford.

Campbell, Beatrix (1980) 'Feminist sexual politics', *Feminist Review*, 5:1–18.

—— (1993) *Goliath: Britain's dangerous places*, Methuen: London.

Canaan, Joyce E. (1996) ' "One thing leads to another": drinking, fighting and working-class masculinities' in M. Mac an Ghaill (ed.) *Understanding maculinities*, Open University Press: Buckingham, pp. 114–25.

Caplan, Pat (1987) 'Introduction' in Pat Caplan (ed.) *The cultural construction of sexuality*, Tavistock: London, pp. 1–30.

Carrigan, Tim, Connell, Bob and Lee, John (1985) 'Toward a new theory of masculinity', *Theory and Society*, 14(5):551–604.

Cashmore, Ernest (1979) *Rastaman,* Allen & Unwin: London.

—— and Troyna, Barry (1982a) 'Black youth in crisis' in E. Cashmore and B. Troyna *Black youth in crisis*, George Allen & Unwin: London, pp. 15–34.

—— —— (eds) (1982b) *Black youth in crisis*, George Allen & Unwin: London.

Cavendish, Ruth (1982) *On the line*, Routledge and Kegan Paul: London.

Chapman, Rowena (1988) 'The great pretender: variations on the new man theme' in R. Chapman and J. Rutherford (eds) *Male order: unwrapping masculinity*, Lawrence and Wishart: London.

Charles, Nickie (1979) 'An analysis of the ideology of women's domestic role and its social effects in modern Britain', unpublished Ph.D. thesis, University of Keele.

—— (1983) 'Women and trade unions in the workplace' in Feminist Review (ed.): *Waged work: a reader*, Virago: London, pp. 160–85.

—— (1993) *Gender divisions and social change*, Harvester Wheatsheaf: Hemel Hempstead.

—— (1995) 'Feminist politics, domestic violence and the state', *Sociological Review*, 43(4):617–40.

—— (1996) 'Feminist practices: identity, difference, power' in N. Charles and F. Hughes-Freeland (eds) *Practising feminism: identity, difference, power*, Routledge: London, pp. 1–37.

—— (2000) *Feminism, the state and social policy*, Macmillan: Basingstoke.

—— and Davies, Charlotte Aull (2000) 'Cultural stereotypes and the gendering of senior management', *The Sociological Review*, 48(4):544–67.

—— and Hintjens, Helen (1998) 'Gender, ethnicity and cultural identity: women's "places"' in N. Charles and H. Hintjens (eds) *Gender, ethnicity and political ideologies*, Routledge: London, pp. 1–26.

—— and Kerr, Marion (1988) *Women, food and families*, Manchester University Press: Manchester.

Chodorow, Nancy (1978) *The reproduction of mothering*, University of California Press: Berkeley, Calif.

Clarke, Cheryl (1996) 'Lesbianism: an act of resistance' in Stevi Jackson and Sue Scott (eds) *Feminism and sexuality: a reader*, Edinburgh University Press: Edinburgh, pp. 155–61.

Clarke, John, Hall, Stuart, Jefferson, Tony, and Roberts, Brian (1976) 'Subcultures, cultures and class: a theoretical overview' in S. Hall and T. Jefferson (eds) *Resistance through rituals*, Hutchinson: London, pp. 9–74.

Clarricoates, Katherine (1980) 'The importance of being Ernest . . . Emma . . . Tom . . . Jane. The perception and categorization of gender conformity and gender deviation in primary schools' in Rosemary Deem (ed.) *Schooling for women's work*, Routledge and Kegan Paul: London, Boston, and Henley, pp. 26–41.

Cockburn, Cynthia (1977) 'When women get involved in community action' in M. Mayo (ed.) *Women in the community*, Routledge and Kegan Paul: London, pp. 61–70.

—— (1983) *Brothers*, Pluto Press: London.

—— (1987) *Two-track training: sex inequalities and the YTS*, Macmillan Education: Basingstoke.

—— (1991) *In the way of women*, Macmillan: Basingstoke.

Cohen, Albert (1955) *Delinquent boys: the culture of the gang*, The Free Press: Glencoe, Ill.

Cohen, Michele (1998) '"A habit of healthy idleness": boys' underachievement in historical perspective' in D. Epstein, J. Elswood, V. Hey, and J. Maw (eds) *Failing boys? Issues in gender and achievement*, Open University Press: Buckingham and Philadelphia, pp. 19–34.

Cohen, Phil (1997) *Rethinking the youth question*, Macmillan: Basingstoke.

Cohen, Stan (1980, first published 1972) *Folk devils and moral panics*, Martin Robertson: Oxford.

Coleman, David and Chandola, Tarani (1999) 'Britain's place in Europe's population' in S. McRae (ed.) *Changing Britain*, Oxford University Press: Oxford, pp. 37–67.

Collins, Patricia Hill (1991) 'Learning from the outsider within: the sociological significance of black feminist thought' in M. M. Fonow and J. A. Cook (eds) *Beyond methodology: feminist scholarship as lived research*, Indiana University Press: Indiana, pp. 35–59.

Coltrane, Scott (1995) 'The future of fatherhood: social, demographic, and economic influences on men's family involvements' in W. Marsiglio (ed.) *Fatherhood: contemporary theory, research, and social policy*, Sage: Thousand Oaks, Calif., pp. 255–74.

Comer, Lee (n.d.) *The myth of motherhood*, Spokesman pamphlet no. 21, The Bertrand Russell Peace Foundation: Nottingham.

Connell, R. W. (1987) *Gender and power*, Polity Press: Cambridge.

—— (1989) 'Cool guys, swots and wimps: the interplay of masculinity and education', *Oxford Review of Education*, 15(3):291–303.

—— (1993a) 'The big picture: masculinities in recent world history', *Theory and Society*, 22(5):597–623.

—— (ed.) (1993b) Special Issue of *Theory and Society* on Masculinities, 22(5).

—— (1995) *Masculinities*, Polity Press: Cambridge.

Coote, Anna (2000) 'Introduction' in A. Coote (ed.) *New gender agenda*, Institute for Public Policy Research: London, pp. 1–12.

Cornwall, Andrea and Lindisfarne, Nancy (eds) (1994) *Dislocating masculinity: comparative ethnographies*, Routledge: London and New York.

Corrigan, Paul (1976) 'Doing nothing' in Stuart Hall and Tony Jefferson (1976) *Resistance through rituals: youth subcultures in post-war Britain*, Hutchinson: London, pp. 103–5.

Cragg, Arnold and Dawson, Tim (1984) *Unemployed women: a study of attitudes and experiences*, Research paper no. 47, Department of Employment, HMSO: London.

Croll, Elizabeth (1981) 'Women in rural production and reproduction in the Soviet Union, China, Cuba and Tanzania: case studies', *Signs*, 7(2):375–99.

Crompton, Rosemary (1986) 'Women and the service class' in R. Crompton and M. Mann (eds) *Gender and stratification*, Polity Press: Cambridge, pp. 119–36.

—— (1997) *Women and work in modern Britain*, Oxford University Press: Oxford.

—— and Harris, Fiona (1998a) 'Explaining women's employment patterns: "orientations" to work revisited', *British Journal of Sociology*, 49(1):118–47.

—— —— (1998b) 'Gender relations and employment: the impact of occupation', *Work, Employment and Society*, 12(2):297–315.

Crowther, Geoffrey (1959) *15 to 18: a report of the central advisory council for education (England)*, vol. 1, HMSO: London.

Cucchiari, Salvatore (1981) 'The gender revolution and the transition from bisexual horde to patrilocal band: the origins of gender hierarchy' in S. B. Ortner and H. Whitehead (eds) *Sexual meanings: the cultural construction of gender and sexuality*, Cambridge University Press: Cambridge, pp. 31–79.

Dalton, Russell J. and Kuechler, Manfred (eds) (1990) *Challenging the political order*, Polity Press: Cambridge.

Darling, John and Glendinning, Anthony (1996) *Gender matters in schools*, Cassell: London and New York.

Dean, Malcolm (1994) 'No need for a man about the house', *Guardian*, 2 July 1994.

Deem, Rosemary (1978) *Women and schooling*, Routledge and Kegan Paul: London, Henley, and Boston.

Delphy, Christine (1984) *Close to home*, Hutchinson: London.

—— (1996) 'Rethinking sex and gender' in D. Leonard and L. Adkins (eds) *Sex in question: French materialist feminism*, Taylor & Francis: London, pp. 30–41.

—— and Leonard, Diana (1992) *Familiar exploitation: a new analysis of marriage in contemporary western societies*, Polity Press: Cambridge.

Dennis, Norman (1989) 'Sociology and the spirit of sixty-eight', *The British Journal of Sociology*, (40)3:418–41.

—— and Erdos, George (1993) *Families without fatherhood*, IEA Health and Welfare Unit: London.

—— Henriques, Fernando, and Slaughter, Clifford (1956) *Coal is our life*, Tavistock: London.

Dennison, Catherine and Coleman, John (2000) *Young people and gender: a review of research*, The women's unit, Cabinet Office and the family policy unit, the Home Office: London.

DeVault, Marjorie L. (1991) *Feeding the family: the social organization of caring as gendered work*, University of Chicago Press: Chicago and London.

Dex, Shirley and McCulloch, Andrew (1997) *Flexible employment in Britain: a statistical analysis*, Equal Opportunities Commission: Manchester.

Donaldson, Mike (1993) 'What is hegemonic masculinity?', *Theory and Society*, 22(5):643–57.

Downes, David (1999) 'Crime and deviance' in S. Taylor (ed.) *Sociology: issues and debates*, Macmillan: Basingstoke, pp. 231–52.

Doyal, Lesley (1981) *The political economy of health*, Pluto Press: London.

Duncan, Simon (1996) 'The diverse worlds of European patriarchy' in M. D Garcia-Ramon and J. Monk (eds) *Women of the European Union*, Routledge: London, pp. 74–110.

Duncombe, Jean and Marsden, Dennis (1993) 'Love and intimacy: the gender division of emotion and "emotion work" ', *Sociology*, 27(2):221–41.

—— —— (1995) ' "Workaholics" and "whingeing women": theorising intimacy and emotion work—the last frontier of gender inequality?', *Sociological Review*, 43(2):150–69.

—— —— (1996) 'Whose orgasm is this anyway? "Sex work" in long-term heterosexual couple relationships' in J. Weeks and J. Holland (eds) *Sexual cultures: communities, values and intimacy*, Explorations in sociology 48, BSA, Macmillan: Basingstoke, pp. 220–38.

Dunne, Gillian (1997) *Lesbian lifestyles: women's work and the politics of sexuality*, Macmillan: Basingstoke.

Dwyer, Daisy and Bruce, Judith (eds) (1988) *A home divided: women and income in the third world*, Stanford University Press: Stanford, Calif.

Dyer, Clare (1994) 'More lesbian parents win', *Guardian*, 6 July 1994.

Elson, Diane and Pearson, Ruth (1981) '"Nimble fingers make cheap workers": an analysis of women's employment in Third World export manufacturing', *Feminist Review*, 7:87–107.

—— —— (1984) 'The subordination of women and the internationalisation of factory production' in K. Young, C. Wolkowitz, and R. McCullagh (eds) *Of marriage and the market*, Routledge & Kegan Paul: London, pp. 18–40.

Engels, Frederick (1972) *The origin of the family, private property and the state*, Lawrence and Wishart: London.

England, Leonard (1950) 'A British sex survey', *The international journal of sociology*, Feb.

Epstein, Debbie (1998) 'Real boys don't work: "underachievement", masculinity and the harassment of "sissies"' in D. Epstein et al. (eds) *Failing boys? Issues in gender and achievement*, Open University Press: Buckingham and Philadelphia, pp. 96–108.

—— (ed.) (1994) *Challenging lesbian and gay inequalities in education*, Open University Press: Buckingham and Philadelphia.

—— and Johnson, Richard (1998) *Schooling sexualities*, Open University Press: Buckingham.

—— Elswood, Jannette, Hey, Valerie, Maw, Janet (1998) 'Schoolboy frictions: feminism and "failing" boys' in D. Epstein et al. (eds) *Failing boys? Issues in gender and achievement*, Open University Press: Buckingham and Philadelphia, pp. 3–18.

Eurobarometer (1993) *Europeans and the family*, Brussels.

Evans, Geoffrey and Norris, Pippa (eds) (1999) *Critical elections: British parties and voters in long-term perspective*, Sage: London.

Eyerman, Ron and Jamison, Andrew (1991) *Social movements: a cognitive approach*, Polity Press: Cambridge.

Featherstone, Mike (1995) *Undoing culture: globalization, postmodernism and identity*, Sage: London.

Feld, Val (2000) 'A new start in Wales: how devolution is making a difference' in A. Coote (ed.) *New gender agenda*, Institute for Public Policy Research: London, pp. 74–80.

Felstead, Alan and Jewson, Nick (eds) (1999) *Global trends in flexible labour*, Macmillan: Basingstoke.

—— —— (2000) *In work, at home: towards an understanding of homeworking*, Routledge: London and New York.

Ferri, Elsa and Smith, Kate (1996) *Parenting in the 1990s*, Joseph Rowntree Foundation: York.

Finch, Janet (1989) *Family obligation and social change*, Polity Press: Cambridge.

—— and Groves, Dulcie (eds) (1983) *A labour of love*, Routledge & Kegan Paul: London.

—— and Mason, Jennifer (1993) *Negotiating family responsibilities*, Tavistock/ Routledge: London and New York.

Foster, Peter, Gomm, Roger, and Hammersley, Martyn (1996) *Constructing educational inequality*, Social research and educational studies series 15, The Falmer Press: London and Washington DC.

Foucault, Michel (1981) *The history of sexuality*, vol. 1, Penguin Books: Harmondsworth.

Franklin, Jane (2000) 'After modernisation: gender, the third way and the new politics' in A. Coote (ed.) *New gender agenda*, Institute for Public Policy Research: London, pp. 15–22.

Frith, Simon (1984) *The sociology of youth*, Causeway Books: Ormskirk.

Fuller, Mary (1980) 'Black girls in a London comprehensive school' in R. Deem (ed.) *Schooling for women's work*, Routledge and Kegan Paul: London, Boston, and Henley, pp. 52–65.

Gagnon, John H. and Parker, Richard G. (1995) 'Conceiving sexualty' in R. G. Parker and J. H. Gagnon (eds) *Conceiving sexuality: approaches to sex research in a postmodern world*, Routledge: New York, pp. 3–16.

Gallagher, Ann (1977) 'Women and community work' in M. Mayo (ed.) *Women in the community*, Routledge & Kegan Paul: London, pp. 121–41.

Gershuny, Jonathan, Godwin, Michael, and Jones, Sally (1994) 'The domestic labour revolution: a process of lagged adaptation' in M. Anderson, F. Bechhofer, and J. Gershuny (eds) *The social and political economy of the household*, Oxford University Press: Oxford, pp. 151–97.

Giddens, Anthony (1992) *The transformation of intimacy: sexuality, love and eroticism in modern societies*, Polity Press: Cambridge.

Gilmore, David (1990) *Manhood in the making: cultural concepts of masculinity*, Yale University Press: New Haven and London.

Gilroy, Paul (1993) *Small acts*, Serpent's tail: London.

Ginn, Jay et al. (1996) 'Feminist fallacies: a reply to Hakim on women's employment', *British Journal of Sociology*, 47(1):167–74.

Gittins, Diana (1985) *The family in question*, Macmillan: Basingstoke.

Glucksmann, Miriam (1995) 'Why "work"? Gender and the "total social organization of labour"', *Gender, work and organization*, 2(2):63–75.

—— (1998) 'Retailing and shopworkers: filling the gap between production and consumption', paper presented to the Work, Employment and Society conference, September, Cambridge University.

—— (2000) *Cottons and Casuals: the gendered organisation of labour in time and space*, Sociology Press: Durham.

Goddard, Victoria (1987) 'Honour and shame: the control of women's sexuality and group identity in Naples' in P. Caplan (ed.) *The cultural construction of sexuality*, Tavistock: London, pp. 166–92.

Goldthorpe, John, Lockwood, David, Bechhofer, Frank, Platt, Jennifer (1968) *The affluent worker: political attitudes and behaviour*, Cambridge University Press: Cambridge.

—— —— —— —— (1969) *The affluent worker in the class structure*, Cambridge University Press: Cambridge.

Goot, Murray and Reid, Elizabeth (1975) *Women and voting studies: mindless matrons or sexist scientism?*, Contemporary political sociology series, 1(6), Sage professional paper, London.

Gorard, Stephen, Rees, Gareth, Salisbury, Jane (1999) 'Reappraising the apparent underachievement of boys at school', *Gender and Education*, 11(4):441–54.

Gottfried, Heidi (1998) 'Beyond Patriarchy? Theorising gender and class', *Sociology*, 32(3):451–68.

Graham, Hilary (1984) *Women, health and the family*, Wheatsheaf Books: Brighton.

—— (1991) 'The concept of caring in social research', *Sociology*, 25(1):61–78.

Green, Eileen, Hebron, Sandra, and Woodward, Diana (1990) *Women's leisure, what leisure?*, Macmillan: Basingstoke.

Gregson, Nicky and Lowe, Michelle (1994) *Servicing the middle classes: class, gender and waged domestic labour in contemporary Britain*, Routledge: London and New York.

Griffin, Christine (1985) *Typical girls? Young women from school to the job market*, Routledge & Kegan Paul: London and New York.

—— (1996) 'Experiencing power: dimensions of gender, "race" and class' in N. Charles and F. Hughes-Freeland (eds) *Practising feminism: identity, difference, power*, Routledge: London, pp. 180–201.

Grimshaw, Damian and Rubery, Jill (2001) *The gender pay gap: a research review*, Equal Opportunities Commission: Manchester.

Guardian newspaper.

Hacker, Helen Mayer (1957) 'The new burdens of masculinity', *Marriage and Family Living*, 19 August: 227–33.

Hakim, Catherine (1987a) *Home-based work in Britain: a report on the 1981 national homeworking survey and the DE research programme on homework*, Research paper no. 60, Department of Employment: London.

—— (1987b) 'Homeworking in Britain: key findings from the national survey of home-based workers', *Employment Gazette*, 95(2):92–104.

—— (1995) 'Five feminist myths about women's employment', *British Journal of Sociology*, 1995:429–455.

Halford, Susan, Savage, Michael, and Witz, Ann (1997) *Gender, careers and organisations*, Macmillan: Basingstoke.

Hall, Stuart and Jefferson, Tony (1976) *Resistance through rituals: youth subcultures in post-war Britain*, Hutchinson: London.

—— Critcher, Chas, Jefferson, Tony, Clarke, John, Roberts, Brian (1978) *Policing the crisis: mugging, the state and law and order*, Macmillan: London.

Halsey, A. H., Heath, A. F., Ridge, J. M. (1980) *Origins and destinations: family, class, and education in modern Britain*, Clarendon Press: Oxford.

Hanmer, Jalna and Maynard, Mary (eds) (1987) *Women, violence and social control*, Explorations in sociology 23, BSA, Macmillan: Basingstoke.

Haraway, Donna (1988) 'Situated knowledges: the science question in feminism and the privilege of partial perspective', *Feminist Studies*, 14(3):575–99.

Harding, Sandra (1986) *The science question in feminism*, Open University Press: Milton Keynes.

Hargreaves, David (1967) *Social relations in a secondary school*, Routledge and Kegan Paul: London.

Harley, Sharon (1997) 'Speaking up: the politics of black women's labor history' in E. Higginbotham and M. Romero (eds) *Women and work: exploring race, ethnicity, and class*, vol. 6, Women and Work, Sage: Thousand Oaks, Calif., London, New Delhi, pp. 28–51.

Harris, C. C. (ed.) (1979) *The sociology of the family: new directions for Britain*, Sociological Review monograph 28, University of Keele: Keele.

—— (1983a) *The family and industrial society*, George Allen & Unwin: London.

—— (1983b) 'Introduction to the abridged edition' in C. Rosser and C. C. Harris *The family and social change*, student edition, Routledge and Kegan Paul: London, pp. xi–xviii.

Hart P. E. (1988) *Youth unemployment in Great Britain*, Cambridge University Press: Cambridge.

Hartmann, Heidi (1986) 'The unhappy marriage of Marxism and feminism: towards a more progressive union' in L. Sargent (ed.) *The unhappy marriage of Marxism and feminism*, Pluto: London, pp. 1–41.

Hartsock, Nancy (1990) 'Foucault on power: a theory for women?' in L. J. Nicholson (ed.) *Feminism/postmodernism*, Routledge: London, pp. 157–75.

Harvey, Penelope and Gow, Peter (eds) (1994) *Sex and violence*, Routledge: London.

Haug, Frigga (ed.) (1983) *Female sexualization*, Verso: London.

Hearn, Jeff (1996) 'Is masculinity dead? A critique of the concept of masculinity/masculinities' in Mairtin Mac an Ghaill (ed.) *Understanding masculinities*, Open University Press: Buckingham and Philadelphia, pp. 202–17.

Hebdige, Dick (1979) *Subculture: the meaning of style*, Methuen: London and New York.

Helie-Lucas, Marie-Aimee (1994) 'The preferential symbol for Islamic identity: women in Muslim Personal Laws' in V. M. Moghadam (ed.) *Identity politics and women: cultural reassertions and feminisms in international perspective*, Westview: Boulder, Col., pp. 391–407.

Henwood, Melanie, Rimmer, Lesley, and Wicks, Malcolm (1987) *Inside the family: changing roles of men and women*, Family Policy Studies Centre: London.

Hester, Marianne and Harne, Lynne (1999) 'Fatherhood, children and violence: placing the UK in an international context' in S. Watson and L. Doyal (eds) *Engendering social policy*, Open University Press: Buckingham, pp. 148–64.

Higginbotham, Elizabeth (1997) 'Introduction' in E. Higginbotham and M. Romero (eds) *Women and work: exploring race, ethnicity, and class*, vol. 6, Women and Work, Sage: Thousand Oaks, Calif., London, New Delhi, pp. xv–xxxii.

Hills, Jill (1981) 'Britain' in J. Lovenduski and J. Hills (eds) *The politics of the second electorate*, Routledge and Kegan Paul: London, pp. 8–32.

Holland, Janet, Ramazanoglu, Caroline, Sharpe, Sue, and Thomson, Rachel (1991) *Pressure, resistance, empowerment: young women and the negotiation of safer sex*, Tufnell Press: London.

Holland, Janet, Ramazanoglu, Caroline, Sharpe, Sue (1993) *Wimp or gladiator: Contradictions in the acquisition of masculine sexuality*, Tufnell Press: London.

—— —— —— (1994) 'Power and desire: the embodiment of female sexuality', *Feminist Review*, 46:21–38.

—— —— —— and Thomson, Rachel (1996a) 'Reputations: journeying into gendered power relations' in J. Weeks and J. Holland (eds) *Sexual cultures: communities, values and intimacy*, Explorations in sociology 48, BSA, Macmillan: Basingstoke, pp. 239–260.

—— —— and Thomson, Rachel (1996b) 'In the same boat? The gendered (in)experience of first heterosex' in Diane Richardson (ed.) *Theorising heterosexuality*, Open University Press: Buckingham, pp. 143–60.

hooks, bell (1996) 'Continued devaluation of black womanhood' in S. Jackson and S. Scott (eds) *Feminism and sexuality: a reader*, Edinburgh University Press: Edinburgh, pp. 216–23.

Humphries, Jane (1977) 'Class struggle and the persistence of the working-class family', *Cambridge Journal of Economics*, 1:241–58.

Hunt, Audrey (1968) *A survey of women's employment*, Government Social Survey, HMSO: London.

Hunt, Pauline (1980) *Gender and class consciousness*, Macmillan: Basingstoke.

ILEA [Inner London Education Authority] (1987) *Ethnic background and examination results*, Research and statistics (ILEA/RS/1120/87): London.

Independent on Sunday newspaper.

Inglehart, Ronald (1990) *Culture shift in advanced society*, Princeton University Press: Princeton, N.J.

Jackson, Brian and Marsden, Dennis (1986, first published 1962) *Education and the working class*, Ark Paperbacks: London and New York.

Jackson, Margaret (1987) '"Facts of life" or the eroticization of women's oppression? Sexology and the social construction of heterosexuality' in Pat Caplan (ed.) *The cultural construction of sexuality*, Tavistock: London, pp. 52–81.

Jackson, Stevi (1993) 'Even sociologists fall in love: an exploration in the sociology of emotions', *Sociology* 27(2):201–20.

—— (1996) 'Heterosexuality and feminist theory' in Diane Richardson (ed.) *Theorising heterosexuality*, Open University Press: Buckingham, pp. 21–38.

—— (1999) *Heterosexuality in question*, Sage: London.

—— and Scott, Sue (1996) 'Sexual skirmishes and feminist factions: twenty-five years of debate on women and sexuality' in S. Jackson and S. Scott (eds) *Feminism and sexuality: a reader*, Edinburgh University Press: Edinburgh, pp. 1–31.

Jamieson, Lynn (1998) *Intimacy: personal relationships in modern societies*, Polity Press: Cambridge.

—— (1999) 'Intimacy transformed? A critical look at the "pure relationship"', *Sociology*, 33(3):477–94.

Jayawardena, Kumari (1986) *Feminism and nationalism in the Third world*, Zed Press: London.

Jeffreys, Sheila (1996) 'Heterosexuality and the desire for gender' in Diane Richardson (ed.) *Theorising heterosexuality*, Open University Press: Buckingham, pp. 75–90.

Jenkins, J. Craig (1995) 'Social movements, political representation, and the state: an agenda and comparative framework' in J. C. Jenkins and B. Klandermans (eds) *The politics of social protest: comparative perspectives on states and social movements*, UCL Press: London, pp. 14–35.

Jephcott, Pearl, Seear, Nancy, and Smith, John H. (1962) *Married women working*, Allen & Unwin: London.

Jones, Stephanie (1997) 'Still a mining community', unpublished Ph.D. thesis, University of Wales Swansea.

Josephides, Sasha (1988) 'Honour, family, and work: Greek Cypriot women before and after migration' in S. Westwood and P. Bhachu (eds) *Enterprising women: ethnicity, economy and gender relations*, Routledge: London and New York, pp. 34–57.

Kabeer, Naila (2000) *The power to choose*, Verso: London.

Kandiyoti, Deniz (1991) 'Introduction' in *Women, Islam and the state*, Macmillan: London, pp. 1–21.

Kelly, Liz (1988) *Surviving sexual violence*, Polity Press: Cambridge.

Kempadoo, Kemala and Doezema, Jo (eds) (1998) *Global sex workers*, Routledge: London and New York.

Kiernan, Kathleen, Land, Hilary, and Lewis, Jane (1998) *Lone motherhood in twentieth-century Britain*, Clarendon Press: Oxford.

Kimmel, Michael (1990) 'After fifteen years: the impact of the sociology of masculinity on the masculinity of sociology' in J. Hearn and D. Morgan (eds) *Men, masculinities and social theory*, Unwin Hyman: London, pp. 93–109.

King, Ronald (1971) 'Unequal access in education—sex and social class', *Social and Economic Administration*, 5:167–75.

Kofman, Eleonore (1998) 'When society was simple: gender and ethnic divisions and the Far and New Right in France' in N. Charles and H. Hintjens (eds) *Gender, ethnicity and political ideologies*, Routledge: London, pp. 91–106.

Lacey, Colin (1970) *Hightown grammar: the school as a social system*, Manchester University Press: Manchester.

Lambart, Audrey M. (1976) 'The sisterhood' in M. Hammersley and P. Woods (eds) *The process of schooling: a sociological reader*, Routledge and Kegan Paul: London and Henley, in asssociation with The Open University Press, pp. 152–9.

Lancaster, Roger N. (1995) ' "That we should all turn queer?": homosexual stigma in the making of manhood and the breaking of a revolution in Nicaragua' in R. G. Parker and J. H. Gagnon (eds) *Conceiving sexuality: approaches to sex research in a postmodern world*, Routledge: New York, pp. 135–56.

Land, Hilary (1994) 'The demise of the male breadwinner—in practice but not in theory: a challenge for social security systems' in S. Baldwin and J. Falkingham (eds) *Social security and social change: new challenges to the Beveridge model*, Harvester Wheatsheaf: London, pp. 100–15.

Land, Hilary (1999) 'The changing worlds of work and families' in S. Watson and L. Doyal (eds) *Engendering social policy*, Open University Press: Buckingham, pp. 12–29.

Lees, Sue (1986) *Losing out: sexuality and adolescent girls*, Hutchinson: London.

Leira, Arnlaug (1998) 'The modernisation of motherhood' in E. Drew, R. Emerek, and E. Mahon (eds) *Women, work and the family in Europe*, Routledge: London and New York, pp. 159–69.

Lewis, Charlie (1986) *Becoming a father*, Open University Press: Milton Keynes and Philadelphia.

Lewis, Jane (1992) *Women in Britain since 1945*, Blackwell: Oxford.

—— (1993) 'Introduction: Women, work, family and social policies in Europe' in J. Lewis (ed.) *Women and social policies in Europe*, Edward Elgar: Aldershot, pp. 1–24.

Liddle, Joanna and Michielsens, Elisabeth (2000) 'Gender, class and political power in Britain' in S. M. Rai (ed.) *International perspectives on gender and democratisation*, Macmillan: Basingstoke.

Lie, John (1996) 'From agrarian patriarchy to patriarchal capitalism: gendered capitalist industrialization in Korea' in V. M. Moghadam (ed.) *Patriarchy and economic development*, Clarendon Press: Oxford, pp. 34–79.

Lim, Linda (1983) 'Capitalism, imperialism and patriarchy: the dilemma of Third World women workers in multinational factories' in J. Nash and M. P. Fernandez-Kelly (eds) *Women, men and the international division of labour*, State University of New York Press: Albany, pp. 70–91.

Llewellyn, Mandy (1980) 'Studying girls at school: the implications of confusion' in R. Deem (ed) *Schooling for women's work*, Routledge and Kegan Paul: London, Boston, and Henley, pp. 42–51.

Lovenduski, Joni (1986) *Women and European politics: contemporary feminism and public policy*, Wheatsheaf Books: Brighton.

—— (1996) 'Sex, gender and British politics' in J. Lovenduski and P. Norris (eds) *Women in politics*, Oxford University Press in association with the Hansard Society: Oxford, pp. 3–18.

—— (1999) 'Sexing political behaviour in Britain' in S. Walby (ed.) *New agendas for women*, Macmillan: Basingstoke, pp. 190–209.

—— and Hills, Jill (1981) 'Introduction' in J. Lovenduski and J. Hills (eds) *The politics of the second electorate*, Routledge and Kegan Paul: London, pp. 1–7.

—— and Randall, Vicky (1993) *Contemporary feminist politics: women and power in Britain*, Oxford University Press: Oxford.

Lowe, Nigel V. (1982) 'The legal status of fathers: past and present' in L. McKee and M. O'Brien (eds) *The father figure*, Tavistock Publications: London, pp. 26–42.

Lummis, Trevor (1982) 'The historical dimension of fatherhood: a case study 1890–1914' in L. McKee and M. O'Brien (eds) *The father figure*, Tavistock Publications: London, pp. 43–56.

Lupton, Deborah and Barclay, Lesley (1997) *Constructing fatherhood: discourses and experiences*, Sage: London.

Mac an Ghaill, Mairtin (1988) *Young, gifted and black*, Open Univerity Press: Milton Keynes.

—— (1994) *The making of men: masculinities, sexualities and schooling*, Open University Press: Buckingham and Philadelphia.

—— (1996) 'Irish masculinities and sexualities in England' in Lisa Adkins and Vicki Merchant (eds) *Sexualizing the social: power and the organization of sexuality*, Explorations in sociology 47, BSA, Macmillan: Basingstoke.

MacCormack, Carol P., and Strathern, Marilyn (eds) (1980) *Nature, culture and gender*, Cambridge University Press: Cambridge.

MacDonald, Madeleine (1980) 'Socio-cultural reproduction and women's education' in R. Deem (ed.) *Schooling for women's work*, Routledge and Kegan Paul: London, Boston, and Henley, pp. 13–25.

MacInnes, John (1998) *The end of masculinity*, Open University Press: Buckingham and Philadelphia.

MacIntyre, Sally (1977) *Single and pregnant*, Croom Helm: London.

Mansfield, Penny and Collard, Jean (1988) *The beginning of the rest of your life?: a portrait of newly-wed marriage*, Macmillan: Basingstoke.

Marshall, Gordon, Rose, David, Newby, Howard, and Vogler, Carolyn (1989) *Social class in modern Britain*, Unwin Hyman: London.

Martin, Jean and Roberts, Ceridwen (1984) *Women and employment: a lifetime perspective*, Department of Employment/OPCS: London.

Martino, Wayne (1999) ' "Cool boys", "party animals", "squids" and "poofters": interrogating the dynamics and politics of adolescent masculinities in school', *British Journal of Sociology*, 20(2):239–63.

Maynard, Mary (1990) 'The re-shaping of sociology? Trends in the study of gender', *Sociology*, 24(2):269–90.

Mayo, Marjorie (1977) 'Introduction' in M. Mayo (ed.) *Women in the community*, Routledge and Kegan Paul: London, pp. ix–xiii.

McCall, Leslie (1992) 'Does gender *fit*? Bourdieu, feminism, and conceptions of social order', *Theory and Society* 21:837–67.

McIntosh, Mary (1968) 'The homosexual role', *Social Problems*, 16(2):182–92.

McKee, Lorna (1982) 'Fathers' participation in infant care: a critique' in L. McKee and M. O'Brien (eds) *The father figure*, Tavistock Publications: London, pp. 120–38.

—— and O'Brien, Margaret (1982) 'The father figure: some current orientations and historical perspectives' in L. McKee and M. O'Brien (eds) *The father figure*, Tavistock Publications: London, pp. 1–25.

McMahon, Anthony (1993) 'Male readings of feminist theory: the psychologization of sexual politics in the masculinity literature', *Theory and Society*, 22(5):675–95.

McMahon, Patrice C. (1994) 'The effect of economic and political reforms on Soviet/Russian women' in N. Aslanbeigui, S. Pressman, and G. Summerfield (eds) *Women in the age of economic transformation*, Routledge: London, pp. 59–73.

McRae, Susan (1999a) 'Introduction: family and household change' in S. McRae (ed.) *Changing Britain*, Oxford University Press: Oxford, pp. 1–33.

McRae, Susan (ed.) (1999b) *Changing Britain*, Oxford University Press: Oxford.

McRobbie, Angela (1991) *Feminism and youth culture*, Macmillan: Basingstoke.

—— and Garber, Jenny (1991, first published 1978) 'Girls and subcultures' in Angela McRobbie (1991) *Feminism and youth culture*, Macmillan: Basingstoke.

Mencher, Joan P. (1988) 'Women's work and poverty: women's contribution to household maintenance in south India' in D. Dwyer and J. Bruce (eds) *A home divided: women and income in the third world*, Stanford University Press: Stanford, Calif., pp. 99–119.

Messner, Michael A. (1993) ' "Changing men" and feminist politics in the United States', *Theory and Society*, 22(5):723–37.

Mies, Maria (1986) *Patriarchy and accumulation on a world scale*, Zed Press: London.

Miller, Walter B. (1958) 'Lower class culture as a generating milieu of gang delinquency', *Journal of Social Issues*, 14(3):5–19.

Millett, Kate (1974) *Sexual politics*, Abacus: London.

Mirza, Heidi Safia (1992) *Young, female and black*, Routledge: London and New York.

Mitchell, Juliet (1974) *Psychoanalysis and feminism*, Allen Lane: London.

Modood, Tariq, Berthoud, Richard, et al. (1997) *Ethnic minorities in Britain: diversity and disadvantage*, The fourth national survey of ethnic minorities, Policy Studies Institute: London.

Moghadam, Valentine M. (1994) 'Introduction: women and identity politics in theoretical and comparative perspective' in V. M. Moghadam (ed.) *Identity politics and women: cultural reassertions and feminisms in international perspective*, Westview Press: Boulder, Col., pp. 3–26.

—— (1995) 'Gender dynamics of restructuring in the semiperiphery' in R. L. Blumberg, C. A. Rakowski, I. Tinker and M. Monteon (eds) *Engendering wealth and well-being*, Westview Press: Boulder, Col., pp. 17–37.

—— (1996) 'Introduction and overview' in V. M. Moghadam (ed.) *Patriarchy and economic development*, Clarendon Press: Oxford, pp. 1–15.

Moi, Toril (1991) 'Appropriating Bourdieu: feminist theory and Pierre Bourdieu's sociology of culture', *New Literary History*, 22:1017–49.

Monk, Janice and Garcia-Ramon, Maria Dolors (1996) 'Placing women of the European Union' in M. D. Garcia-Ramon and J. Monk (eds) *Women of the European Union*, Routledge: London, pp. 1–30.

Morgan, David (1979) 'New directions in family research and theory' in C. C. Harris (ed.) *The sociology of the family: new directions for Britain*, Sociological Review monograph 28, University of Keele: Keele, pp. 3–18.

—— (1996) *Family connections*, Polity Press: Oxford.

Morris, Jenny (1991) *Pride against prejudice: a personal politics of disability*, The Women's Press: London.

Morris, Lydia (1990) *The workings of the household*, Polity Press: Cambridge.

Mort, Frank (1996) *Cultures of Consumption: masculinities and social space in late 20th century Britain*, Routledge: London and New York.

Mosley, Jane and Thomson, Elizabeth (1995) 'Fathering behavior and child outcomes: the role of race and poverty' in W. Marsiglio (ed.) *Fatherhood: contemporary theory, research, and social policy*, Sage: Thousand Oaks, Calif., pp. 148–65.

Muncie, John (1984) *'The trouble with kids today': youth and crime in post-war Britain*, Hutchinson: London.

—— (1999) *Youth and crime: a critical introduction*, Sage: London.

Murphy, Patricia and Elwood, Jannette (1998) 'Gendered learning outside and inside school: influences on achievement' in Debbie Epstein et al. (eds) *Failing boys? Issues in gender and achievement*, Open University Press: Buckingham and Philadelphia, pp. 162–81.

Murray, Charles (1990) *The emerging British underclass*, Institute of Economic Affairs: London.

Myrdal, Alva and Klein, Viola (1956) *Women's two roles: home and work*, Routledge and Kegan Paul: London.

Neale, Bren and Smart, Carol (1997) 'Experiments with parenthood?', *Sociology*, 31(2):201–91.

Nelson, Barbara J. and Chowdhury, Najma (eds) (1994) *Women and politics worldwide*, Yale University Press: New Haven and London.

Newsom, John (1963) *Half our Future: a Report of the Central Advisory Council for Education (England)*, HMSO: London.

Newson, John and Newson, Elizabeth (1965, first published 1963) *Patterns of infant care in an urban community*, Penguin Books: Harmondsworth.

Norris, Pippa (1996) 'Women politicians: transforming Westminster?' in J. Lovenduski and P. Norris (eds) *Women in politics*, Oxford University Press in association with the Hansard Society: Oxford, pp. 91–104.

—— (1997) *Electoral change since 1945*, Blackwell: Oxford.

—— (1999) 'Gender: a gender-generation gap?' in G. Evans and P. Norris (eds) *Critical elections: British parties and voters in long-term perspective*, Sage: London, pp. 148–80.

—— and Lovenduski, Joni (1993) 'Gender and party politics in Britain' in J. Lovenduski and P. Norris (eds) *Gender and party politics*, Sage: London, pp. 35–59.

—— —— (1995) *Political recruitment: gender, race and class in the British Parliament*, Cambridge University Press: Cambridge.

Norwood, Cyril (1943) *Curriculum and examinations in secondary schools*, Report of the Committee of the Secondary School Examinations Council Appointed by the President of the Board of Education in 1941, HMSO: London.

Oakley, Ann (1972) *Sex, gender and society*, Temple Smith: London.

—— (1974) *The sociology of housework*, Martin Robertson: London.

—— (1981) *From here to maternity: becoming a mother*, Penguin Books: Harmondsworth.

—— (1989) 'Women's studies in British sociology: to end at our beginning?', *British Journal of Sociology*, (40)3:442–470.

O'Connor, Pat (1995) 'Understanding variation in marital sexual pleasure: an impossible task?', *Sociological Review*, 43(1):342–62.

O'Donnell, Mike and Sharpe, Sue (2000) *Uncertain masculinities: youth, ethnicity and class in contemporary Britian*, Routledge: London and New York.

Oerton, Sarah (1997) ' "Queer housewives?": some problems in theorising the division of domestic labour in lesbian and gay households', *Women's Studies International Forum*, 20(3):421–30.

Offe, Claus (1985) 'New social movements: challenging the boundaries of institutional politics', *Social Research*, 52(4):817–68.

Ong, Aihwa (1990) 'Japanese factories, Malay workers: class and sexual metaphors in West Malaysia' in J. M. Atkinson and S. Errington (eds) *Power and difference: gender in island South East Asia*, Stanford University Press: Stanford, Calif., pp. 385–422.

ONS (2001) *Social Trends*, 2001 edn., no. 31, The Stationery Office: London.

Ortner, Sherry B. (1974) 'Is female to male as nature is to culture?' in M. Z. Rosaldo and L. Lamphere (eds) *Woman, culture and society*, Stanford University Press: Stanford, Calif., pp. 67–88.

Pahl, Jan (1989) *Money and marriage*, Macmillan: Basingstoke.

Pahl, Ray (1984) *Divisions of labour*, Basil Blackwell: Oxford.

Paechter, Carrie (1998) *Education the other: gender, power and schooling*, The Falmer Press: London and Washington, DC.

Parsons, Talcott and Bales, Robert F. (1955) *Family, socialization and interaction process*, Free Press: Glencoe, Ill.

Paterson, Sheila (1963) *Dark strangers*, Tavistock Publications: London.

—— (1968) *Immigrants in industry*, Oxford University Press: London.

Pearson, Ruth (2000) 'Moving the goalposts: gender and globalisation in the twenty-first century', *Gender and Development*, 8(1):10–19.

Perrigo, Sarah (1996) 'Women and change in the Labour Party 1979–1995' in J. Lovenduski and P. Norris (eds) *Women in politics*, Oxford University Press in association with the Hansard Society: Oxford, pp. 118–31.

Peterson, V. Spike and Runyan, Anne Sisson (1993) *Global gender issues*, Westview Press: Boulder, Col.

Pettman, Jan Jindy (1996) 'An international political economy of sex?' in E. Kofman and G. Youngs (eds) *Globalization: theory and practice*, Pinter: London, pp. 191–208.

Phillips, Ann (1991) *Engendering democracy*, Polity Press: Cambridge.

Phizacklea, Annie (1983) 'In the frontline' in A. Phizacklea (ed.) *One way ticket: migration and female labour*, Routledge and Kegan Paul: London.

—— (1988) 'Entrepreneurship, ethnicity, and gender' in S. Westwood and P. Bhachu (eds) *Enterprising women: ethnicity, economy and gender relations*, Routledge: London and New York, pp. 20–33.

—— (1990) *Unpacking the fashion industry: gender, racism and class in production*, Routledge: London.

—— (1999) 'Gender and transnational labour migration' in R. Barot, H. Bradley and S. Fenton (eds) *Ethnicity, gender and social change*, Macmillan: Basingstoke and St Martin's Press, Inc: New York.

—— and Wolkowitz, Carol (1995) *Homeworking women: gender, racism and class at work*, Sage: London, Thousand Oaks, Calif., New Delhi.

Phoenix, Ann (1988) 'Narrow definitions of culture: the case of early motherhood' in S. Westwood and P. Bhachu (eds) *Enterprising women: ethnicity, economy and gender relations*, Routledge: London and New York, pp. 153–76.

Piachaud, David (1984) *Round about 50 hours a week*, Child Poverty Action Group: London.

Pilcher, Jane (1999) *Women in contemporary Britain*, Routledge: London and New York.

Pollert, Anna (1981) *Girls, wives factory lives*, Macmillan: Basingstoke.

—— (1996) 'Gender and class revisited; or, the poverty of "patriarchy"', *Sociology*, 30(4):639–59.

Preston, Peter (2000) 'My daughter is just fine', *Guardian*, 31 January 2000.

Pringle, Rosemary (1989) *Secretaries talk*, Verso: London.

Pryce, Ken (1986, first edition 1979) *Endless pressure*, Bristol Classical Press: Bristol.

Ramazanoglu, Caroline (ed.) (1993) *Up against Foucault*, Routledge: London.

—— and Holland, Janet (1993) 'Women's sexuality and men's appropriation of desire' in C. Ramazanoglu (ed.) *Up against Foucault*, Routledge: London, pp. 239–64.

Randall, Vicky (1987) *Women and politics*, 2nd edn., Macmillan Education: Basingstoke.

Raphael Reed, Lynn (1999) 'Troubling boys and disturbing discourses on masculinity and schooling: a feminist exploration of current debates and interventions concerning boys in school', *Gender and Education*, 11(1):93–110.

Rapoport, Rhona, Rapoport, Robert N., Strelitz, Ziona, with Kew, Stephen (1977) *Fathers, mothers and others*, Routledge and Kegan Paul: London and Henley.

Rees, Teresa (1992) *Women and the labour market*, Routledge: London.

—— (1999) *Women and work: 25 years of equality legislation in Wales*, University of Wales Press: Cardiff.

Rex, John (1982) 'West Indian and Asian youth' in E. Cashmore and B. Troyna (eds) *Black youth in crisis*, George Allen & Unwin: London, pp. 53–71.

Reynolds, David and Sullivan, Michael (1987) *The comprehensive experiment*, Falmer Press: London.

Rich, Adrienne (1980) 'Compulsory heterosexuality and lesbian existence', *Signs*, 5(4):631–60.

Richards, Martin P. M. (1982) 'How should we approach the study of fathers?' in L. McKee and M. O'Brien (eds) *The father figure*, Tavistock Publications: London, pp. 57–71.

Richardson, Diane (1993) *Women, motherhood and childrearing*, Macmillan: Basingstoke.

Riddell, Sheila (1992) *Gender and the politics of the curriculum*, Routledge: London and New York.

—— (1998) 'Boys and underachievement: the Scottish dimension', *International Journal of Inclusive Education*, 2(2):169–86.

Robertson, Roland (1992) *Globalization: social theory and global culture*, Sage: London.

Rogers, Marigold (1994) 'Growing up lesbian: the role of the school' in D. Epstein (ed.) *Challenging lesbian and gay inequalities in education*, Open University Press: Buckingham and Philadelphia, pp. 31–48.

Rosaldo, Michelle Z. (1974) 'Woman, culture and society: a theoretical overview' in M. Z. Rosaldo and L. Lamphere (eds) *Woman, culture and society*, Stanford University Press: Stanford, Calif., pp. 17–42.

Rose, Hilary (1994) 'Gay brains, gay genes and feminist science theory' in J. Weeks and J. Holland (eds) *Sexual cultures: communities, values and intimacy*, explorations in sociology 48, BSA, Macmillan: Basingstoke, pp. 53–72.

Roseneil, Sasha (1995a) *Disarming patriarchy: feminism and political action at Greenham*, Open University Press: Milton Keynes.

—— (1995b) 'The coming of age of feminist sociology: some issues of practice and theory for the next twenty years', *British Journal of Sociology*, 46(2):191–205.

Rosser, Colin and Harris, C. C. (1983, first published 1965) *The family and social change*, Routledge and Kegan Paul: London.

Rubin, Gayle (1975) 'The traffic in women: notes on the "political economy" of sex' in R. R. Reiter (ed.) *Toward an anthropology of women*, Monthly Review Press: New York, pp. 157–210.

Rudolph, Hedwig, Appelbaum, Eileen, and Maier, Friederike (1994) 'Beyond socialism: the uncertain prospects for East German women in a unifed Germany' in N. Aslanbeigui, S. Pressman and G. Summerfield (eds) *Women in the age of economic transformation*, Routledge: London, pp. 11–26.

Runyan, Anne Sisson (1996) 'The places of women in trading places: gendered, global/regional regimes and internationalized feminist resistance' in E. Kofman and G. Youngs (eds) *Globalization: theory and practice*, Pinter: London, pp. 238–52.

Rutter, Michael, Giller, Henri, and Hagell, Ann (1998) *Antisocial behaviour by young people*, Cambridge University Press: Cambridge.

Safa, Helen I. (1990) 'Women's social movements in Latin America', *Gender and society*, 4(3):354–69.

Saggar, Shamit and Heath, Anthony (1999) 'Race: towards a multicultural electorate?' in G. Evans and P. Norris (eds) *Critical elections: British parties and voters in long-term perspective*, Sage: London, pp. 102–23.

Saifullah Khan, Verity (1979) 'Work and network: South Asian women in South London' in S. Harding (ed.) *Ethnicity at Work*, Macmillan: London and Basingstoke, pp. 115–33.

Savage, Mike (1992) 'Women's expertise, men's authority: gendered organizations and the contemporary middle class' in M. Savage and A. Witz (eds) *Gender and bureaucracy*, Blackwell/The Sociological Review: Oxford, pp. 124–51.

Sayers, Janet (1982) *Biological politics*, Tavistock Publications: London and New York.

Schmude, Jurgen (1996) 'Contrasting developments in female labour force participation in East and West Germany since 1945' in M. D. Garcia-Ramon and J. Monk (eds) *Women of the European Union*, Routledge: London, pp. 156–85.

Scott, Alan (1997) 'Introduction' in A. Scott (ed.) *The limits of globalization*, Routledge: London.

Scott, Alison McEwen (1994) 'Gender segregation and the SCELI research' in A. M. Scott (ed.) *Gender segregation and social change*, Oxford University Press: Oxford, pp. 1–38.

Scott, Jacqueline, Alwin, Duane F., and Braun, Michael (1996) 'Generational changes in gender-role attitudes: Britain in a cross-national perspective', *Sociology*, 30(3):471–92.

—— Braun, Michael, and Alwin, Duane (1993) 'The family way' in R. Jowell, L. Brook, L. Dowds, and D. Ahrendt (eds) *International Social Attitudes*, the 10th BSA report, SPCR, Dartmouth: Aldershot, pp. 23–4.

Seccombe, Wally (1993) *Weathering the storm: working-class families from the industrial revolution to the fertility decline*, Verso: London, New York.

Segal, Lynne (1987) *Is the future female?*, Verso: London.

—— (1990) *Slow motion: changing masculinities, changing men*, Virago: London.

—— (1993) 'Changing men: masculinities in context', *Theory and Society*, 22(5): 625–41.

—— (1997) 'Feminist sexual politics and the heterosexual predicament' in L. Segal (ed.) *New sexual agendas*, Macmillan: Basingstoke, pp 77–89.

Sewell, Tony (1998) 'Loose cannons: exploding the myth of the "black macho" lad' in D. Epstein et al. (eds) *Failing boys? Issues in gender and achievement*, Open University Press: Buckingham and Philadelphia, pp. 111–27.

Shacklady Smith, Lesley (1978) 'Sexist assumptions and female delinquency' in C. Smart and B. Smart (eds) *Women, sexuality and social control*, Routledge and Kegan Paul: London.

Shah, Samir (1975) *Immigrants and employment in the clothing industry: the rag trade in London's East End*, Runnymede Trust: London.

Sharpe, Sue (1976) *Just like a girl*, Penguin: Harmondsworth.

Shelton, Beth Anne and John, Daphne (1993) 'Ethnicity, race, and difference: a comparison of white, black and Hispanic men's household labor time' in J. Hood (ed.) *Men, work and family*, Sage: Newbury Park, Calif., pp. 131–50.

Shepherd, Gill (1987) 'Rank, gender and homosexuality: Mombasa as a key to understanding sexual options' in P. Caplan (ed.) *The cultural construction of sexuality*, Tavistock: London, pp. 240–70.

Sherwin, Susan et al. (1998) *The politics of women's health*, Temple University Press: Philadelphia.

Short, Clare (1996) 'Women and the Labour Party' in J. Lovenduski and P. Norris (eds) *Women in politics*, Oxford University Press in association with the Hansard Society: Oxford, pp. 19–27.

Siltanen, Janet (1994) *Locating gender: occupational segregation, wages and domestic responsibilities*, UCL Press: London.

—— and Stanworth, Michelle (1984) 'The politics of private woman and public man' in J. Siltanen and M. Stanworth (eds) *Women and the public sphere: a critique of sociology and politics*, Hutchinson: London, pp. 185–208.

Simms, Madeleine and Smith, Christopher (1982) 'Young fathers: attitudes to marriage and family life' in L. McKee and M. O'Brien (eds) *The father figure*, Tavistock Publications: London, pp. 139–52.

Simon, William and Gagnon, John H. (1969) 'On psychosexual development' in D. A. Goslin (ed) *Handbook of socialization theory and research*, Rand McNally: Chicago, Ill., pp. 733–52.

Skeggs, Beverley (1997) *Formations of gender and class*, Sage Publications: London.

Skelton, Christine (1997) 'Primary boys and hegemonic masculinities', *British Journal of Sociology of Education*, 18(3):349–69.

Smart, Carol (1996) 'Desperately seeking post-heterosexual woman' in J. Holland and L. Adkins (eds) *Sex, sensibility and the gendered body*, Explorations in sociology 46, BSA, Macmillan: Basingstoke, pp. 222–41.

Smith, Dorothy E. (1988) *The everyday world as problematic*, Open University Press: Milton Keynes.

Social Justice (Commission on Social Justice) (1994) *Social justice: strategies for national renewal*, Report of the Commission on Social Justice, Vintage: London.

Social Trends (1970) *Social Trends*, HMSO: London.

Speak, Suzanne, Cameron, Stuart, and Gilroy, Rose (1997) *Young single fathers: participation in fatherhood—barriers and bridges*, Family Policy Studies Centre: London.

Spelman, Elizabeth V. (1990) *Inessential woman: problems of exclusion in feminist thought*, London: The Women's Press.

Squires, Judith (1999) 'Rethinking the boundaries of political representation' in S. Walby (ed.) *New agendas for women*, Macmillan: Basingstoke, pp. 169–89.

Stacey, Judith (1993) 'Towards kinder, gentler uses for testosterone', *Theory and Society*, 22(5):711–21.

Stacey, Margaret (1981) 'The division of labour revisited or overcoming the two Adams' in P. Abrams et al. (eds) *Practice and progress: British sociology 1950–1980*, Allen & Unwin: London, pp. 172–90.

—— and Price, Marion (1981) *Women, power, and politics*, Tavistock Publications: London.

Staggenborg, Suzanne (1991) *The pro-choice movement: organization and activism in the abortion conflict*, Oxford University Press: New York.

Stanley, Liz (1995) *Sex surveyed 1949–1994*, Taylor & Francis: London.

Stanworth, Michelle (1983) *Gender and schooling: a study of sexual divisions in the classroom*, Hutchinson in association with the Explorations in Feminism Collective: London.

Stead, Jean (1987) *Never the same again: women and the miners' strike*, The Women's Press: London.

Stephenson, Mary-Ann (1998) *The glass trapdoor: women, politics and the media during the 1997 general election*, Fawcett: London.

Stier, Haya and Tienda, Marta (1993) 'Are men marginal to the family? Insights from Chicago's inner city' in J. Hood (ed.) *Men, work and family*, Sage: Newbury Park, Calif., pp. 23–44.

Stockman, Norman, Bonney, Norman, and Xuewen, Sheng (1995) *Women's work in East and West*, UCL Press: London.

Summerfield, Penny (1989, first published 1984) *Women workers in the Second World War: production and patriarchy in conflict*, Routledge: London and New York.

Swarup, Hem Lata, Sinha, Niroj, Ghosh, Chitra and Rajput, Pam (1994) 'Women's political engagement in India: some critical issues' in B. J. Nelson and N. Chowdhury (eds) (1994) *Women and politics worldwide*, Yale University Press: New Haven and London, pp. 361–79.

Tabet, Paola (1996) 'Natural fertility, forced reproduction' in D. Leonard and L. Adkins (eds) *Sex in question: French materialist feminism*, Taylor & Francis: London, pp. 109–77.

Thorogood, Nicki (1987) 'Race, class and gender: the politics of housework' in J. Brannen and G. Wilson (eds) *Give and take in families*, Allen & Unwin: London, pp. 18–41.

Tilly, Charles (1984) 'Social movements and national politics' in C. Bright and S. Harding (eds) *State making and social movements: essays in history and theory*, University of Michigan Press: Ann Arbor, pp. 297–317.

Tilly, Louise A. and Scott, Joan W. (1987) *Women, work and family*, Methuen: New York and London.

TUC (1955) *Women in the trade union movement*, Trades Union Congress: London.

Travis, Alan (1999) *Guardian*, 29 December 1999.

United Nations (1995) *The world's women 1995: trends and statistics*, United Nations: New York.

—— (1999) *1999 World survey on the role of women in development: globalization, gender and work*, Department of Economic and Social Affairs, United Nations: New York.

—— (2000) *Progress of the world's women 2000*, UNIFEM biennial report, United Nations Development Fund for Women: New York.

Vaiou, Dina (1996) 'Women's work and everyday life in southern Europe in the context of European integration' in M. D. Garcia-Ramon and J. Monk (eds) *Women of the European Union*, Routledge: London, pp. 61–73.

Valentine, Gill (1996) 'An equal place to work? Anti-lesbian discrimination and sexual citizenship in the European Union' in M. D. Garcia-Ramon and J. Monk (eds) *Women of the European Union*, Routledge: London, pp. 111–25.

VanEvery, Jo (1995) *Heterosexual women changing the family: refusing to be a 'wife'!*, Taylor & Francis: London.

—— (1997) 'Understanding inequality: reconceptualizing housework', *Women's Studies International Forum*, 20(3):411–20.

Vogel, Lise (1983) *Marxism and the oppression of women*, Pluto: London.

Vogler, Carolyn and Pahl, Jan (1993) 'Social and economic change and the organisation of money within marriage', *Work, employment and society*, 7(1):71–95.

Waddington, David, Wykes, Maggie, and Critcher, Chas (1991) *Split at the seams?*, Open University Press: Milton Keynes.

Wajcman, Judy (1998) *Managing like a man*, Polity Press: Cambridge.

Walby, Sylvia (1986) *Patriarchy at work*, Polity: Cambridge.

—— (1990) *Theorizing patriarchy*, Basil Blackwell: Oxford.

—— (1994) 'Is citizenship gendered?', *Sociology*, 28(2):379–95.

—— (1996) 'The "declining significance" or the "changing forms" of patriarchy?' in V. M. Moghadam (ed) *Patriarchy and development*, Clarendon Press: Oxford, pp. 19–33.

—— (1997) *Gender transformations*, Routledge: London and New York.

Walkerdine, Valerie (1989) *Counting girls out*, Virago: London.

Weedon, Chris (1987) *Feminist practice and poststructuralist theory*, Blackwell: Oxford.

Weeks, Jeffrey (1987) 'Questions of identity' in P. Caplan (ed.) *The cultural construction of sexuality*, Tavistock: London and New York, pp. 31–51.

—— (1989) *Sex, politics and society*, 2nd edn., Longman: London.

Weiner, Gaby, Arnot, Madeleine, and David, Miriam (1997) 'Is the future female? Female success, male disadvantage, and changing gender patterns in education' in A. H. Halsey, H. Lauder, P. Brown, and A. Stuart Wells (eds) *Education: culture, economy, society*, Oxford University Press: Oxford, New York, pp. 620–30.

Wellings, Kaye, Field, Julia, Johnson, Anne M., and Wadsworth, Jane (1994) *Sexual behaviour in Britain: the national survey of sexual attitudes and lifestyles*, Penguin Books: London.

Werbner, Pnina (1988) 'Taking and giving: working women and female bonds in a Pakistani immigrant neighbourhood' in S. Westwood and P. Bhachu (eds) *Enterprising women: ethnicity, economy and gender*, Routledge: London and New York, pp. 177–202.

Weston, Kath (1991) *Families we choose*, Columbia University Press: New York.

Westwood, Sallie (1985) *All day every day: factory and family in the making of women's lives*, Pluto Press: London.

—— (1988) 'Workers and wives: continuities and discontinuities in the lives of Gujarati women' in S. Westwood and P. Bhachu (eds) *Enterprising women: ethnicity, economy and gender*, Routledge: London and New York, pp. 103–31.

—— and Bhachu, Parminder (eds) (1988) *Enterprising women: ethnicity, economy and gender*, Routledge: London and New York.

—— and Phizacklea, Annie (2000) *Trans-nationalism and the politics of belonging*, Routledge: London and New York.

Wheelock, Jane (1990) *Husbands at home*, Routledge: London.

Wight, Daniel (1996) 'Beyond the predatory male: the diversity of young Glaswegian men's discourses to describe heterosexual relationships' in L. Adkins and V. Merchant (eds) *Sexualizing the social: power and the organization of sexuality*, Explorations in sociology 47, BSA, pp. 145–170.

Williams, Christine (ed.) (1993) *Doing 'women's work': men in nontraditional occupations*, Sage: London.

Williams, Fiona (1989) *Social policy: a critical introduction*, Polity Press: Cambridge.

—— (1998) 'Troubled masculinities in social policy discourses: fatherhood' in J. Popay, J. Hearn and J. Edwards (eds) *Men, gender divisions and welfare*, Routledge: London and New York.

Willis, Paul (1977) *Learning to labour*, Gower: Aldershot.

—— (1984a) 'Youth unemployment: 1. A new social state', *New Society*, 29 March: 475–7.

—— (1984b) 'Youth unemployment: 2. Ways of living', *New Society*, 5 April: 13–15.

Wilson, Elizabeth (1977) *Women and the welfare state*, Tavistock: London.

Wilson, R. A. (1994) 'Sectoral and occupational change: prospects for women's employment' in R. Lindley (ed.) *Labour market structures and prospects for women*, Equal Opportunities Commission: Manchester.

Witz, Anne (1992) *Professions and patriarchy*, Routledge: London.

—— and Savage, Mike (1992) 'The gender of organizations' in M. Savage and A. Witz (eds) *Gender and bureaucracy*, Blackwell/The Sociological Review: Oxford, pp. 3–62.

Wolf, Diane L. (1991) 'Female autonomy, the family and industrialisation in Java' in R. Blumberg (ed.) *Gender, family and economy: the triple overlap*, Sage: London, pp. 128–48.

Wolpe, AnnMarie (1978) 'Education and the sexual division of labour' in A. Kuhn and A. Wolpe (eds) *Feminism and Materialism*, Routledge and Kegan Paul: London, Boston, and Henley, pp. 290–328.

—— (1988) *Within school walls: the role of discipline, sexuality and the curriculum*, Routledge: London and New York.

Worsley, Peter (1974) 'The state of theory and the status of theory', *Sociology*, 8:1–17.

Yates, Lyn (1997) 'Gender equity and the boys debate: what sort of challenge is it?', *British Journal of Sociology of Education*, 18(3):337–47.

Young, Michael and Wilmott, Peter (1962) *Family and kinship in East London*, Pelican: Harmondsworth.

—— —— (1973) *The symmetrical family*, Routledge and Kegan Paul: London.

Younger, Mike and Warrington, Molly (1996) 'Differential achievement of girls and boys at GCSE: some observations from the perspective of one school', *British Journal of Sociology of Education*, 17(3):299–313.

—— —— and Williams, Jacquetta (1999) 'The gender gap and classroom interactions: reality and rhetoric?', *British Journal of Sociology of Education*, 20(3):325–41.

Yuval-Davis, Nira (1995) 'The Cairo conferences, women and transversal politics', *Women against fundamentalism journal*, 6:19–21.

Zimmeck, Meta (1992) 'Marry in haste, repent at leisure: women, bureaucracy and the post office, 1870–1920' in M. Savage and A. Witz (eds) *Gender and bureaucracy*, Blackwell/The Sociological Review: Oxford, pp. 65–93.

Index